Grade 1

Addison-Wesley Mathematics

Robert E. Eicholz   Phares G. O'Daffer   Randall I. Charles
Sharon L. Young   Carne S. Barnett   Charles R. Fleenor

Stanley R. Clemens   Carol A. Thornton
Andy Reeves   Joan E. Westley

▲▼ Addison-Wesley Publishing Company

Menlo Park, California ■ Reading, Massachusetts ■ New York
Don Mills, Ontario ■ Wokingham, England ■ Amsterdam ■ Bonn
Sydney ■ Singapore ■ Tokyo ■ Madrid ■ San Juan

Program Advisors

John A. Dossey
Professor of Mathematics
Illinois State University
Normal, Illinois

Freddie Renfro
K-12 Mathematics Coordinator
La Porte Independent School
　District
La Porte, Texas

Bonnie Armbruster
Associate Professor
Center for the Study of
　Reading
University of Illinois
Champaign, Illinois

David C. Brummett
Educational Consultant
Palo Alto, California

William J. Driscoll
Chairman
Department of Mathematical Sciences
Central Connecticut State University
Burlington, Connecticut

Betty C. Lee
Assistant Principal
Ferry Elementary School
Detroit, Michigan

Irene Medina
Mathematics Coordinator
Tom Browne Middle School
Corpus Christi, Texas

Rosalie C. Whitlock
Educational Consultant
Stanford, California

Contributing Writers

Betsy Franco
Marilyn Jacobson
Marny Sorgen
Judith K. Wells

Mary Heinrich
Ann Muench
Connie Thorpe

Penny Holland
Gini Shimabukuro
Sandra Ward

Executive Editor

Diane H. Fernández

Cover Photograph
Steven Hunt/The Image Bank

ISBN 0-201-27100-1

10 11 12 - WC - 95 94

 Text printed on recycled paper.

Contents

Letter to Student   x

Chapter 1   Classification, Patterns, and Numbers to 9

Classification   1
My Pattern Book   3
Number Patterns to 4   5
Number Patterns to 6   7
Introduction to Problem Solving   9
Using Critical Thinking   10
Number Patterns to 9   11
   Midchapter Review/Quiz   12
Nickels and Pennies   13

Order to 9   15
Counting Before and After   17
   Mixed Review   18
Problem Solving: Finding Data from a Story   19
Problem Solving Strategy: Look for a Pattern   20
Wrap Up   21
Chapter Review/Test   22
Enrichment: Identifying Patterns   23
Cumulative Review   24

Chapter 2   Numbers to 20 and Graphing

Numbers 10 to 12   25
Numbers 13 to 16   27
Numbers 17 to 20   29
Dimes, Nickels, and Pennies   31
Problem Solving: Understanding the Operations 33
Estimation   34
Making and Reading Graphs   35
   Midchapter Review/Quiz   36
Graphing and Comparing Numbers   37

Order to 20   39
   Mixed Review   40
Problem Solving: Retelling a Story   41
Problem Solving Strategy: Act It Out   42
Wrap Up   43
Chapter Review/Test   44
Enrichment: Reading Number Names   45
Cumulative Review   46

Chapter 3   Understanding Addition

Addition   47
Addition Sentences   49
My Addition Book   51
Different Ways to Show a Sum   53
   Midchapter Review/Quiz   54
Problem Solving: Understanding the Operations 55
Probability   56
Turnaround Facts and Adding 0   57
Adding in Horizontal and Vertical Forms   59
   Mixed Review   60
Money Sums   61
Problem Solving: Acting Out the Story   63
Problem Solving Strategy: Use Objects   64
Wrap Up   65
Chapter Review/Test   66
Enrichment: Probability   67
Cumulative Review   68

Chapter 4   Understanding Subtraction

Subtraction   69
Subtraction Sentences   71
Problem Solving: Understanding the Operations   73
Calculator   74
Subtracting in Horizontal and Vertical Forms   75
Crossing Out to Subtract   77
   Midchapter Review/Quiz   78
Zero in Subtraction   79
Related Subtraction Facts   81

Mixed Review   82
Fact Families   83
Problem Solving: Asking a Question   85
Problem Solving Strategy: Choose
   the Operation   86
Wrap Up   87
Chapter Review/Test   88
Enrichment: Ordering Events   89
Cumulative Review   90

Chapter 5   Addition Facts: Count Ons and Zeros

Counting On 1 or 2 and Zero Addition Facts   91
Counting On with Turnaround Facts   93
Counting On 3   95
Counting On 1, 2, or 3   97
   Midchapter Review/Quiz   98
Problem Solving: Understanding the Operations   99
Informal Algebra   100
Fact Practice and Probability   101
   Mixed Review   102
Fact Practice and Graphing   103
Problem Solving: Telling a Story   105
Problem Solving Strategy: Guess and Check   106
Wrap Up   107
Chapter Review/Test   108
Enrichment: Missing Addends   109
Cumulative Review   110

Chapter 6   Addition Facts: Sums to 12

Small Doubles   111
Sums of 10   113
Fact Practice   115
Problem Solving: Understanding the Operations   117
Mental Math   118
Doubles Plus One   119
Fact Practice   121
   Midchapter Review/Quiz   122
Making 10, Adding Extra   123

Mixed Review   124
Adding 3 Numbers   125
Problem Solving: Showing Data   127
Problem Solving Strategy: Make a Table   128
Wrap Up   129
Chapter Review/Test   130
Enrichment: Comparing Quantity   131
Cumulative Review   132

Chapter 7   Measurement

Estimating and Measuring Length:
  Nonstandard Units   133
Estimating and Measuring Length: Inches   135
Using a Ruler: Inches   137
  Mixed Review   138
Using a Ruler: Feet   139
  Midchapter Review/Quiz   140
Ordering by Length and Height   141
Problem Solving: Understanding the Operations   143
Estimating Area   144
Estimating and Measuring Length: Centimeters   145
Estimating and Measuring Length: Decimeters   147
Estimating and Measuring Capacity   149
Estimating and Measuring Weight   150
Problem Solving: Determining
  Reasonable Answers   151
Problem Solving Strategy: Draw a Picture   152
Chapter Review/Test: Customary   153
Chapter Review/Test: Metric   154
Enrichment: Odd and Even Numbers   155
Cumulative Review   156

Chapter 8   Subtraction Facts: Count Backs, Zeros, and Doubles

Counting Back 1 or 2   157
Counting Back 3   159
Counting Back 1, 2, or 3   161
  Midchapter Review/Quiz   162
Problem Solving: Understanding the Operations   163
Calculator   164
Zero Subtraction Facts   165
Adding to Check Subtraction   167
Subtraction Doubles   169
Fact Practice   171
  Mixed Review   172
Problem Solving: Asking the Question   173
Problem Solving Strategy: Choose
  the Operation   174
Wrap Up   175
Chapter Review/Test   176
Enrichment: Finding 1-Foot Units   177
Cumulative Review   178

Chapter 9   Geometry

Sorting Solids   179
Graphing Solids   181
Plane Figures and Solids   183
Sides and Corners   185
  Midchapter Review/Quiz   186
My Geometry Book   187
Problem Solving: Understanding the Operations   189
Using Critical Thinking   190
Inside, Outside, and On   191
Symmetric Figures   193
Congruent Figures   195
  Mixed Review   196
Problem Solving: Finding Data from a Map   197
Problem Solving Strategy: Look for a Pattern   198
Wrap Up   199
Chapter Review/Test   200
Enrichment: Making Shapes   201
Cumulative Review   202

Chapter 10   Subtraction Facts to 12

Subtracting from 9 and 10   203
Fact Practice   205
Problem Solving: Understanding the Operations   207
Data Analysis   208
Counting Up to Subtract   209
Fact Practice   211
  Midchapter Review/Quiz   212
Adding to Check Subtraction   213
Fact Families   215

Fact Practice   217
  Mixed Review   218
Problem Solving: Telling a Story   219
Problem Solving Strategy: Use Logical
  Reasoning   220
Wrap Up   221
Chapter Review/Test   222
Enrichment: Finding All Ways   223
Cumulative Review   224

Chapter 11   Place Value

Grouping by Tens   225
Showing Tens and Ones   227
Decade Numbers and Names   229
Showing and Writing 2-Digit Numbers   231
  Midchapter Review/Quiz   232
Tens and Ones   233
Problem Solving: Understanding the Operations   235
Informal Algebra   236
Trading Dimes and Pennies   237

Dimes and Pennies   239
  Mixed Review   240
Problem Solving: Making Estimates   241
Problem Solving Strategy: Make a List   242
Wrap Up   243
Chapter Review/Test   244
Enrichment: Temperature   245
Cumulative Review   246

Chapter 12   Number Relationships and Counting Patterns

Counting to 50	247
Counting to 100	249
Counting On and Back	251
Numbers Before, After, and Between	253
Comparing Numbers	255
Midchapter Review/Quiz	256
Problem Solving: Understanding the Operations	257
Calculator	258
Counting Patterns for 10s	259
Mixed Review	260
Counting Patterns for 2s and 5s	261
Ordinal Numbers	263
Problem Solving: Finding Extra Data	265
Problem Solving Strategy: Make a Table	266
Wrap Up	267
Chapter Review/Test	268
Enrichment: Making and Reading a Pictograph	269
Cumulative Review	270

Chapter 13   Money

Counting Dimes and Pennies	271
Counting Nickels and Pennies	273
Counting Dimes and Nickels	275
Counting Dimes, Nickels, and Pennies	277
Counting and Comparing Money	279
Midchapter Review/Quiz	280
Problem Solving: Understanding the Operations	281
Calculator	282
Counting Quarters and Other Coins	283
Mixed Review	284
Problem Solving: Using Data from a Newspaper Ad	285
Problem Solving Strategy: Guess and Check	286
Wrap Up	287
Chapter Review/Test	288
Enrichment: Dollar Bill	289
Cumulative Review	290

Chapter 14   Time

Clock Parts	291
Time on the Hour	293
Mixed Review	294
Problem Solving: Understanding the Operations	295
Estimation	296
Time on the Half Hour	297
Midchapter Review/Quiz	298
The Mouse Family's Time Book	299
Calendar	301
Problem Solving: Using Data from a Chart	303
Problem Solving Strategy: Make a List	304
Wrap Up	305
Chapter Review/Test	306
Enrichment: Finding Patterns on a Calendar	307
Cumulative Review	308

Chapter 15   Addition Facts: Sums to 18

Adding 9	309
Doubles Through 9 + 9	311
Fact Practice	313
Adding Three Numbers	315
Problem Solving: Understanding the Operations	317
Mental Math	318
Doubles Plus One Through 8 + 9	319
Midchapter Review/Quiz	320
Sums to 18	321
Fact Practice	323
Mixed Review	324
Problem Solving: Determining Reasonable Answers	325
Problem Solving Strategy: Use Objects	326
Wrap Up	327
Chapter Review/Test	328
Enrichment: Exploring Addition	329
Cumulative Review	330

Chapter 16   Addition and Subtraction Facts to 18

Subtraction Doubles to 18	331
Subtracting 9	333
Fact Practice	335
Problem Solving: Understanding the Operations	337
Informal Algebra	338
Using Addition to Subtract 4, 5, and 6	339
Midchapter Review/Quiz	340
Using Addition to Subtract 7 and 8	341
Related Subtraction Facts	343
Fact Families	345
Mixed Review	346
Problem Solving: Using a Number Sentence	347
Problem Solving Strategy: Use Objects	348
Wrap Up	349
Chapter Review/Test	350
Enrichment: Using a Number Line to Add or Subtract	351
Cumulative Review	352

Chapter 17   Understanding 2-Digit Addition and Subtraction

Counting On by Ones	353
Making a Ten	355
Problem Solving: Understanding the Operations	357
Data Analysis	358
Counting On by Tens	359
Adding Tens and Ones	361
Counting Back by Ones	363
Midchapter Review/Quiz	364
Counting Back by Tens	365
Subtracting Tens and Ones	367
Mixed Review	368
Problem Solving: Choosing a Calculation Method	369
Problem Solving Strategy: Draw a Picture	370
Wrap Up	371
Chapter Review/Test	372
Enrichment: Finding Another Solution	373
Cumulative Review	374

Chapter 18   Extending Number Ideas

Multiplying Equal Groups of Two   375
Multiplying Equal Groups of Five   377
Problem Solving: Understanding the Operations   379
Probability   380
Understanding Division: Sharing   381
Understanding Division: Separating   383
   Midchapter Review/Quiz   384
Fractions: Halves   385
Fractions: Thirds and Fourths   387
   Mixed Review   388
Fractions: Using Sets   389
Problem Solving: Finding Missing Data   391
Problem Solving Strategy: Use Logical
   Reasoning   392
Wrap Up   393
Chapter Review/Test   394
Enrichment: Relating Multiplication
   and Division   395
Cumulative Review   396

Resource Bank and Glossary

Contents   397
Data Bank   398
Calculator Bank   401
Computer Bank   405
More Practice Bank   409
Glossary   433

Dear Girls and Boys,

What will you do inside this book?

You will talk about numbers.

You will find patterns.

two   **four**   **six**

2   4   6

You will write numbers and math words.

You will work in groups or with a partner.

You will see how math can be used everyday.

You will learn about shapes and measuring.

You will do many things during math.

You will think about math and have fun. We know you will like your book.

From your friends at Addison-Wesley.

1
Classification, Patterns, and Numbers to 9

Workmat

Classification

Ring what belongs.

1.

2.

3.

4.

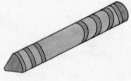

PROBLEM SOLVING

5. Which is not like the others?
Tell why. Give two answers.

Name _____

My Pattern Book

Color to continue the pattern.

Dear Family:
Ask your child to tell how he or she chose what color to use.

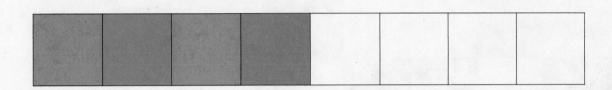

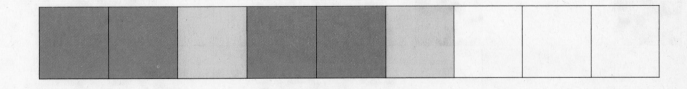

Color to continue the pattern.

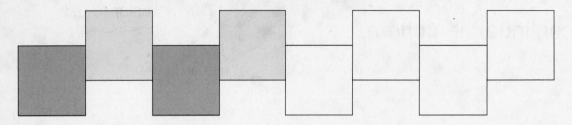

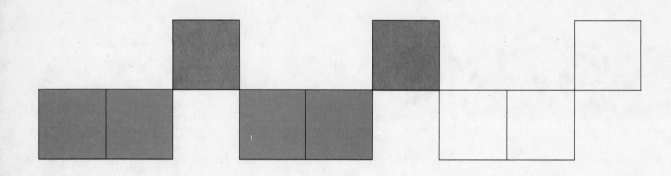

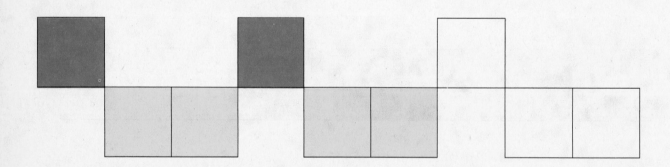

Color your own pattern.

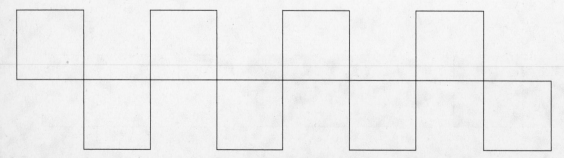

More Practice, page 409, set B

Name _____

Number Patterns to 4

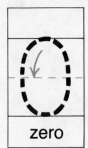 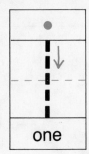  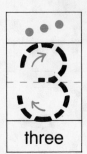 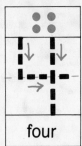

| zero | one | two | three | four |

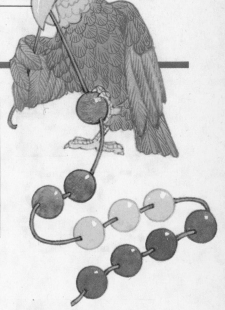

Write how many birds. Practice.

1.

_____

2.

_____

3.

_____

4.

_____

5.

_____

Continue the number pattern. Color to match.

1.

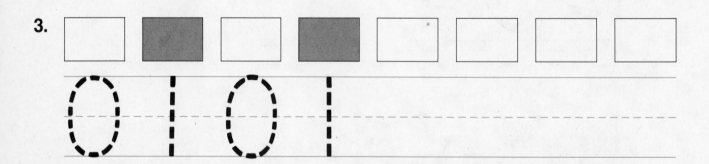

2 3 2 3 _____

2.

3 4 3 4 _____

3.

0 1 0 1 _____

TALK ABOUT IT

4. What is the next number?
Tell why. Write it.

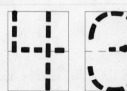

4 3 2

Number Patterns to 6

I more each time

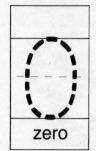 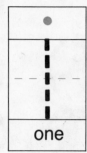   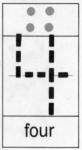  

| zero | one | two | three | four | five | six |

Write how much money.

1.

_____ ¢

2.

_____ ¢

3.

_____ ¢

4.

_____ ¢

1. Write how much money.
Talk about the patterns you see.

5¢ 6¢ ____¢ ____¢ ____¢ ____¢

MAKE AN ESTIMATE

2. About how many will fit?

_____   _____

my guess _____   my count _____

Introduction to Problem Solving

Listen to the story.

UNDERSTAND
FIND DATA
PLAN
ESTIMATE
SOLVE
CHECK

Chapter 1

(nine)   9

Using Critical Thinking

Tell how each car is different from
the one before.
Draw and color the next car.

1.

2.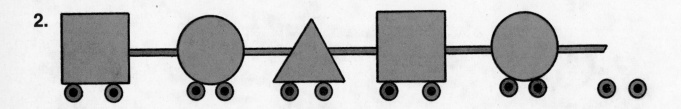

3.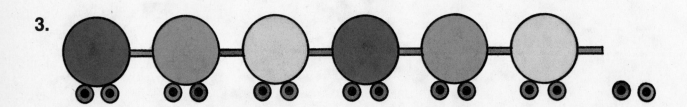

4. Draw and color a one-difference train.

Number Patterns to 9

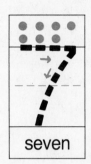  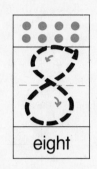

seven eight nine

0 1 2 3 4 5 6 7 8 9

Write how many animals.

1.  _____

2.  _____

3.  _____

4.  _____

5.  _____

Continue the number pattern.
Color to match.

7 8 9 7 8 9 _____

MIDCHAPTER REVIEW/QUIZ

1. Color to continue the pattern.

Write how many.

2.

3.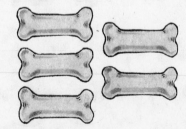

Nickels and Pennies

5 pennies

5¢

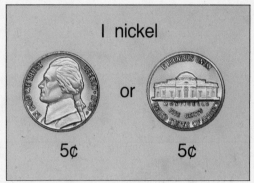

I nickel

or

5¢   5¢

Game

Work with a partner.
Take turns.
Spin.
Take that many pennies.
Trade when you can.

Spinner

Write how much money.

5¢

---

1.  _ _ _ _ _ ¢

2. _ _ _ _ _ ¢

3. _ _ _ _ _ ¢

WRITE ABOUT IT

Write the word for each coin.

4.  _ _ _ _ _ _ _ _ _ _

5. _ _ _ _ _ _ _ _ _ _

penny   nickel

Order to 9

1. Write the numbers in order.
Tally to match.

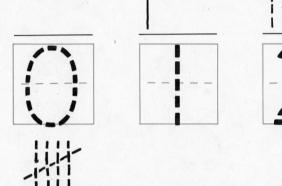

0	1	2		

5				

2. Connect the dots in order.
Start at ★.

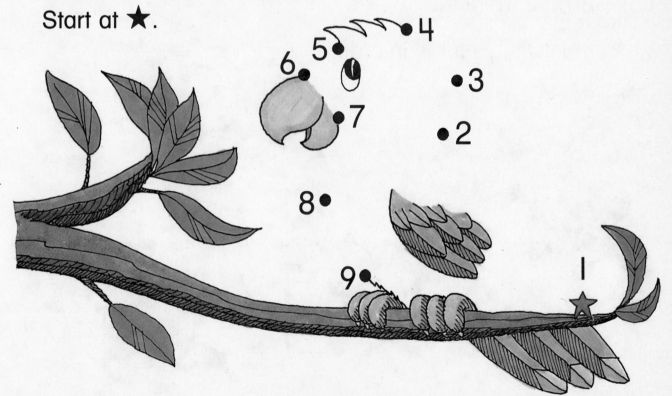

I. Write the numbers in order.

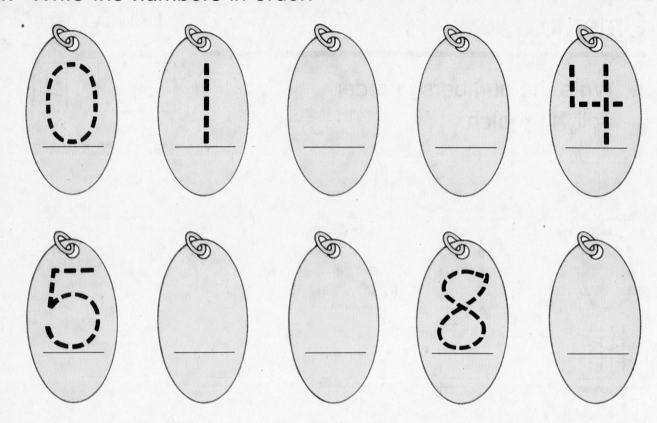

USE CRITICAL THINKING

2. Number the pictures in order.

Name _____

Counting Before and After

Write the number that comes after.

1.

2.

3.

4.

5.

6.

7.

8.

Write the missing numbers.

9. 0 1 ___ 3 ___ 5 6 ___

Write the number that comes before.

1.  2 3 4 5

2.  __ 1 2 3

3. 7 8 9

4. 5 6 7

5. 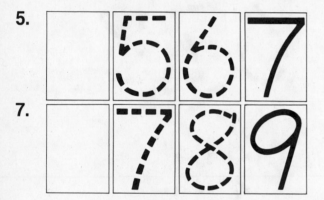 __ 5 6 7

6. 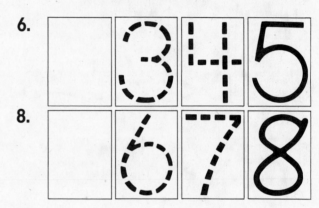 __ 3 4 5

7. __ 7 8 9

8. __ 6 7 8

MIXED REVIEW

Write how many.

9.  _____

10.  _____

11. Write the numbers in order.

 0

Problem Solving
Finding Data from a Story

UNDERSTAND
FIND DATA
PLAN
ESTIMATE
SOLVE
CHECK

Listen to the story.

Tally the pets.

Write the number for each tally.

PET PARADE

Chapter 1

(nineteen) 19

Problem Solving Strategy
Look for a Pattern

UNDERSTAND
FIND DATA
PLAN
ESTIMATE
SOLVE
CHECK

Cut out the animals. Listen to the story.
Paste the next animal in the pattern.
Talk about the patterns you see.

1. Jenny's shelf

2. Steph's shelf

3. your shelf
Make your own pattern.
Ask your partner what comes next.

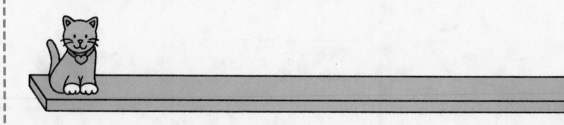

Name _____

Wrap Up

MATH WORDS

Ring what belongs. Tell why.

1.   7   IIIII I

2.   1¢

3. 4   ▪▪ ▪   ▪▪▪▪   IIII

4. ▪ ▪   2   III   ▪▪

MATH REASONING

Write the missing numbers.
Talk about the pattern.

5.

2, ____, ____, 4, ____, ____, ____, ____

Name _____

Chapter Review/Test

1. Ring what belongs.

2. Ring what comes next.

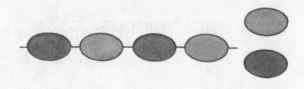

3. Write numbers to continue the pattern.

0	1	2	0	1	2			
7	8	9	7	8	9			

Write how much money.

4.  _____ ¢

5.  _____ ¢

6. Connect the dots in order. Start at ★.

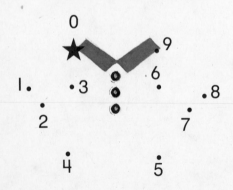

Write the missing numbers.

7.
2	3	

8.
	6	5

ENRICHMENT
Identifying Patterns

Continue the pattern.
Talk about the patterns you see.

1.

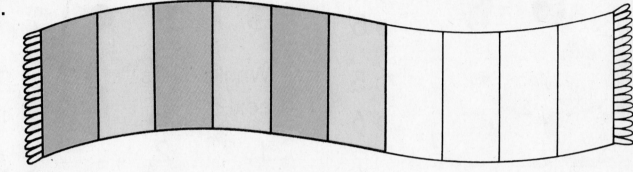

2.

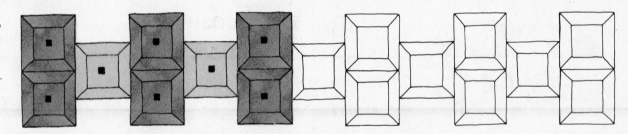

3. Color to make your own pattern.

4. Draw and color a pattern you see.

Name _____

CUMULATIVE REVIEW

How many are there?

1.
○ 3
○ 4
○ 5

2.
○ 5
○ 6
○ 7

3.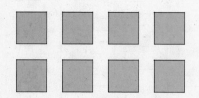
○ 8
○ 9
○ 10

4. How much money is there?

○ 4¢
○ 7¢
○ 8¢

5. Choose which one belongs.

○ △
○ ○
○ □

6. What comes next?

1, 2, 1, 2, 1, ____
○ 2
○ 1
○ 3

7. Choose the number that is right after.

| 5 | 6 | 7 | |
○ 9
○ 4
○ 8

8. Choose the number that is right before.

| | 7 | 8 | 9 |
○ 6
○ 8
○ 5

9. Ted saw ⊥⊥⊥⊥ I .

He saw ⊥⊥⊥⊥ III .

How many did Ted see?

○ 7

○ 8

○ 9

Chapter 1 Cumulative Review

2
Numbers to 20 and Graphing

Workmat

Numbers 10 to 12

Use counters.

Ten   **Ones**

1. Fill the .

Write **10** in all.

2. Fill the .
   Put down 1 extra counter.

Write **11** in all.

3. Fill the .
   Put down 2 extra counters.

Write **12** in all.

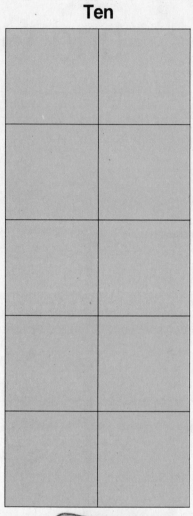

WRITE ABOUT IT

1 dozen eggs

4. Count all the eggs.
   Write the number and the word.

_____ eggs in a **dozen** .

| 13 | 14 | 15 | 16 |

Numbers 13 to 16

Use 16 counters.
Fill the blue 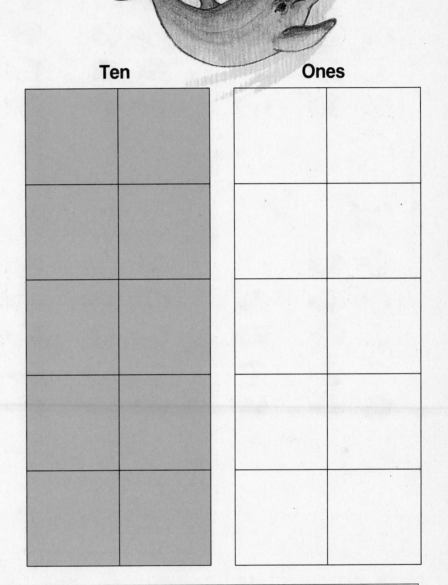.
Put some in the other.
Find how many in all.

Ten   **Ones**

1. 10 and _____   _____ in all

2. 10 and _____   _____ in all

3. _____ and _____   _____ in all

4. _____ and _____   _____ in all

Ring 10. Write the number in all.

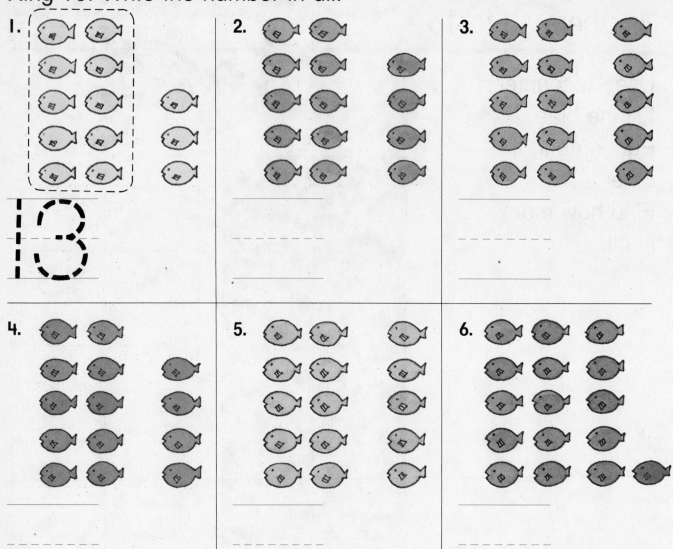

1. 13

2. _____

3. _____

4. _____

5. _____

6. _____

USE CRITICAL THINKING

7. Write the numbers.

Page
before is
_____

14   15

Page
after is
_____

| 17 | 18 | 19 | 20 |

Numbers 17 to 20

Use 20 counters.
Fill the blue ▥.
Put some in the
other ▥.
Find how many
in all.

Ten

Ones

1. 1O and _____ _____ in all

2. 1O and _____ _____ in all

3. _____ and _____ _____ in all

4. _____ and _____ _____ in all

Ring 10. Write the number in all. Practice.

1.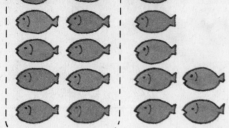

2.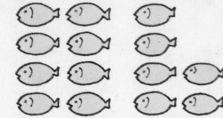

3.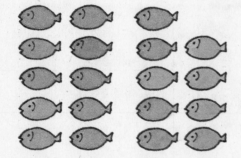

4.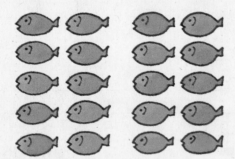

MENTAL MATH

5. Write the number.

More Practice, page 410, set C

Dimes, Nickels, and Pennies

10 pennies

10¢

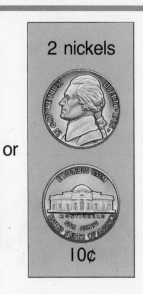

2 nickels

or

10¢

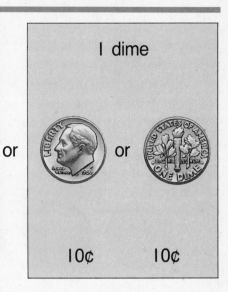

1 dime

or

or

10¢   10¢

Game

Work with a partner.
Take turns.
Spin.
Take that many
pennies.
Trade when you can.

Spinner

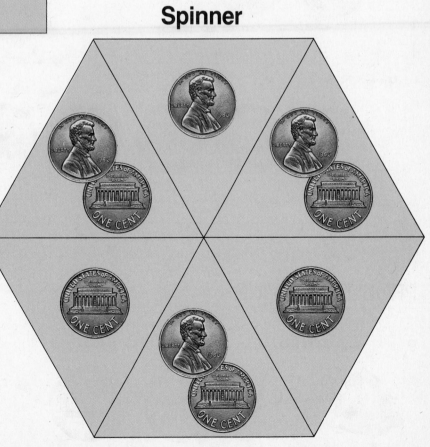

Write how much money.

1.

_____

_____ ¢

2.

_____

_____ ¢

3.

_____

_____ ¢

4.

_____

_____ ¢

PROBLEM SOLVING

5. I want this.　　　I have this.　　　Can I buy it?

yes

no

Name _____

Problem Solving
Understanding the Operations

UNDERSTAND
FIND DATA
PLAN
ESTIMATE
SOLVE
CHECK

Listen to the story. Use counters to show it.
Write the answer.

1. the story

_____

- - - - - - -

_____ dolphins

2. the  story

_____

- - - - - - -

_____ eggs

3. the story

_____

- - - - - - -

_____ fish

4. the story

_____

- - - - - - -

_____ jewels

Chapter 2

ESTIMATION

About how many will fit?
Ring what you think.
Use objects to check.

1.

about 3 5 10

2.

about 3 5 10

3.

about 3 6 15

4.

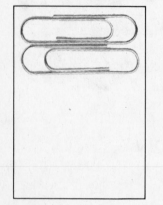

about 3 6 15

5.

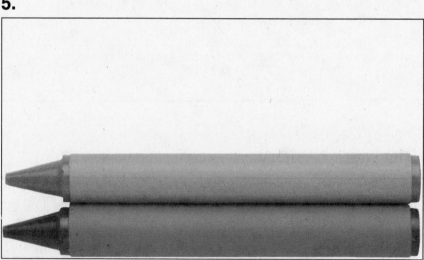

about 3 5 15

Making and Reading Graphs

Count the boats.
Color a box for each boat.

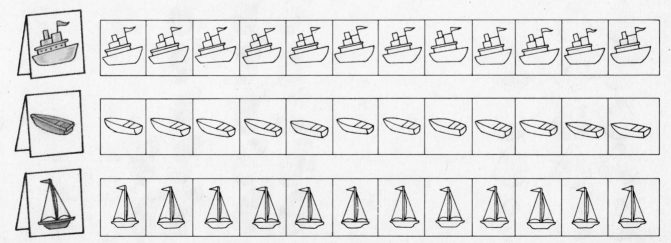

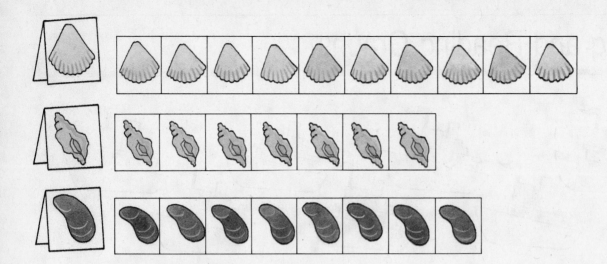

1. Ring the one with more.

2. Ring the one with fewer.

MIDCHAPTER REVIEW/QUIZ

Ring 10. Write the number in all.

1.

_____

_ _ _ _ _ _ _ _

_____

2.

_____

_ _ _ _ _ _ _ _

_____

Graphing and Comparing Numbers

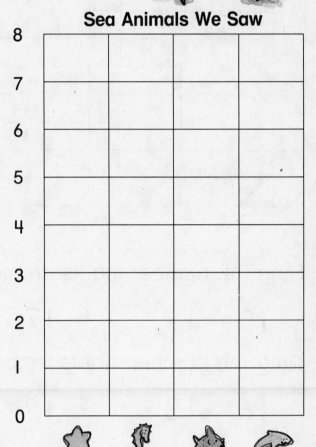

1 tally I	5 tallies ⵀ

A class counted the sea animals they saw.

  or 7

 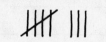 or 8

  or 5

  or 6

Sea Animals We Saw

1. Color the graph to show how many the class saw.

2. How many more than ? _____ more

3. How many fewer than ? _____ fewer

4. How many more than ? _____ more

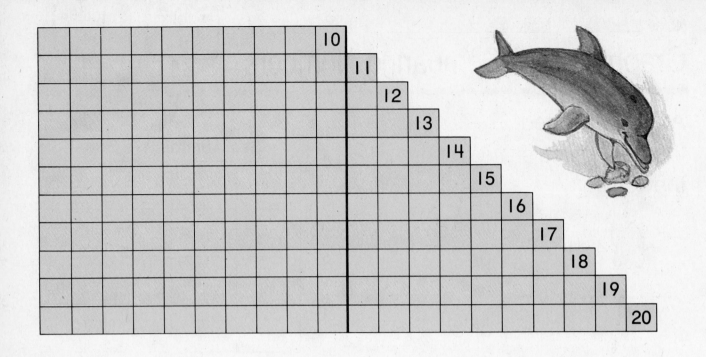

Ring the number that is greater.

1. 10 (14)   2. 17 13   3. 14 18

Ring the number that is less.

4. 16 13   5. 12 19   6. 15 11

FIND THE DATA

7. **Data Hunt** Ask 8 friends the question.
   Show their answers on the graph.

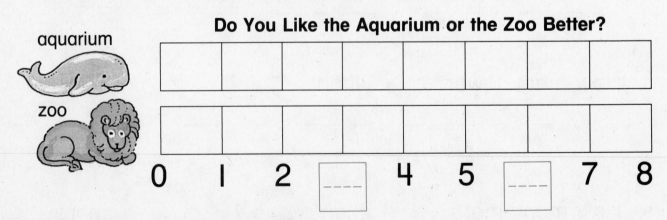

8. Write the missing numbers.

Order to 20

8 9 10 11 12 13 14 15 16 17 18 19 20

before

between

after

14

15

16

When you count on, the number that is **less** comes **before**.

When you count on, the number that is **greater** comes **after**.

Write the numbers.

1. before   between   after

11   12   [ ]

2. before   between   after

[ ]   18   19

3. before   between   after

8   [ ]   10

4. before   between   after

[ ]   16   17

5. before   between   after

18   19   [ ]

6. before   between   after

13   [ ]   15

Write the missing numbers.

1.

2.

3.

4.

MIXED REVIEW

5. Write numbers to continue the pattern.

1, 3, 5, 1, 3, 5, 1, 3, ____, ____, ____

6. Connect the dots in order.
Start at 0.

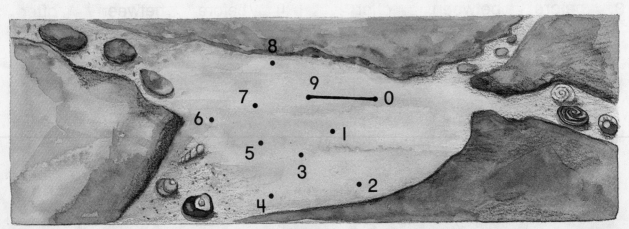

Name ________________________________

UNDERSTAND
FIND DATA
PLAN
ESTIMATE
SOLVE
CHECK

Problem Solving
Retelling a Story

Listen to the story.
Write the number you hear.
Retell the story with a number you pick.
Write your number.
Ring the number that is greater.

1.

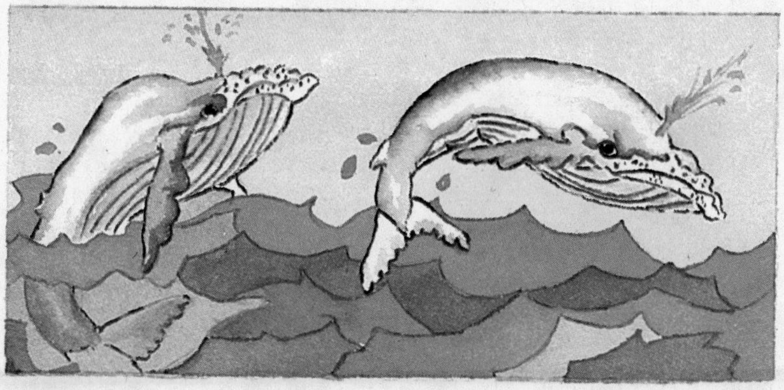

number you hear ______

your number ______

2.

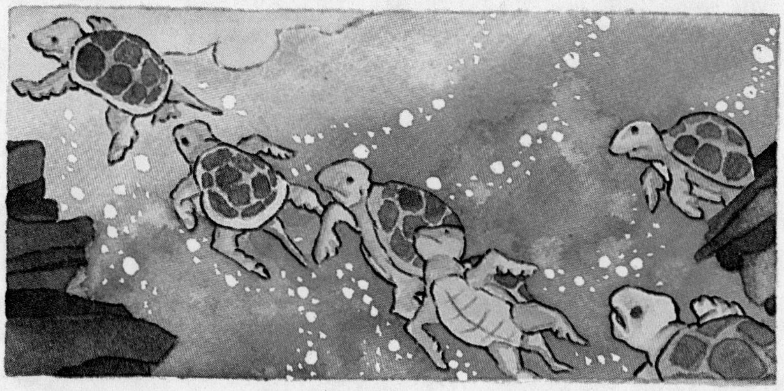

number you hear ______

your number ______

3.

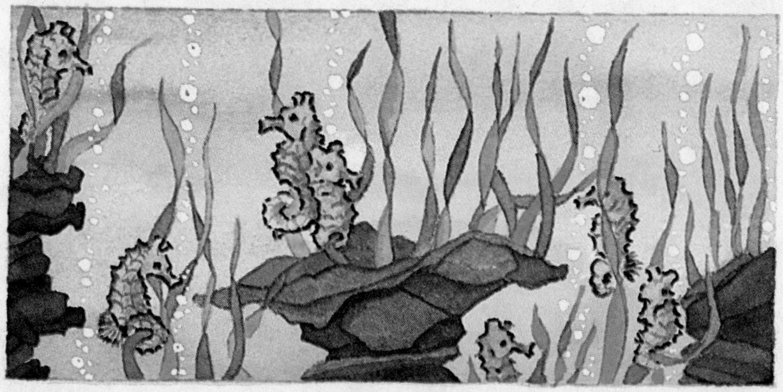

number you hear ______

your number ______

UNDERSTAND
FIND DATA
PLAN
ESTIMATE
SOLVE
CHECK

Problem Solving Strategy
Act It Out

Listen to the story.

Act it out.

Paste fish to show the story.

WRAP UP

MATH WORDS

1. Ring the numbers that come after 12.

 15 10 13 9 20 11

2. Ring the numbers that come before 15.

 19 12 14 16 18 10

3. Ring the numbers that come between 12 and 16.

 13 11 17 15 18 14

MATH REASONING

I have 14¢.

I have 18¢.

I have 16¢.

Is each sentence correct? Ring **yes** or **no.**

4. All have more than 12¢.　　yes　　no

5. All have less than 17¢.　　yes　　no

6. One has less than 15¢.　　yes　　no

Name _____

CHAPTER REVIEW/TEST

Ring 10. Write how many in all.

1. 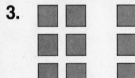 _ _ _ _ _ _ _ _ _ _

2. 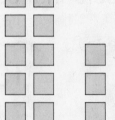 _ _ _ _ _ _ _ _ _ _

3.  _ _ _ _ _ _ _ _ _ _

4. _ _ _ _ _ _ _ _ _ _

5. Write how much money.

      _ _ _ _ _ _ _ _ _ ¢

6. Count. Write how many. Ring
   the number that is greater.

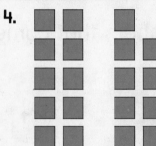

Sticker Graph

0 1 2 3 4 5 6 7 8

 _ _ _ _ _ _ _   _ _ _ _ _ _ _

7. Write the missing numbers.

| 12 | 13 | | | | 15 | | | 17 | | | | 19 | 20 |

ENRICHMENT
Reading Number Names

Connect the red dots in order.
Start at zero. Count on. Connect
the blue dots in order. Start
at ten. Count back.

0	zero	6	six
1	one	7	seven
2	two	8	eight
3	three	9	nine
4	four	10	ten
5	five		

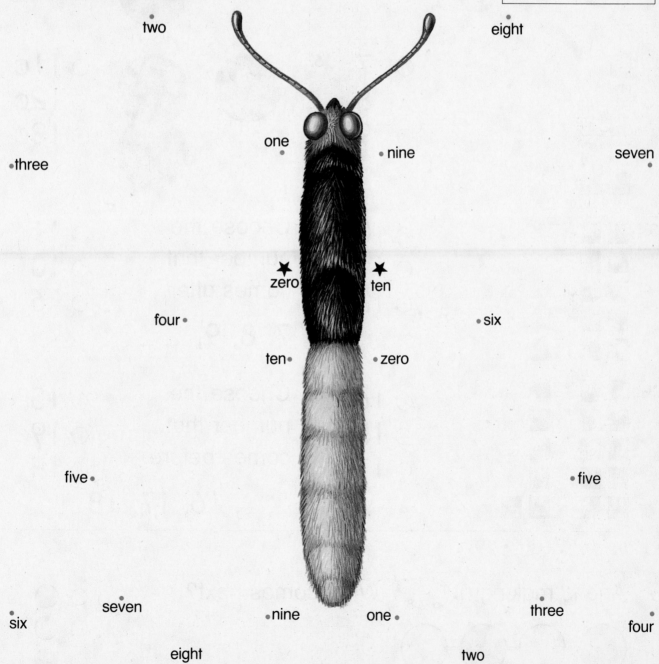

CUMULATIVE REVIEW

How many are there?

1.
- ○ 5
- ○ 6
- ○ 4

2.
- ○ 7
- ○ 8
- ○ 9

3.
- ○ 10
- ○ 11
- ○ 12

4.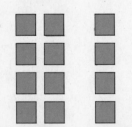
- ○ 16
- ○ 15
- ○ 17

How much money is there?

5.
- ○ 3¢
- ○ 5¢
- ○ 7¢

6.
- ○ 11¢
- ○ 12¢
- ○ 13¢

7. Choose the number that comes after.
- ○ 11
- ○ 10
- ○ 6

7, 8, 9, ____

8. Choose the number that comes before.
- ○ 15
- ○ 19
- ○ 14

____, 16, 17, 18

9. Ana is making a . What comes next?

- ○
- ○
- ○

3
Understanding Addition

Workmat

Addition

Put in 3.
Put in 2.
There are
5 in all.

Use counters.
Put some in a pile.
Put some more in the pile.
Find how many in all.

1. _____ + _____ = _____

    put in   put in   in all

2. _____ + _____ = _____

    put in   put in   in all

3. _____ + _____ = _____

    put in   put in   in all

4. _____ + _____ = _____

    put in   put in   in all

PROBLEM SOLVING

5. Tell your partner an addition
   story about putting counters
   into a box. Use counters to
   show the story. Draw it here.

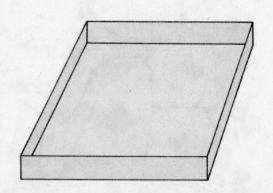

Addition Sentences

Get 6 two-color counters.

Put some of your counters in your hand.

Shake them. Pour your counters onto the tent.

Write the addition sentence.

1. [ ] + [ ] = sum [ ]

in all

2. [ ] + [ ] = sum [ ]

in all

3. [ ] + [ ] = sum [ ]

in all

Draw ● to show the numbers.
Write the sum.

1.

$2 + 3 = \underline{5}$

2.

$2 + 1 = \underline{}$

3.

$1 + 3 = \underline{}$

4.

$2 + 2 = \underline{}$

5.

$1 + 1 = \underline{}$

6.

$1 + 4 = \underline{}$

WRITE ABOUT IT

7.

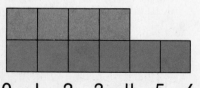

0 1 2 3 4 5 6

more
fewer

There are _____ blue than red.

There are _____ red than blue.

My Addition Book

Dear Family:
Ask your child to read this book to you.

Paste some animal punchouts to tell a story.
Write the number sentence.
Paste ⊞ or ⊟ .

_____ Paste here. _____ = _____
                                in all

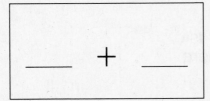 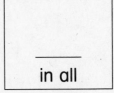

_____ + _____   Paste here.   _____
                                in all

| _____ | Paste here. | _____ | = | _____ in all |

| _____ + _____ | Paste here. | _____ in all |

Different Ways to Show a Sum

Work with a partner.

Share 5 cubes of one color.

Share 5 cubes of a different color.

Put some cubes of one color on the circus train.

Finish the train with cubes of the other color.

Color to show what you did.

Write the number sentence.

I.

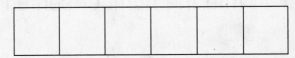

___ + ___ ⋯ ___

sum

2.

___ + ___ ⋯ ___

sum

3.

___ + ___ ⋯ ___

sum

4.

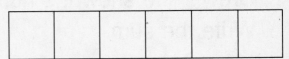

___ + ___ ⋯ ___

sum

Use two colors.
Show different ways to make a sum of 7.
Write the number sentences.

1.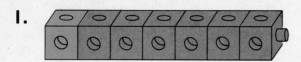
$\underline{1} + \underline{6} = \underline{7}$

2.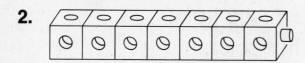
$\underline{} + \underline{} = \underline{7}$

3.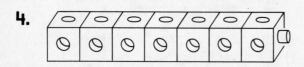
$\underline{} + \underline{} = \underline{}$

4.
$\underline{} + \underline{} = \underline{}$

MIDCHAPTER REVIEW/QUIZ

1. Write the number sentence.

$\underline{} + \underline{} = \underline{}$ $\underline{} + \underline{} = \underline{}$

2. Draw ○ to show the numbers.
   Write the sum.

   ○   ○

   ○

$1 + 2 = \underline{}$ $2 + 2 = \underline{}$

UNDERSTAND
FIND DATA
PLAN
ESTIMATE
SOLVE
CHECK

Problem Solving
Understanding the Operations

Listen to the story.
Use counters to show it.
Answer the question.
Write the number sentence.

1. the  story

$4 + 2 = $ _____

_____ elephants in all

2. the story

$1 + 5 = $ _____

_____ dogs in all

3. the story

$2 + 3 + 2 = $ _____

_____ chimps in all

Probability

Guess what you will spin. Color to show
your guess. Use your spinner.
Color to show your spin.

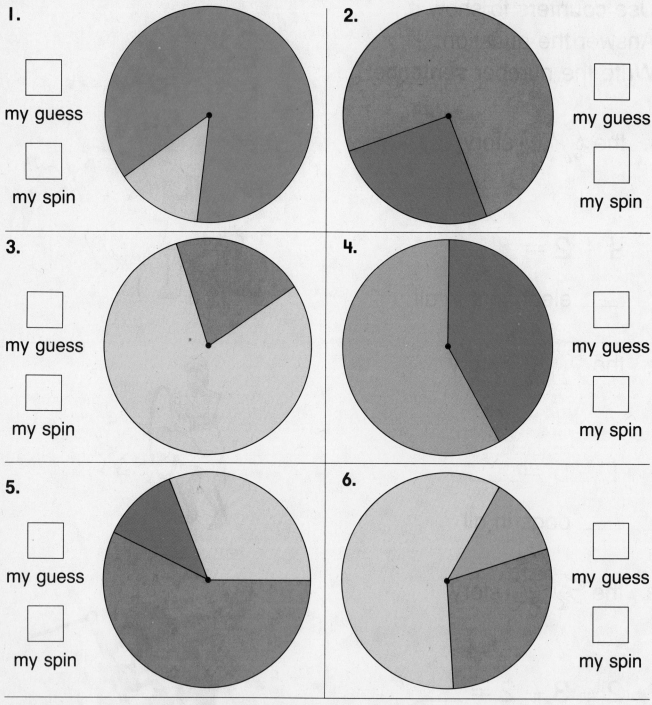

1.

my guess

my spin

2.

my guess

my spin

3.

my guess

my spin

4.

my guess

my spin

5.

my guess

my spin

6.

my guess

my spin

7. How many times did you guess right?
Tell how you decided what to guess.

Turnaround Facts and Adding 0

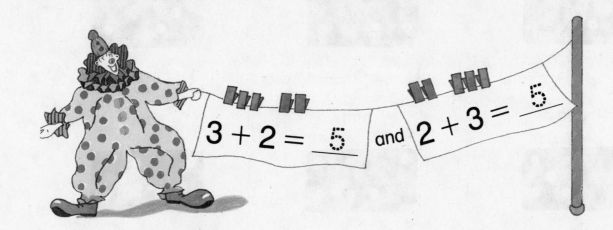

$3 + 2 = \underline{5}$ and $2 + 3 = \underline{5}$

Add. Write the sum
for the turnaround fact.

1. $1 + 3 = \underline{}$ and $3 + 1 = \underline{}$

2. $2 + 4 = \underline{}$ and $4 + 2 = \underline{}$

3. $1 + 4 = \underline{}$ and $4 + 1 = \underline{}$

4. $2 + 0 = \underline{}$ and $0 + 2 = \underline{}$

Add. Write the turnaround fact.

1.

$5 + 0 = \underline{5}$

and

$\underline{0} + \underline{5} = \underline{5}$

2.

$4 + 2 = \underline{}$

and

$\underline{} + \underline{} = \underline{}$

3.

$3 + 2 = \underline{}$

and

$\underline{} + \underline{} = \underline{}$

4.

$0 + 6 = \underline{}$

and

$\underline{} + \underline{} = \underline{}$

5.

$1 + 4 = \underline{}$

and

$\underline{} + \underline{} = \underline{}$

6.

$3 + 0 = \underline{}$

and

$\underline{} + \underline{} = \underline{}$

USE MENTAL MATH

Write the number that is 2 more.

7. $5 \rightarrow \underline{7}$ **8.** $8 \rightarrow \underline{}$ **9.** $6 \rightarrow \underline{}$ **10.** $9 \rightarrow \underline{}$

Adding in Horizontal and Vertical Forms

1 + 2 = 3

$$\begin{array}{r} 1 \\ + 2 \\ \hline 3 \end{array}$$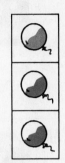

Use two colors. Color what you see.
Add.

1. 1 + 3 = ___

$$\begin{array}{r} 1 \\ + 3 \\ \hline \end{array}$$

2. 1 + 1 = ___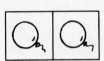

$$\begin{array}{r} 1 \\ + 1 \\ \hline \end{array}$$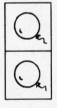

3. 3 + 2 = ___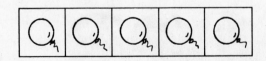

$$\begin{array}{r} 3 \\ + 2 \\ \hline \end{array}$$

Write what you see. Add.

1.  $\begin{array}{r} 3 \\ +\ 4 \\ \hline 7 \end{array}$

2. 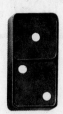 $\begin{array}{r} \\ +\ \\ \hline \end{array}$

3.  $\begin{array}{r} \\ +\ \\ \hline \end{array}$

4.  $\begin{array}{r} \\ +\ \\ \hline \end{array}$

5.  $\begin{array}{r} \\ +\ \\ \hline \end{array}$

6. $\begin{array}{r} \\ +\ \\ \hline \end{array}$

7.  $\begin{array}{r} \\ +\ \\ \hline \end{array}$

8.  $\begin{array}{r} \\ +\ \\ \hline \end{array}$

9.  $\begin{array}{r} \\ +\ \\ \hline \end{array}$

MIXED REVIEW
Write how much money.

10.  ____¢

11.  ____¢

12. Write the numbers before and after.

___ , 14, ___

13. Write the number between.

18, ___ , 20

Name _____

Money Sums

Game

Work with a partner.
Take turns.
Spin.
Take that many
pennies.
Find the sum.

Spinner

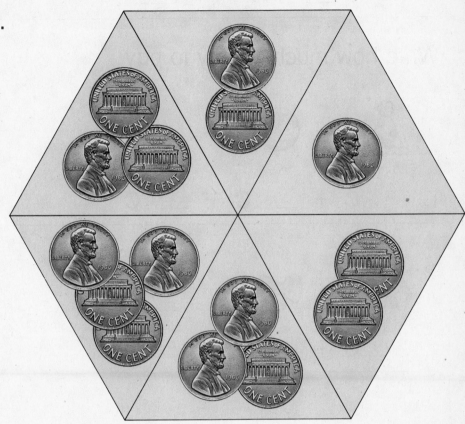

1. ____¢ + ____¢ = ____¢
   spin   spin   sum

2. ____¢ + ____¢ = ____¢
   spin   spin   sum

3. ____¢ + ____¢ = ____¢
   spin   spin   sum

4. ____¢ + ____¢ = ____¢
   spin   spin   sum

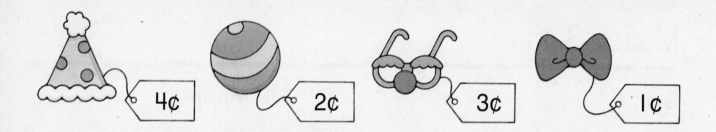

4¢   2¢   3¢   1¢

Write how much money to pay.

1. ____ ¢ + ____ ¢ = ____ ¢

2. ____ ¢ + ____ ¢ = ____ ¢

3. ____ ¢ + ____ ¢ = ____ ¢

PROBLEM SOLVING

4. You will spend

Ring what you can buy.

Problem Solving
Acting Out the Story

UNDERSTAND
FIND DATA
PLAN
ESTIMATE
SOLVE
CHECK

Listen to the story.
Act it out.
Write the number sentence.

1.

_____ + _____ ===== _____

_____ monkeys in all

2.

_____ + _____ ===== _____

_____ seals in all

3.

_____ + _____ ===== _____

_____ horses in all

4.

_____ + _____ ===== _____

_____ lions in all

Bo

Flo

Jo

Mo

| UNDERSTAND |
| FIND DATA |
| PLAN |
| ESTIMATE |
| SOLVE |
| CHECK |

Problem Solving Strategy
Use Objects

Cut out the clowns. Listen
to the first story. Use the clowns
to act it out. Listen to the second
story. Paste the clowns to show it.

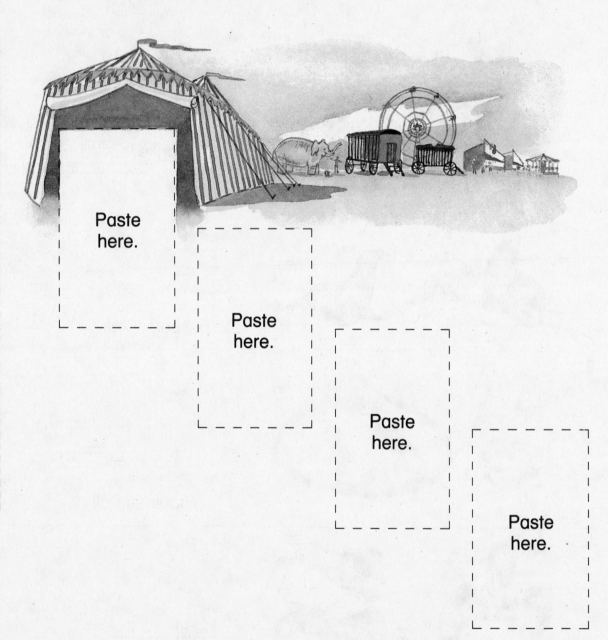

Paste
here.

Paste
here.

Paste
here.

Paste
here.

Paste
here.

WRAP UP

MATH WORDS

Ring the ones that make the same sum.

1.  |

2.  |

3. |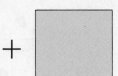

MATH REASONING

4. Make two number sentences.
   Use all the numbers.

 + =

☐ + ☐ = ☐

Name _____

CHAPTER REVIEW/TEST

Draw ● to show the number.
Write the sum.

1.

$3 + 2 =$ ___

2.

$4 + 1 =$ ___

3. Use two colors. Show two different
ways to name a sum of 6. Write
the number sentences.

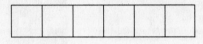   ___ + ___ = ___

   ___ + ___ = ___

Add. Write the turnaround fact.

4.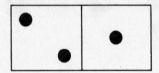

$2 + 1 =$ ___   ___ + ___ = ___

Write what you see. Add.

5. 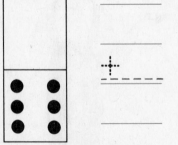   _____

6. 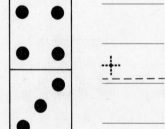   _____

7. 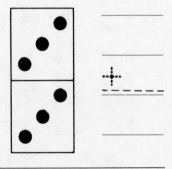   _____

8. Add.

$3¢ + 2¢ =$ ___ ¢ $2¢ + 4¢ =$ ___ ¢

ENRICHMENT
Probability

Which spinner should you use to
spin each? Ring the spinner.

1. always yellow

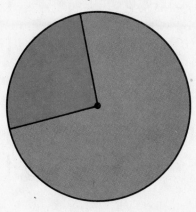 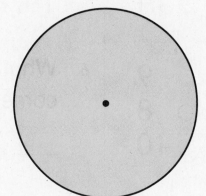 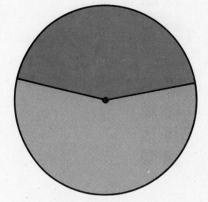

2. never yellow

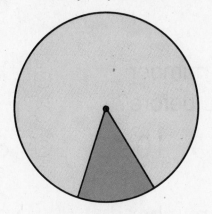 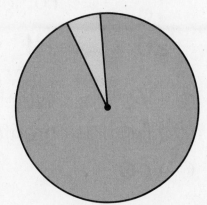 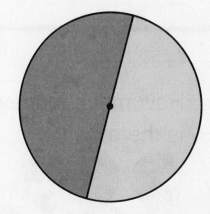

3. sometimes yellow

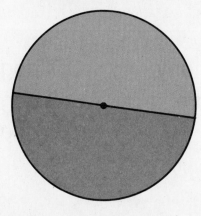 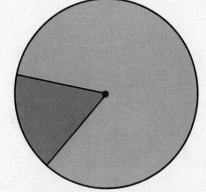 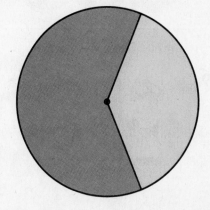

CUMULATIVE REVIEW

How many are there?

1. ○ 15
   ○ 16
   ○ 14

2. ○ 9
   ○ 8
   ○ 10

3. ○ 19
   ○ 18
   ○ 20

4. How much money is there?
   ○ 7¢
   ○ 15¢
   ○ 16¢
   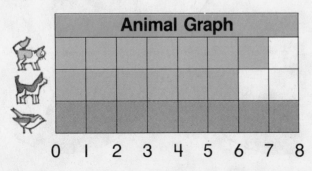

5. What number comes after?
   14, 15, ___
   ○ 11
   ○ 17
   ○ 16

6. What number comes before?
   ___, 9, 10
   ○ 6
   ○ 11
   ○ 8

7. What number comes between?
   14, ___, 16
   ○ 13
   ○ 15
   ○ 17

8. Which is greater than 16?
   ○ 15
   ○ 17
   ○ 14

9.

Animal Graph

0 1 2 3 4 5 6 7 8

How many dogs are there?
○ 7 dogs
○ 8 dogs
○ 6 dogs

4
Understanding Subtraction

Workmat

Subtraction

Get 6 counters.
Put some in a pile.
Take away some from the pile.
Find how many are left.

Put 5 in a pile.
Take away 2.
3 are left.

1. _____   _____   _____
    in the pile   take away   are left

2. _____   _____   _____
    in the pile   take away   are left

3. _____   _____   _____
    in the pile   take away   are left

4. _____   _____   _____
    in the pile   take away   are left

USE MENTAL MATH

5. **Write the number.**

You say it if you
count on from 9.

You say it if you
count back from 11.

The number is ____.

Subtraction Sentences

Get 6 counters.

Put some counters in the tent.
Take away some.
Write the subtraction sentence.

1. _____ ----- _____ ::::: _____
   put in   take away   are left

2. _____ ----- _____ ::::: _____
   put in   take away   are left

3. _____ ----- _____ ::::: _____
   put in   take away   are left

4. _____ ----- _____ ::::: _____
   put in   take away   are left

Subtract.

$$5 - 4 = \underline{1}$$

1.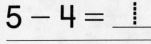

$$4 - 2 = \underline{}$$

2.

$$5 - 1 = \underline{}$$

3.

$$4 - 3 = \underline{}$$

4.

$$5 - 2 = \underline{}$$

5.

$$3 - 2 = \underline{}$$

6.

$$4 - 1 = \underline{}$$

SHOW WITH COUNTERS

7. Show each with counters.

Color  the ones that are correct.

Cross out the rest.

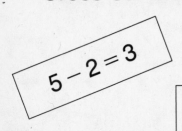

$$5 - 2 = 3$$

$$5 - 3 = 2$$

$$4 - 1 = 2$$

$$6 - 2 = 3$$

More Practice, page 413, set A

Problem Solving
Understanding the Operations

Listen to the story. Use counters to show it.
Finish the number sentence.

1. the 🐸 story

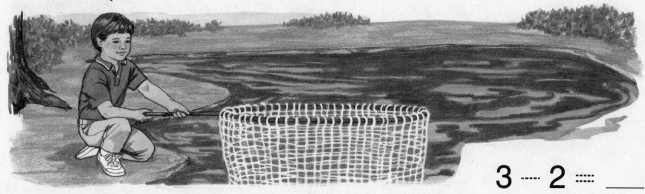

$3 - 2 = $ ____

2. the 🐢 story

$4 - 1 = $ ____

3. the 🦆 story

$5 - 4 = $ ____

Calculator

 Use a .

Write the number you subtract to get the target number.

Start with	Subtract	Target Number
9	–	= 6

I think I'll try 3 as my subtract number. It works!

ON/C	9	–	3	=	6

Start with	Subtract	Target Number

1. 9 – [ ] = 7

2. 9 – [ ] = 8

3. 9 – [ ] = 9

4. 8 – [ ] = 2

5. 8 – [ ] = 4

6. 8 – [ ] = 6

Subtracting in Horizontal and Vertical Forms

$3 - 1 = \underline{2}$ and

$$\begin{array}{r} 3 \\ -1 \\ \hline 2 \end{array}$$

Subtract.

1. $4 - 2 = \underline{}$ and
$$\begin{array}{r} 4 \\ -2 \\ \hline \end{array}$$

2. $5 - 1 = \underline{}$ and
$$\begin{array}{r} 5 \\ -1 \\ \hline \end{array}$$

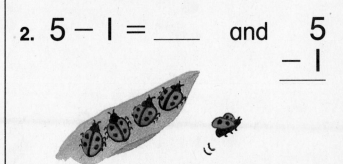

3. $5 - 3 = \underline{}$ and $\quad 5$

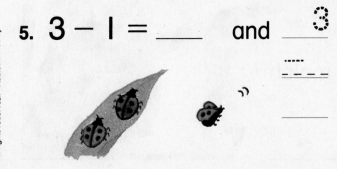

4. $4 - 3 = \underline{}$ and $\quad 4$

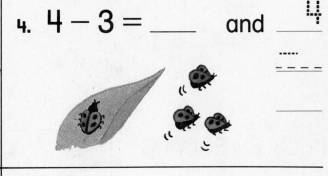

5. $3 - 1 = \underline{}$ and $\quad 3$

6. $5 - 2 = \underline{}$ and $\quad 5$

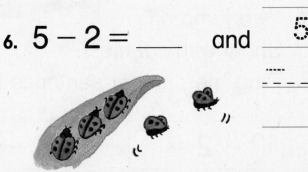

Subtract.

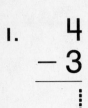

The bird
had 4.

1. $\begin{array}{r} 4 \\ -3 \\ \hline \end{array}$

2. $\begin{array}{r} 5 \\ -2 \\ \hline \end{array}$

3. $\begin{array}{r} 4 \\ -1 \\ \hline \end{array}$

4. $\begin{array}{r} 4 \\ -2 \\ \hline \end{array}$

5. $\begin{array}{r} 3 \\ -2 \\ \hline \end{array}$

6. $\begin{array}{r} 5 \\ -3 \\ \hline \end{array}$

7. $\begin{array}{r} 6 \\ -2 \\ \hline \end{array}$

8. $\begin{array}{r} 3 \\ -1 \\ \hline \end{array}$

9. $\begin{array}{r} 6 \\ -4 \\ \hline \end{array}$

PROBLEM SOLVING

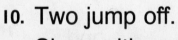

10. Two jump off.
Show with counters.
Ring the number sentence to match.

$3 - 2 = 1$ $3 - 1 = 2$

Crossing Out to Subtract

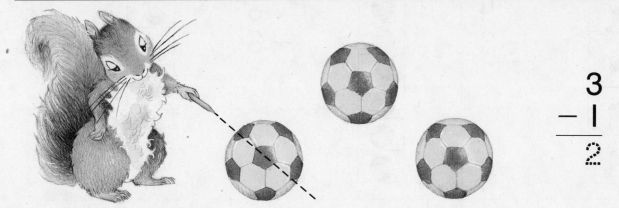

$$\begin{array}{r} 3 \\ -\ 1 \\ \hline 2 \end{array}$$

Cross out. Subtract.

1.

$$\begin{array}{r} 3 \\ -\ 2 \\ \hline \end{array}$$

2.

$$\begin{array}{r} 4 \\ -\ 1 \\ \hline \end{array}$$

3.

$$\begin{array}{r} 5 \\ -\ 3 \\ \hline \end{array}$$

4.

$$\begin{array}{r} 4 \\ -\ 3 \\ \hline \end{array}$$

5.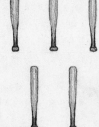

$$\begin{array}{r} 5 \\ -\ 2 \\ \hline \end{array}$$

6.

$$\begin{array}{r} 4 \\ -\ 2 \\ \hline \end{array}$$

7. Tell your partner a story for  6.

Cross out. Subtract.

1. 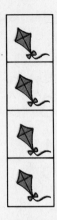 $\begin{array}{r} 4 \\ -3 \\ \hline \end{array}$

2.  $\begin{array}{r} 6 \\ -3 \\ \hline \end{array}$

3.  $\begin{array}{r} 5 \\ -2 \\ \hline \end{array}$

4. 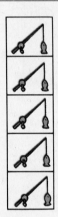 $\begin{array}{r} 5 \\ -1 \\ \hline \end{array}$

5. 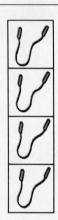 $\begin{array}{r} 4 \\ -2 \\ \hline \end{array}$

6.  $\begin{array}{r} 6 \\ -4 \\ \hline \end{array}$

MIDCHAPTER REVIEW/QUIZ

Subtract.

1.

$5 - 2 = \underline{\hphantom{00}}$

2. $\begin{array}{r} 3 \\ -1 \\ \hline \end{array}$

3.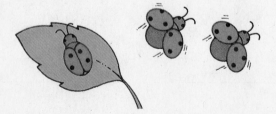

$3 - 2 = \underline{\hphantom{00}}$

4. 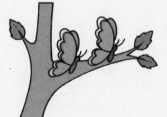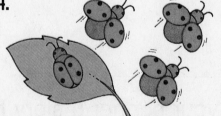 $\begin{array}{r} 4 \\ -3 \\ \hline \end{array}$

Zero in Subtraction

Listen to the story.
Cross out when needed.
Finish the number sentence.

$$2 - 2 = 0$$

1.

$$3 - 3 = 0$$

2.

$$2 - 0 = 2$$

3.

$$4 - 4 = \underline{\hspace{1cm}}$$

4.

$$3 - 0 = \underline{\hspace{1cm}}$$

5.

$$\begin{array}{r} 4 \\ -\ 0 \\ \hline \end{array}$$

6.

$$\begin{array}{r} 5 \\ -\ 5 \\ \hline \end{array}$$

$3 - 3 = 0$

$\begin{array}{r} 4 \\ -2 \\ \hline 2 \end{array}$

Subtract.

1. $4 - 3 =$ ___ $\qquad$ $2 - 0 =$ ___ $\qquad$ $5 - 2 =$ ___

2. $4 - 4 =$ ___ $\qquad$ $3 - 2 =$ ___ $\qquad$ $2 - 0 =$ ___

3.
$\begin{array}{r} 3 \\ -1 \\ \hline \end{array}$
$\quad$
$\begin{array}{r} 2 \\ -1 \\ \hline \end{array}$
$\quad$
$\begin{array}{r} 4 \\ -0 \\ \hline \end{array}$
$\quad$
$\begin{array}{r} 5 \\ -5 \\ \hline \end{array}$
$\quad$
$\begin{array}{r} 4 \\ -1 \\ \hline \end{array}$
$\quad$
$\begin{array}{r} 2 \\ -2 \\ \hline \end{array}$

4.
$\begin{array}{r} 5 \\ -3 \\ \hline \end{array}$
$\quad$
$\begin{array}{r} 5 \\ -0 \\ \hline \end{array}$
$\quad$
$\begin{array}{r} 5 \\ -1 \\ \hline \end{array}$
$\quad$
$\begin{array}{r} 6 \\ -3 \\ \hline \end{array}$
$\quad$
$\begin{array}{r} 3 \\ -3 \\ \hline \end{array}$
$\quad$
$\begin{array}{r} 4 \\ -2 \\ \hline \end{array}$

FIND THE DATA

5. **Data Hunt** Ask 8 friends the question.
   Color the graph to show the data.

Would You Like a Dog or a Cat More?

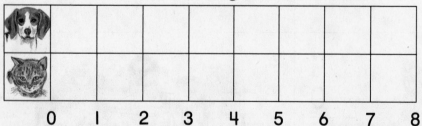

0 1 2 3 4 5 6 7 8

6. Which has more? Ring one.

7. How many more? ___ more

Related Subtraction Facts

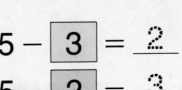
Part is left.

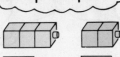 whole   Snap off part.

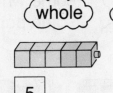

5   3   2

$5 - \boxed{3} = 2$

$5 - \boxed{2} = 3$

Use cubes. Make a train. Snap off part.
Finish each number sentence.

1.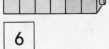

6

$6 - \boxed{4} = 2$

$6 - \boxed{2} = \underline{}$

2.

5

$5 - \boxed{4} = \underline{}$

$5 - \boxed{1} = \underline{}$

3.

7

$7 - \boxed{5} = \underline{}$

$7 - \boxed{2} = \underline{}$

4.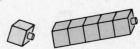

6

$6 - \boxed{1} = \underline{}$

$6 - \boxed{5} = \underline{}$

5.

8

$8 - \boxed{5} = \underline{}$

$8 - \boxed{3} = \underline{}$

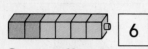 6

Snap off part.

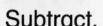 2   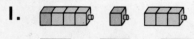 4

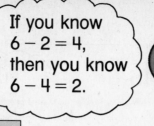 If you know
6 − 2 = 4,
then you know
6 − 4 = 2.

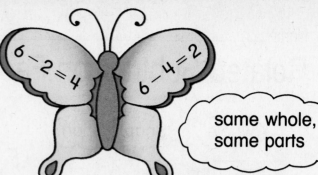 6 − 2 = 4   6 − 4 = 2

same whole,
same parts

Subtract.

1.

| 4 | 1 | 3 |

$4 - 1 = \underline{3}$

$4 - 3 = \underline{}$

2.

| 5 | 2 | 3 |

$5 - 2 = \underline{}$

$5 - 3 = \underline{}$

3.

| 7 | 2 | 5 |

$7 - 2 = \underline{}$

$7 - 5 = \underline{}$

4.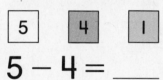

| 5 | 4 | 1 |

$5 - 4 = \underline{}$

$5 - 1 = \underline{}$

5.

| 6 | 1 |  5 |

$6 - 1 = \underline{}$

$6 - 5 = \underline{}$

6.

| 3 | 2 | 1 |

$3 - 2 = \underline{}$

$3 - 1 = \underline{}$

MIXED REVIEW

7. Add. Write the turnaround fact.

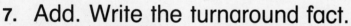

$2 + 3 = \underline{}$ and $\underline{} + \underline{} = \underline{}$

8. Write how many.

Animals in the Park

 $\underline{}$ $\underline{}$

Fact Families

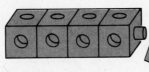

a 6 train

Work with a partner.
Share 6 cubes.

Make a train.　　　Snap it.

Finish the number sentences.

1. Make a 6 train.

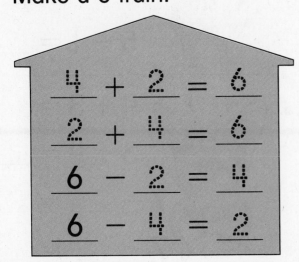

$4 + 2 = 6$

$2 + 4 = 6$

$6 - 2 = 4$

$6 - 4 = 2$

2. Make a 4 train.

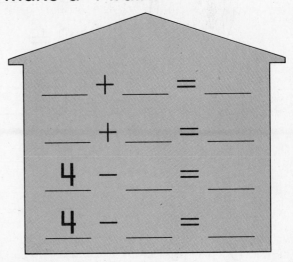

$\underline{} + \underline{} = \underline{}$

$\underline{} + \underline{} = \underline{}$

$4 - \underline{} = \underline{}$

$4 - \underline{} = \underline{}$

3. Make a 5 train.

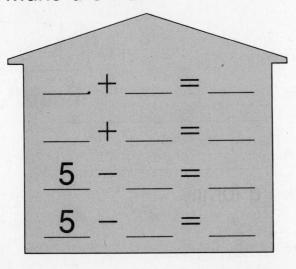

$\underline{} + \underline{} = \underline{}$

$\underline{} + \underline{} = \underline{}$

$5 - \underline{} = \underline{}$

$5 - \underline{} = \underline{}$

4. Make a 3 train.

$\underline{} + \underline{} = \underline{}$

$\underline{} + \underline{} = \underline{}$

$3 - \underline{} = \underline{}$

$3 - \underline{} = \underline{}$

Make a fact family. Add or subtract.

1.
$$5 + 2 = \underline{}$$
$$2 + 5 = \underline{}$$
$$7 - 5 = \underline{}$$
$$7 - 2 = \underline{}$$

2.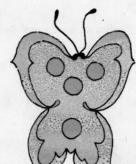
$$3 + 1 = \underline{}$$
$$1 + 3 = \underline{}$$
$$4 - 3 = \underline{}$$
$$4 - 1 = \underline{}$$

3.
$$3 + 2 = \underline{}$$
$$2 + 3 = \underline{}$$
$$5 - 3 = \underline{}$$
$$5 - 2 = \underline{}$$

4.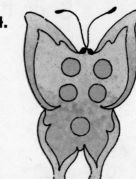
$$4 + 1 = \underline{}$$
$$1 + 4 = \underline{}$$
$$5 - 4 = \underline{}$$
$$5 - 1 = \underline{}$$

5.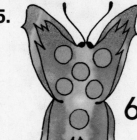
$$5 + 1 = \underline{}$$
$$1 + 5 = \underline{}$$
$$6 - \underline{} = \underline{}$$
$$6 - \underline{} = \underline{}$$

6.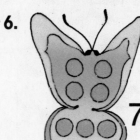
$$4 + 3 = \underline{}$$
$$3 + 4 = \underline{}$$
$$7 - \underline{} = \underline{}$$
$$7 - \underline{} = \underline{}$$

WRITE ABOUT IT

family

7. $4 + 4 = \underline{}$ and $8 - 4 = \underline{}$

These two facts make a small \underline{}.
Write two more facts that make a family.

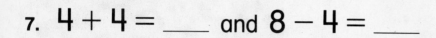
$\underline{3} + \underline{3} = \underline{}$ and $6 - \underline{} = \underline{}$

Name _____

UNDERSTAND
FIND DATA
PLAN
ESTIMATE
SOLVE
CHECK

Problem Solving
Asking a Question

Use counters to show the story.
Ring the question you would ask.
Write the number sentence.

1. Five birds sit   Two fly away.
   on a wire.

 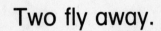  

Ring one.

How many birds are there in all?

How many birds are left?
_____ ◯ _____ = _____

---

2. Four ducks swim   Two more
   in a pond.   join them.

Ring one.

How many ducks are there in all?

How many ducks are left?   _____ ◯ _____ = _____
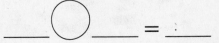

Problem Solving Strategy
Choose the Operation

UNDERSTAND
FIND DATA
PLAN
ESTIMATE
SOLVE
CHECK

Listen to the stories. Think about the action. Match the picture to the action.

Addition
Put together

Subtraction
Take away

WRAP UP

MATH WORDS

Write the number of cubes.
Match the whole to its parts.

whole   parts

1.   ▪

   _____

2.   ▪

   _____

3.   ▪

   _____

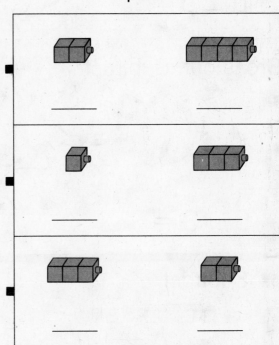

MATH REASONING

4. Look for a pattern.
   Write the next two facts.

$$
\begin{array}{cccc}
6 & 6 & 6 & 6 \\
-0 & -1 & -2 & -3 \\
\hline
6 & 5 & 4 & 3
\end{array}
$$

6   6

Name _____

CHAPTER REVIEW/TEST

Subtract.

1.

$4 - 2 =$ ____

2.

$5 - 1 =$ ____

Cross out. Subtract.

3.

$5 - 3 =$ ____

4.

$$\begin{array}{r} 3 \\ -3 \\ \hline \end{array}$$

5. Subtract.

 6
2  4

$6 - 2 =$ ____ and

$6 - 4 =$ ____

6. Make a fact family.
Add or subtract.

$4 + 2 =$ ____

$2 + 4 =$ ____

$6 -$ ____ $=$ ____

$6 -$ ____ $=$ ____

7. Ring the words that tell the action.

put together

take away

ENRICHMENT
Ordering Events

Number the pictures in order.

A.

B.

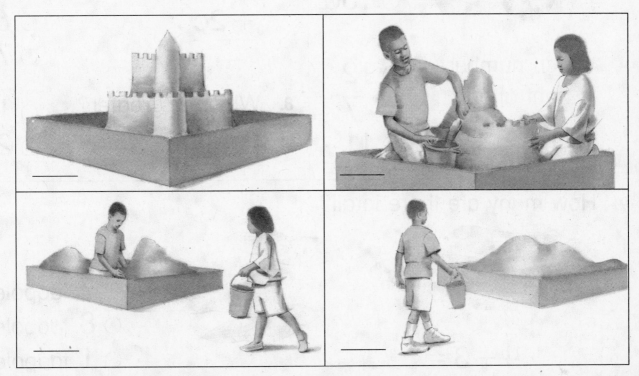

CUMULATIVE REVIEW

How many are there?

1.
   - ○ 10
   - ○ 9
   - ○ 11

2.
   - ○ 16
   - ○ 18
   - ○ 17

3. Count how much money.

   - ○ 14¢
   - ○ 5¢
   - ○ 15¢

4. Which number is right after?

   9, 10, ___
   - ○ 12
   - ○ 7
   - ○ 11

Add.

5.

   $3 + 3 = $ ___
   - ○ 6
   - ○ 5
   - ○ 7

6.

   $\begin{array}{r} 3 \\ + 0 \\ \hline \end{array}$
   - ○ 0
   - ○ 4
   - ○ 3

7. $\begin{array}{r} 4¢ \\ + 2¢ \\ \hline \end{array}$
   - ○ 5¢
   - ○ 6¢
   - ○ 7¢

8. Which is greater?

   12, 20
   - ○ 12
   - ○ 20

9. How many are there in all?

   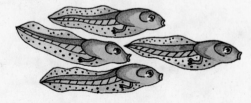 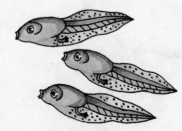

   $4 + 3 = $ ___
   - ○ 7 tadpoles
   - ○ 8 tadpoles
   - ○ 1 tadpoles

5
Addition Facts
Count Ons and Zeros

Workmat

Counting On 1 or 2 and Zero Addition Facts

Start with the number on the brick. $\underline{5} + \underline{2} = \underline{7}$
Add 0 or count on. Use counters.

1. 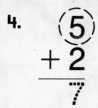 4 $+ \underline{1} =$ _____
   1 more   in all

2. 3 $+ \underline{2} =$ _____
   2 more   in all

3. 5 $+ \underline{0} =$ _____
   0 more   in all

Ring the greater number.
Add 0 or count on.

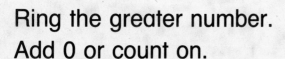

4. $\begin{array}{r} ⑤ \\ +2 \\ \hline 7 \end{array}$
   $\begin{array}{r} 1 \\ +9 \\ \hline \end{array}$
   $\begin{array}{r} 2 \\ +6 \\ \hline \end{array}$
   $\begin{array}{r} 8 \\ +0 \\ \hline \end{array}$
   $\begin{array}{r} 4 \\ +2 \\ \hline \end{array}$
   $\begin{array}{r} 0 \\ +5 \\ \hline \end{array}$

5. $\begin{array}{r} 2 \\ +3 \\ \hline \end{array}$
   $\begin{array}{r} 0 \\ +4 \\ \hline \end{array}$
   $\begin{array}{r} 7 \\ +2 \\ \hline \end{array}$
   $\begin{array}{r} 4 \\ +1 \\ \hline \end{array}$
   $\begin{array}{r} 1 \\ +8 \\ \hline \end{array}$
   $\begin{array}{r} 6 \\ +1 \\ \hline \end{array}$

6. $\begin{array}{r} 1 \\ +2 \\ \hline \end{array}$
   $\begin{array}{r} 5 \\ +1 \\ \hline \end{array}$
   $\begin{array}{r} 2 \\ +8 \\ \hline \end{array}$
   $\begin{array}{r} 7 \\ +0 \\ \hline \end{array}$
   $\begin{array}{r} 7 \\ +1 \\ \hline \end{array}$
   $\begin{array}{r} 0 \\ +9 \\ \hline \end{array}$

FIND THE DATA

7. Count the sums above.
   Tally them here.

Sums of 7	Sums of 9

Name _____

Counting On with Turnaround Facts

Count on to add. Start
with the greater number.
Write the turnaround fact.

$4 + 2 = \underline{6}$

$\underline{2} + \underline{4} = \underline{6}$

two ways,
same sum

1. $2 + 3 = \underline{5}$ and $\underline{} + \underline{} = \underline{}$

2. $8 + 2 = \underline{}$ and $\underline{} + \underline{} = \underline{}$

3. $5 + 1 = \underline{}$ and $\underline{} + \underline{} = \underline{}$

4. $2 + 6 = \underline{}$ and $\underline{} + \underline{} = \underline{}$

5. $4 + 2 = \underline{}$ and $\underline{} + \underline{} = \underline{}$

6. $1 + 9 = \underline{}$ and $\underline{} + \underline{} = \underline{}$

1. Count on to add. Draw lines to match the turnaround facts.

$$\begin{array}{r} 6 \\ + 2 \\ \hline \end{array} \qquad \begin{array}{r} 2 \\ + 9 \\ \hline \end{array} \qquad \begin{array}{r} 2 \\ + 6 \\ \hline \end{array} \qquad \begin{array}{r} 9 \\ + 2 \\ \hline \end{array}$$

Add. Ring if the sum matches the red number.

2.	10	9 + 2	9 + 1	8 + 2	1 + 9
3.	8	2 + 6	1 + 7	5 + 2	6 + 2
4.	9	9 + 0	7 + 2	2 + 4	2 + 7

SHOW WITH COUNTERS

5. Add. Use counters to check.

$$\begin{array}{r} 8 \\ + 2 \\ \hline \end{array} \qquad \begin{array}{r} 1 \\ + 5 \\ \hline \end{array} \qquad \begin{array}{r} 9 \\ + 2 \\ \hline \end{array}$$

Counting On 3

Work in a group. Use your spinner.
Spin. Write that number on the bag.
Count on 3¢. Write how much in all.

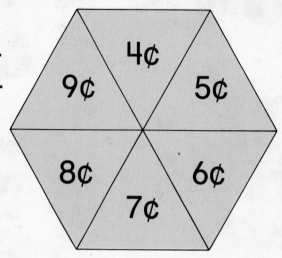

7¢   <u>10</u> ¢
in all

1.

___¢   _____ ¢
in all

2.

___¢   _____ ¢
in all

3.

___¢   _____ ¢
in all

4.

___¢   _____ ¢
in all

5.

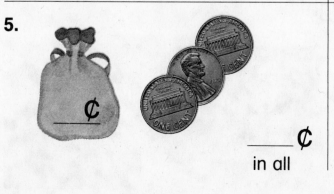

___¢   _____ ¢
in all

6.

___¢   _____ ¢
in all

same as

Add.

1.
$$5¢ + 3¢ = 8¢$$

$$2¢ + 5¢ = \_$$

2.
$$1¢ + 5¢ = \_$$

$$3¢ + 5¢ = \_$$

3.

$2¢$	$2¢$	$3¢$	$4¢$	$7¢$	$0¢$
$+6¢$	$+9¢$	$+0¢$	$+3¢$	$+2¢$	$+5¢$

4.

$7¢$	$5¢$	$3¢$	$2¢$	$4¢$	$6¢$
$+3¢$	$+1¢$	$+6¢$	$+8¢$	$+0¢$	$+2¢$

PROBLEM SOLVING

5. I spent 10¢. Ring what I bought.

Counting On 1, 2, or 3

Start with the greater number. Count on fast.

$$\begin{array}{r} 8 \\ +1 \\ \hline 9 \end{array}$$ ⑨

$$\begin{array}{r} 2 \\ +6 \\ \hline 8 \end{array}$$ 7, 8

$$\begin{array}{r} 9 \\ +3 \\ \hline 12 \end{array}$$ 10, 11, 12

Add. Look at the sums.
Continue the pattern.

1.

$$\begin{array}{r} 6 \\ +2 \\ \hline \end{array}$$
$$\begin{array}{r} 3 \\ +6 \\ \hline \end{array}$$
$$\begin{array}{r} 5 \\ +3 \\ \hline \end{array}$$
$$\begin{array}{r} 2 \\ +7 \\ \hline \end{array}$$
$$\begin{array}{r} 7 \\ +1 \\ \hline \end{array}$$

2.

$$\begin{array}{r} 8 \\ +1 \\ \hline \end{array}$$
$$\begin{array}{r} 3 \\ +7 \\ \hline \end{array}$$
$$\begin{array}{r} 2 \\ +7 \\ \hline \end{array}$$
$$\begin{array}{r} 8 \\ +2 \\ \hline \end{array}$$
$$\begin{array}{r} 1 \\ +8 \\ \hline \end{array}$$

3.

$$\begin{array}{r} 4 \\ +2 \\ \hline \end{array}$$
$$\begin{array}{r} 2 \\ +6 \\ \hline \end{array}$$
$$\begin{array}{r} 1 \\ +5 \\ \hline \end{array}$$
$$\begin{array}{r} 3 \\ +5 \\ \hline \end{array}$$
$$\begin{array}{r} 3 \\ +3 \\ \hline \end{array}$$

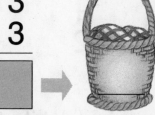

4.

$$\begin{array}{r} 4 \\ +3 \\ \hline \end{array}$$
$$\begin{array}{r} 3 \\ +8 \\ \hline \end{array}$$
$$\begin{array}{r} 5 \\ +2 \\ \hline \end{array}$$
$$\begin{array}{r} 2 \\ +9 \\ \hline \end{array}$$
$$\begin{array}{r} 1 \\ +6 \\ \hline \end{array}$$

Add.

1.
$$\begin{array}{r} 3 \\ +7 \\ \hline \end{array}$$
$$\begin{array}{r} 1 \\ +3 \\ \hline \end{array}$$
$$\begin{array}{r} 0 \\ +4 \\ \hline \end{array}$$
$$\begin{array}{r} 4 \\ +1 \\ \hline \end{array}$$
$$\begin{array}{r} 8 \\ +0 \\ \hline \end{array}$$
$$\begin{array}{r} 7 \\ +3 \\ \hline \end{array}$$

2.
$$\begin{array}{r} 6 \\ +3 \\ \hline \end{array}$$
$$\begin{array}{r} 0 \\ +5 \\ \hline \end{array}$$
$$\begin{array}{r} 7 \\ +2 \\ \hline \end{array}$$
$$\begin{array}{r} 0 \\ +3 \\ \hline \end{array}$$
$$\begin{array}{r} 2 \\ +9 \\ \hline \end{array}$$
$$\begin{array}{r} 8 \\ +2 \\ \hline \end{array}$$

3.
$$\begin{array}{r} 7 \\ +0 \\ \hline \end{array}$$
$$\begin{array}{r} 9 \\ +3 \\ \hline \end{array}$$
$$\begin{array}{r} 5 \\ +2 \\ \hline \end{array}$$
$$\begin{array}{r} 6 \\ +1 \\ \hline \end{array}$$
$$\begin{array}{r} 2 \\ +3 \\ \hline \end{array}$$
$$\begin{array}{r} 4 \\ +2 \\ \hline \end{array}$$

MIDCHAPTER REVIEW/QUIZ

1. Ring the greater number.
   Write the sum.

$$\begin{array}{r} 4 \\ +2 \\ \hline \end{array}$$
$$\begin{array}{r} 1 \\ +6 \\ \hline \end{array}$$
$$\begin{array}{r} 3 \\ +2 \\ \hline \end{array}$$
$$\begin{array}{r} 2 \\ +9 \\ \hline \end{array}$$
$$\begin{array}{r} 8 \\ +1 \\ \hline \end{array}$$
$$\begin{array}{r} 5 \\ +1 \\ \hline \end{array}$$

2. Add. Write the turnaround fact.

$3 + 7 =$ ___ $5 + 2 =$ ___ $2 + 8 =$ ___

and | and | and

___ + ___ = ___ | ___ + ___ = ___ | ___ + ___ = ___

Problem Solving
Understanding the Operations

UNDERSTAND
FIND DATA
PLAN
ESTIMATE
SOLVE
CHECK

Listen to the story. Use counters to
show it. Write + or − in the ○ .
Finish the number sentence.

1. the 🐸 story

$4 \bigcirc 1 = \underline{\hspace{1cm}}$

$\underline{\hspace{1cm}}$ flies

2. the 👧 story

$2 \bigcirc 3 = \underline{\hspace{1cm}}$

$\underline{\hspace{1cm}}$ flowers

3. the 🐱 story

$2 \bigcirc 4 = \underline{\hspace{1cm}}$

$\underline{\hspace{1cm}}$ rabbits

Informal Algebra

Work with a partner. Listen to the story.
Use counters to show it.
Write the numbers in the boxes.
Ring the greater sum.

1. the 🐻 story

   3 + ☐

   3 + ☐

2. the 🐿 story

   7 + ☐

   7 + ☐

3. the 🐿 story

   6 + ☐

   6 + ☐

4. the 🐰 story

   4 + ☐

   4 + ☐

Fact Practice and Probability

Toss two number cubes. Add the numbers.
Mark the sum on the graph.

$4 + 3 = \underline{7}$

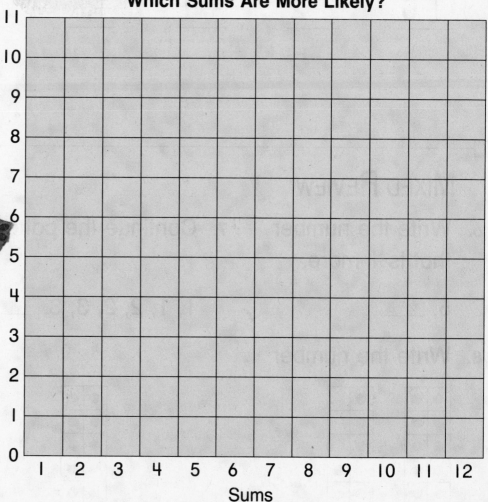

Which Sums Are More Likely?

Sums

Add.

1. $3 + 6 = \underline{9}$ $4 + 2 = \underline{}$

2. $9 + 3 = \underline{}$ $0 + 9 = \underline{}$

3. $7 + 1 = \underline{}$ $5 + 2 = \underline{}$

4.
$\begin{array}{r}3\\+4\\\hline\end{array}$
$\begin{array}{r}6\\+0\\\hline\end{array}$
$\begin{array}{r}3\\+8\\\hline\end{array}$
$\begin{array}{r}5\\+3\\\hline\end{array}$
$\begin{array}{r}3\\+0\\\hline\end{array}$
$\begin{array}{r}2\\+9\\\hline\end{array}$

5.
$\begin{array}{r}5\\+0\\\hline\end{array}$
$\begin{array}{r}8\\+2\\\hline\end{array}$
$\begin{array}{r}4\\+1\\\hline\end{array}$
$\begin{array}{r}0\\+7\\\hline\end{array}$
$\begin{array}{r}3\\+3\\\hline\end{array}$
$\begin{array}{r}8\\+0\\\hline\end{array}$

MIXED REVIEW

6. Write the number that is 1 more.

5, _____

7. Continue the pattern.

1, 1, 2, 2, 3, 3, _____, _____, _____

8. Write the number.

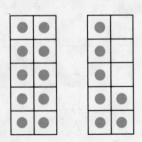   _____

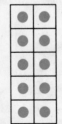   _____

Fact Practice and Graphing

Add.

1. $\begin{array}{r} 6 \\ +3 \\ \hline \end{array}$ $\begin{array}{r} 2 \\ +5 \\ \hline \end{array}$ $\begin{array}{r} 9 \\ +2 \\ \hline \end{array}$ $\begin{array}{r} 6 \\ +0 \\ \hline \end{array}$ $\begin{array}{r} 1 \\ +8 \\ \hline \end{array}$ $\begin{array}{r} 5 \\ +2 \\ \hline \end{array}$

2. $\begin{array}{r} 9 \\ +0 \\ \hline \end{array}$ $\begin{array}{r} 7 \\ +2 \\ \hline \end{array}$ $\begin{array}{r} 3 \\ +6 \\ \hline \end{array}$ $\begin{array}{r} 0 \\ +7 \\ \hline \end{array}$ $\begin{array}{r} 8 \\ +2 \\ \hline \end{array}$ $\begin{array}{r} 3 \\ +6 \\ \hline \end{array}$

3. $\begin{array}{r} 2 \\ +7 \\ \hline \end{array}$ $\begin{array}{r} 2 \\ +9 \\ \hline \end{array}$ $\begin{array}{r} 3 \\ +4 \\ \hline \end{array}$ $\begin{array}{r} 7 \\ +3 \\ \hline \end{array}$ $\begin{array}{r} 5 \\ +2 \\ \hline \end{array}$ $\begin{array}{r} 3 \\ +9 \\ \hline \end{array}$

4. Look above.   Tally sums of 7. _____

    Tally sums of 9. _____   Tally sums of 11. _____

5. Color the graph to show the data.

How Many of Each Sum?

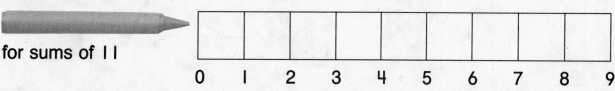

for sums of 7

for sums of 9

for sums of 11

0 1 2 3 4 5 6 7 8 9

Add.

1. $3 + 3 =$ ___ $8 + 2 =$ ___ $0 + 6 =$ ___

2. $2 + 9 =$ ___ $9 + 3 =$ ___ $7 + 3 =$ ___

3. $5 + 3 =$ ___ $2 + 4 =$ ___ $0 + 8 =$ ___

4. $3 + 7 =$ ___ $2 + 8 =$ ___ $6 + 3 =$ ___

5. Look above. Tally sums of 6. _____

   Tally sums of 8. _____   Tally sums of 10. _____

6. Color the graph to show the data.

How Many of Each Sum?

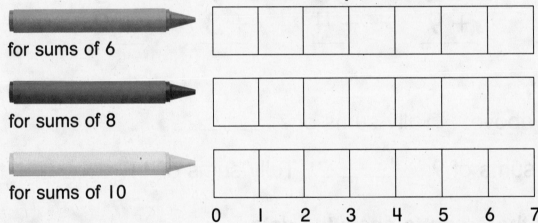

for sums of 6

for sums of 8

for sums of 10

0   1   2   3   4   5   6   7

USE MENTAL MATH

7. Work with a partner. Use punchout 🐝.
   Put one 🐝 on the ☐.
   Say the sum.

☐ + 2 + 1 = Say the sum.

Name _____

Problem Solving
Telling a Story

UNDERSTAND
FIND DATA
PLAN
ESTIMATE
SOLVE
CHECK

Tell a story about the picture.
Finish the number sentence for the story.

1.

___ + ___ = ___

2.

___ − ___ = ___

3.

___ − ___ = ___

4.

___ + ___ = ___

Problem Solving Strategy
Guess and Check

UNDERSTAND
FIND DATA
PLAN
ESTIMATE
SOLVE
CHECK

Guess how many bikes and trikes are in each race. Write the number in the guess box. Cut out the bikes and trikes. Use them to check. Paste.

A bike has two wheels.

Bike and Trike Races

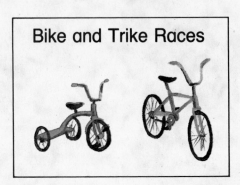

A trike has three wheels.

1. **7 Wheel Race**

Guess	
Check. Paste Here.	

2. **11 Wheel Race**

Guess	
Check. Paste here.	

Chapter 5

WRAP UP

MATH WORDS

Match the turnaround
facts. Write the sums.

1. $3 + 2 =$ _____ .

2. $2 + 4 =$ _____ .

3. $1 + 5 =$ _____ .

4. $4 + 1 =$ _____ .

5. $2 + 5 =$ _____ .

. $4 + 2 =$ _____

. $1 + 4 =$ _____

. $5 + 2 =$ _____

. $2 + 3 =$ _____

. $5 + 1 =$ _____

MATH REASONING

Finish the number sentences.
Use the numbers on
the balloons.

6. _____ $+ 0 =$ _____

7. _____ $+ 1 =$ _____

8. _____ $+ 2 =$ _____

CHAPTER REVIEW/TEST

1. Ring the greater number. Add.

$$\begin{array}{r} 5 \\ +2 \\ \hline \end{array} \qquad \begin{array}{r} 1 \\ +7 \\ \hline \end{array} \qquad \begin{array}{r} 6 \\ +0 \\ \hline \end{array} \qquad \begin{array}{r} 8 \\ +1 \\ \hline \end{array} \qquad \begin{array}{r} 0 \\ +9 \\ \hline \end{array} \qquad \begin{array}{r} 2 \\ +8 \\ \hline \end{array}$$

Count on to add.
Write the turnaround fact.

2. $6 + 2 =$ ___ and ___ $+$ ___ $=$ ___

3. $1 + 9 =$ ___ and ___ $+$ ___ $=$ ___

Count on 3¢. Write how much in all.

4.  ___

5.  ___

6. Add.

$$\begin{array}{r} 0 \\ +7 \\ \hline \end{array} \qquad \begin{array}{r} 9 \\ +2 \\ \hline \end{array} \qquad \begin{array}{r} 5 \\ +1 \\ \hline \end{array} \qquad \begin{array}{r} 4¢ \\ +3¢ \\ \hline \end{array} \qquad \begin{array}{r} 6¢ \\ +3¢ \\ \hline \end{array} \qquad \begin{array}{r} 8¢ \\ +1¢ \\ \hline \end{array}$$

7. Tom spent 8¢.
Ring what he bought.

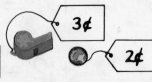

Name _____

ENRICHMENT
Missing Addends

Count on to find how many are
in the bag. Write the missing
number. Then draw to show it.

1. 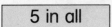 5 in all

$$\underline{2} + 3 = 5$$

2. 3 in all

$$1 + \underline{} = 3$$

3. 8 in all

$$5 + \underline{} = 8$$

4. 7 in all

$$\underline{} + 6 = 7$$

5. 10 in all

$$\underline{} + 7 = 10$$

6. 6 in all

$$5 + \underline{} = 6$$

Name _____

CUMULATIVE REVIEW

Add.

1.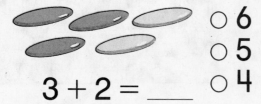

$3 + 2 =$ ___

○ 6
○ 5
○ 4

2.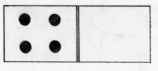

$4 + 0 =$ ___

○ 7
○ 4
○ 0

3.

1
+3

○ 5
○ 6
○ 4

4.

2¢
+1¢

○ 4¢
○ 5¢
○ 3¢

Subtract.

5.

$6 - 2 =$ ___

○ 3
○ 4
○ 5

6.

$4 - 4 =$ ___

○ 4
○ 1
○ 0

7.

7
−5

○ 4
○ 2
○ 3

8.

7
−2

○ 4
○ 3
○ 5

9. Choose the question you would ask.

Three chimps are playing.
Two more join them.

○ How many chimps are left?

○ How many chimps are playing in all?

○ How many chimps go away?

6
Addition Facts
Sums to 12

Name _____

Small Doubles

Use cubes to show each double
fact. Add and match.

1.

| 4 + 4 = $\underset{\text{(8)}}{}$ | 6 + 6 = ___ | 5 + 5 = ___ |

  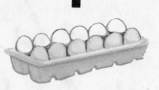

Ring the double facts. Then add all.

2.
$$\begin{array}{cccccc} \boxed{\begin{array}{c}5\\+5\end{array}} & \begin{array}{c}3\\+4\end{array} & \begin{array}{c}2\\+2\end{array} & \begin{array}{c}1\\+7\end{array} & \begin{array}{c}6\\+6\end{array} & \begin{array}{c}4\\+4\end{array} \end{array}$$

3.
$$\begin{array}{cccccc} \begin{array}{c}6\\+2\end{array} & \begin{array}{c}1\\+1\end{array} & \begin{array}{c}2\\+7\end{array} & \begin{array}{c}6\\+6\end{array} & \begin{array}{c}3\\+9\end{array} & \begin{array}{c}3\\+3\end{array} \end{array}$$

4.
$$\begin{array}{cccccc} \begin{array}{c}6\\+6\end{array} & \begin{array}{c}3\\+6\end{array} & \begin{array}{c}5\\+5\end{array} & \begin{array}{c}2\\+8\end{array} & \begin{array}{c}4\\+4\end{array} & \begin{array}{c}5\\+2\end{array} \end{array}$$

WRITE ABOUT IT

5. Write the answer.

4 + 4 = ___ is the _ _ _ _ _ _ _ _ fact.

spider

Sums of 10

Work with a partner.

Share punchouts $\boxed{1}$ to $\boxed{9}$.

Share 10 two-color counters.

Take turns. Pick a card.
Use the number to write a
10 sum. Your partner uses
counters and ▥ to check it.

Write 10 sums here.

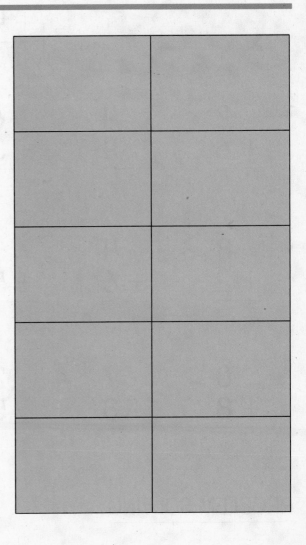

1.
$$\begin{array}{r} 6 \\ +\ 4 \\ \hline 10 \end{array}$$
  +   +   +   +   +

2.
  +   +   +   +   +   +

Add. Ring sums of 10.

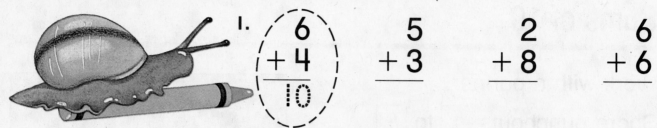

1. (6 + 4 = 10)　　5 + 3　　2 + 8　　6 + 6

2. 2 + 6　　4 + 4　　6 + 3　　2 + 9　　3 + 7　　3 + 9

3. 8 + 2　　4 + 6　　5 + 5　　8 + 3　　1 + 9　　9 + 0

4. 0 + 8　　7 + 3　　2 + 5　　2 + 7　　9 + 1　　3 + 4

PROBLEM SOLVING

5. Maria spent 10¢. What two things did she buy? Ring with 🖍.

6. Ali spent 12¢. What two things did he buy? Ring with 🖍.

4¢　5¢　6¢　3¢　6¢

Fact Practice

Add.

3. $4 + 4 = $ ___

2. $3 + 7 = $ ___

$0 + 2 = $ ___

1. $6 + 4 = 10$

$3 + 3 = $ ___

$6 + 6 = $ ___

$5 + 5 = $ ___

$4 + 6 = $ ___

$3 + 8 = $ ___

$0 + 0 = $ ___

$2 + 2 = $ ___

$9 + 1 = $ ___

4.
$$\begin{array}{cccccc}5 & 6 & 7 & 3 & 5 & 3 \\ +2 & +2 & +2 & +4 & +3 & +6\end{array}$$

5.
$$\begin{array}{c}1 \\ +6\end{array}$$

The sums in 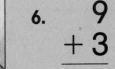 make a number pattern.

6.
$$\begin{array}{c}9 \\ +3\end{array}$$

7. Write the number pattern in .

___ , ___ , ___ , ___ , ___ , ___

Ring the ways to make the sum.

1. **10** (5 + 5) 3 + 7 6 + 3 6 + 4

2. **12** 3 + 9 6 + 6 8 + 3 2 + 9

3. **8** 4 + 4 6 + 2 5 + 3 2 + 7

4. **9** 6 + 2 1 + 8 0 + 9 3 + 6

5. **10** 4 + 6 2 + 8 5 + 5 3 + 7

Add.

6.
$$\begin{array}{r} 2 \\ +3 \\ \hline \end{array} \quad \begin{array}{r} 3 \\ +3 \\ \hline \end{array} \quad \begin{array}{r} 3 \\ +8 \\ \hline \end{array} \quad \begin{array}{r} 6 \\ +6 \\ \hline \end{array} \quad \begin{array}{r} 3 \\ +6 \\ \hline \end{array} \quad \begin{array}{r} 1 \\ +5 \\ \hline \end{array}$$

MAKE AN ESTIMATE

7. Ring sums in ☆6☆ that are close to 10.

8. Write another sum that is close to 10.

$$\begin{array}{r} \underline{} \\ + \\ \hline \end{array}$$

Problem Solving
Understanding the Operations

Listen to the story. Use counters to
show it. Finish the number sentence.

1. the story

$2 \bigcirc 4 = $ ___

___ lizards

2. the story

$4 \bigcirc 2 = $ ___

___ caterpillars

3. the story

$6 \bigcirc 6 = $ ___

___ ants

4. the story

$7 \bigcirc 3 = $ ___

___ grasshoppers

Mental Math

Use punchouts $\boxed{0}$ to $\boxed{12}$.
Show each clue.
Write the number.

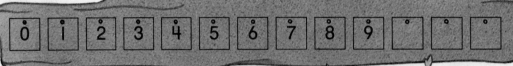

Turn over cards you do not want.

less than
5 + 5

1.

I am less than 5 + 5.

I am greater than 4 + 4.

I am ___9___.

2.

I am greater than 6 + 4.

I am less than 9 + 3.

I am ____.

3.

I am the sum of a double.
I am greater than 9.
I am less than 12.
I am ____.

4.

I am on a 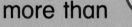.
I am less than 3 + 7.
I am greater than 8.

I am ____.

5.

I am
more than .
I am less than 6¢ + 6¢.

I am ____ ¢.

Doubles Plus One

Add.

I more

1. $\begin{array}{r} 4 \\ +4 \\ \hline 8 \end{array}$ $\begin{array}{r} 4 \\ +5 \\ \hline 9 \end{array}$ $\begin{array}{r} 5 \\ +4 \\ \hline 9 \end{array}$

I more

2. $\begin{array}{r} 5 \\ +5 \\ \hline \end{array}$ $\begin{array}{r} 5 \\ +6 \\ \hline \end{array}$ $\begin{array}{r} 6 \\ +5 \\ \hline \end{array}$

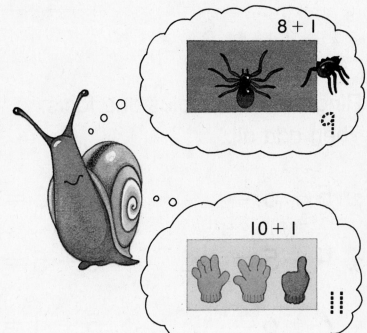

8 + 1

9

10 + 1

11

Ring the double-plus-one facts.
Then add all.

3. $\boxed{4 + 5} =$ ___ $5 + 4 =$ ___ $5 + 2 =$ ___

4. $0 + 5 =$ ___ $5 + 6 =$ ___ $5 + 5 =$ ___

5. $5 + 6 =$ ___ $7 + 3 =$ ___ $5 + 4 =$ ___

6. $6 + 4 =$ ___ $3 + 1 =$ ___ $4 + 1 =$ ___

7. $4 + 5 =$ ___ $6 + 6 =$ ___ $6 + 5 =$ ___

Write the double that helps. Add.

1.
$$5 + 4 = 9$$ $$4 + 4 = 8$$

$$6 + 5$$ $$+$$

$$4 + 5$$ $$+$$

Ring the double-plus-one facts.
Then add all.

2. $(5 + 6) =$ ___ $2 + 8 =$ ___ $9 + 0 =$ ___

3. $4 + 5 =$ ___ $6 + 5 =$ ___ $7 + 2 =$ ___

4. $6 + 6 =$ ___ $5 + 4 =$ ___ $5 + 6 =$ ___

5. $4 + 4 =$ ___ $3 + 6 =$ ___ $6 + 4 =$ ___

FIND THE DATA   DATA BANK

Data Bank (See page 398.)

6. How far is it from Tip's house to Rip's? ___ blocks

7. How far is it from Pip's house to Kip's? ___ blocks

8. How far is it from Flip's house to Pip's? ___ blocks

Fact Practice

Match.

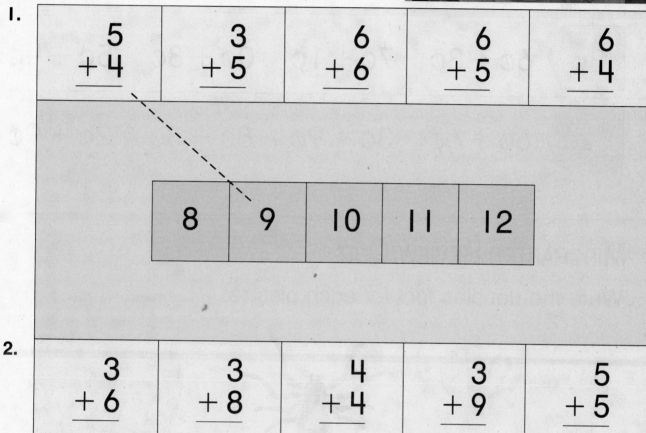

1.

$\begin{array}{r}5\\+4\\\hline\end{array}$	$\begin{array}{r}3\\+5\\\hline\end{array}$	$\begin{array}{r}6\\+6\\\hline\end{array}$	$\begin{array}{r}6\\+5\\\hline\end{array}$	$\begin{array}{r}6\\+4\\\hline\end{array}$

8	9	10	11	12

2.

$\begin{array}{r}3\\+6\\\hline\end{array}$	$\begin{array}{r}3\\+8\\\hline\end{array}$	$\begin{array}{r}4\\+4\\\hline\end{array}$	$\begin{array}{r}3\\+9\\\hline\end{array}$	$\begin{array}{r}5\\+5\\\hline\end{array}$

Add.

3.

$\begin{array}{r}7¢\\+3¢\\\hline\end{array}$	$\begin{array}{r}6¢\\+2¢\\\hline\end{array}$	$\begin{array}{r}1¢\\+4¢\\\hline\end{array}$	$\begin{array}{r}9¢\\+3¢\\\hline\end{array}$	$\begin{array}{r}6¢\\+5¢\\\hline\end{array}$	$\begin{array}{r}1¢\\+6¢\\\hline\end{array}$

4.

$\begin{array}{r}5¢\\+4¢\\\hline\end{array}$	$\begin{array}{r}0¢\\+6¢\\\hline\end{array}$	$\begin{array}{r}4¢\\+3¢\\\hline\end{array}$	$\begin{array}{r}8¢\\+2¢\\\hline\end{array}$	$\begin{array}{r}2¢\\+5¢\\\hline\end{array}$	$\begin{array}{r}2¢\\+9¢\\\hline\end{array}$

Cross out all the ways that
do not make the sum.

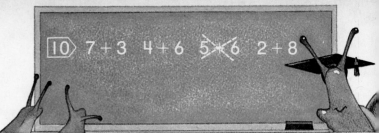

1.
 10¢ ⟩ 7¢ + 3¢   4¢ + 6¢   5̶¢̶ ̶+̶ ̶6̶¢̶   2¢ + 8¢

2.
8¢ ⟩ 6¢ + 3¢   7¢ + 1¢   0¢ + 8¢   5¢ + 4¢

3.
12¢ ⟩ 6¢ + 6¢   3¢ + 9¢   8¢ + 3¢   2¢ + 9¢

Midchapter Review/Quiz

1. Write the doubles fact for each picture.

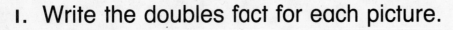

___ + ___ = ___   ___ + ___ = ___   ___ + ___ = ___

2. Add. Ring sums of 10.

3	4	7	8	5	1
+ 5	+ 6	+ 3	+ 1	+ 5	+ 9

3. Add.

5 + 4 = ___   2 + 3 = ___   6 + 5 = ___

Name _____

Making 10, Adding Extra

Put in 7. Then put in as many of the 5 as you can.

You have 10 and 2 extra. That makes 12.

$7 + 5 =$ ___12___

Work with a partner.
Use counters and ▦.
Put in counters for the
greater number. Use the
other number to make
10 and add extra.

1. $\begin{array}{r} 7 \\ +4 \\ \hline \end{array}$ $\begin{array}{r} 4 \\ +7 \\ \hline \end{array}$

2. $\begin{array}{r} 5 \\ +7 \\ \hline \end{array}$ $\begin{array}{r} 7 \\ +5 \\ \hline \end{array}$

3. $\begin{array}{r} 8 \\ +4 \\ \hline \end{array}$ $\begin{array}{r} 4 \\ +8 \\ \hline \end{array}$

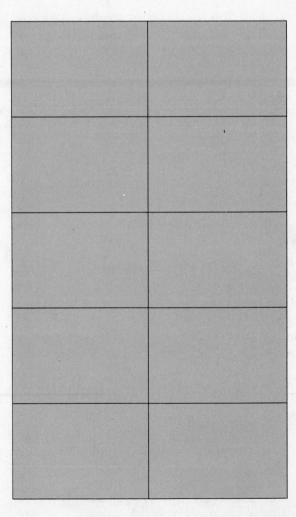

1. Draw ◯ to show the fact.
   Finish the number sentence.

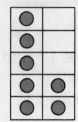   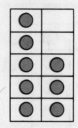   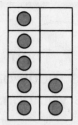

$7 + 5 = $ ___ $8 + 4 = $ ___ $7 + 4 = $ ___

Add.

2.
$$\begin{array}{r} 8 \\ +4 \\ \hline \end{array} \qquad \begin{array}{r} 5 \\ +2 \\ \hline \end{array} \qquad \begin{array}{r} 6 \\ +5 \\ \hline \end{array} \qquad \begin{array}{r} 8 \\ +3 \\ \hline \end{array} \qquad \begin{array}{r} 4 \\ +7 \\ \hline \end{array} \qquad \begin{array}{r} 3 \\ +5 \\ \hline \end{array}$$

3.
$$\begin{array}{r} 4 \\ +6 \\ \hline \end{array} \qquad \begin{array}{r} 7 \\ +5 \\ \hline \end{array} \qquad \begin{array}{r} 0 \\ +2 \\ \hline \end{array} \qquad \begin{array}{r} 7 \\ +4 \\ \hline \end{array} \qquad \begin{array}{r} 2 \\ +9 \\ \hline \end{array} \qquad \begin{array}{r} 6 \\ +6 \\ \hline \end{array}$$

4.
$$\begin{array}{r} 5 \\ +7 \\ \hline \end{array} \qquad \begin{array}{r} 5 \\ +6 \\ \hline \end{array} \qquad \begin{array}{r} 2 \\ +8 \\ \hline \end{array} \qquad \begin{array}{r} 4 \\ +4 \\ \hline \end{array} \qquad \begin{array}{r} 8 \\ +4 \\ \hline \end{array} \qquad \begin{array}{r} 5 \\ +5 \\ \hline \end{array}$$

MIXED REVIEW

5. Subtract.

$5 - 2 = $ ___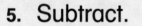

6. Cross out. Subtract.

$3 - 2 = $ ___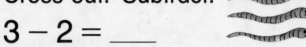

7. Finish the fact family.

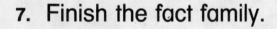 $2 + 1 = $ ___ $3 - 1 = $ ___

   $1 + 2 = $ ___ $3 - 2 = $ ___

More Practice, page 415, set B   Chapter 6

Adding Three Numbers

Work in a group. Share
punchouts $\boxed{0}$ to $\boxed{4}$.
Take turns. Pick a card.
Write the number below.
Add. Use counters to help.

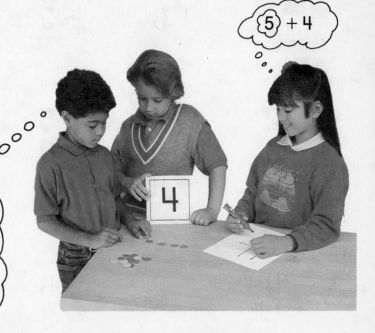

$$\begin{array}{r} 3 \\ 2 \\ + 4 \\ \hline 9 \end{array} \quad 5$$

1.
$$\begin{array}{r} 3 \\ 2 \\ + \\ \hline \end{array} \quad 5 \qquad \begin{array}{r} 2 \\ 3 \\ + \\ \hline \end{array} \quad 5 \qquad \begin{array}{r} 4 \\ 2 \\ + \\ \hline \end{array} \quad 6 \qquad \begin{array}{r} 1 \\ 5 \\ + \\ \hline \end{array} \quad 6 \qquad \begin{array}{r} 1 \\ 3 \\ + \\ \hline \end{array} \quad 4$$

2.
$$\begin{array}{r} 2 \\ 4 \\ + \\ \hline \end{array} \qquad \begin{array}{r} 2 \\ 2 \\ + \\ \hline \end{array} \qquad \begin{array}{r} 5 \\ 1 \\ + \\ \hline \end{array} \qquad \begin{array}{r} 3 \\ 2 \\ + \\ \hline \end{array} \qquad \begin{array}{r} 4 \\ 0 \\ + \\ \hline \end{array} \qquad \begin{array}{r} 4 \\ 1 \\ + \\ \hline \end{array}$$

3.
$$\begin{array}{r} 3 \\ 3 \\ + \\ \hline \end{array} \qquad \begin{array}{r} 6 \\ 0 \\ + \\ \hline \end{array} \qquad \begin{array}{r} 4 \\ 2 \\ + \\ \hline \end{array} \qquad \begin{array}{r} 3 \\ 1 \\ + \\ \hline \end{array} \qquad \begin{array}{r} 1 \\ 5 \\ + \\ \hline \end{array} \qquad \begin{array}{r} 3 \\ 2 \\ + \\ \hline \end{array}$$

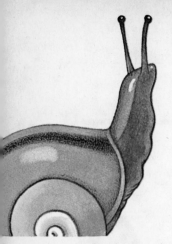

Add.

1.
```
  4      5      5      4      3
  1      5      1      0      1
+ 0    + 2    + 4    + 5    + 5
```

2.
```
  2      4      5      6      6      3
  3      1      0      6      3      2
+ 4    + 4    + 6    + 0    + 3    + 5
```

3.
```
  4      2      3      5      2      4
  4      2      3      1      4      2
+ 2    + 5    + 6    + 5    + 2    + 5
```

TRY A CALCULATOR

4. Guess one number that could go in all the boxes.

$$\boxed{} + \boxed{} + \boxed{} = 18$$

my guess _____

Use a to check your guess.

Write the correct number in each box.

More Practice, page 415, set C   Chapter 6

Problem Solving
Showing Data

UNDERSTAND
FIND DATA
PLAN
ESTIMATE
SOLVE
CHECK

Draw more or cross out to show the story.

1. Ed has 6 🐛.
    Bay has 6 🐛.

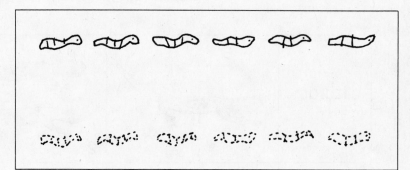

2. Fay had 8 ✹.
    She lost 2 ✹.

3. Bill has 4 🐞.
    Ty has 2 🐞.
    Clara has 4 🐞.

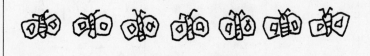

4. Li-Chen
    had 7 🦋.
    She gave
    away 3 🦋.

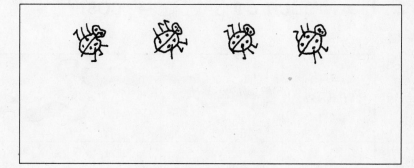

Problem Solving Stategy
Make a Table

Use the table to answer the question.

1. How much do 3 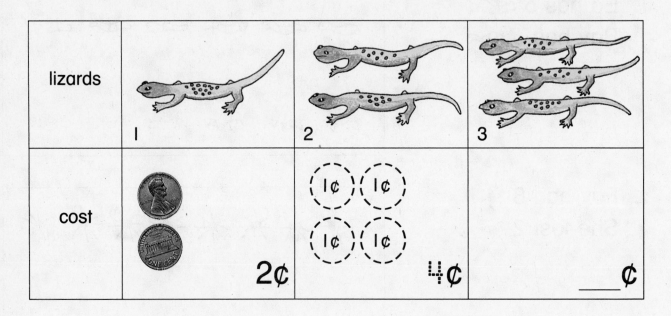 cost?

lizards 2¢ each

lizards	1	2	3
cost	2¢	4¢	___¢

2. How much do 3 worms cost?

worms 3¢ each

worms	1	2	3
cost	3¢	6¢	___¢

More Practice, page 416, set A   Chapter 6

WRAP UP

MATH WORDS

Ring examples of each.

1.	doubles	$5 + 3$	$4 + 4$	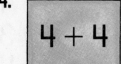
2.	doubles plus one		$3 + 4$	$6 + 5$
3.	sums of 10	$6 + 4$		$3 + 7$

MATH REASONING

Ring the fact that has the greater sum. Tell how you know.

4. $4 + 4$ or $5 + 5$

5. $3 + 3$ or $2 + 2$

6. $3 + 4$ or $3 + 3$

7. $2 + 2$ or $2 + 3$

8. $2 + 3$ or $2 + 4$

9. $3 + 5$ or $4 + 3$

CHAPTER REVIEW/TEST

1. Ring double facts. Then add all.

$$\begin{array}{r} 3 \\ +7 \\ \hline \end{array} \qquad \begin{array}{r} 6 \\ +6 \\ \hline \end{array} \qquad \begin{array}{r} 7 \\ +4 \\ \hline \end{array} \qquad \begin{array}{r} 1 \\ +9 \\ \hline \end{array} \qquad \begin{array}{r} 4 \\ +4 \\ \hline \end{array} \qquad \begin{array}{r} 5 \\ +5 \\ \hline \end{array}$$

2. Add. Ring sums of 10.

$$\begin{array}{r} 5 \\ +6 \\ \hline \end{array} \qquad \begin{array}{r} 5 \\ +5 \\ \hline \end{array} \qquad \begin{array}{r} 2 \\ +8 \\ \hline \end{array} \qquad \begin{array}{r} 7 \\ +3 \\ \hline \end{array} \qquad \begin{array}{r} 5 \\ +7 \\ \hline \end{array} \qquad \begin{array}{r} 4 \\ +7 \\ \hline \end{array}$$

3. Ring double-plus-one facts.
Then add all.

$$\begin{array}{r} 4 \\ +5 \\ \hline \end{array} \qquad \begin{array}{r} 5 \\ +6 \\ \hline \end{array} \qquad \begin{array}{r} 4 \\ +6 \\ \hline \end{array} \qquad \begin{array}{r} 8 \\ +4 \\ \hline \end{array} \qquad \begin{array}{r} 9 \\ +1 \\ \hline \end{array} \qquad \begin{array}{r} 6 \\ +5 \\ \hline \end{array}$$

4. Add.

$$\begin{array}{r} 5 \\ 2 \\ +4 \\ \hline \end{array} \qquad \begin{array}{r} 4 \\ 1 \\ +5 \\ \hline \end{array} \qquad \begin{array}{r} 2 \\ 4 \\ +5 \\ \hline \end{array} \qquad \begin{array}{r} 5 \\ 1 \\ +6 \\ \hline \end{array} \qquad \begin{array}{r} 3 \\ 4 \\ +5 \\ \hline \end{array} \qquad \begin{array}{r} 4 \\ 3 \\ +4 \\ \hline \end{array}$$

5. Draw more or cross out to show the story.

Sally has 4 .

Tony has 3 .

Name _____

ENRICHMENT
Comparing Quantity

Work with a partner. Use counters.
Compare the number in each group.
Tell and write how many more or fewer.
Ring the one with more or fewer.

1.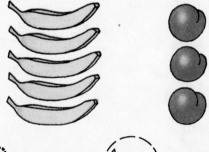

__2__ more

2.

_____ more

3.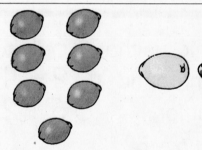

_____ more

4.

_____ fewer

5.

_____ fewer

6.

_____ fewer

CUMULATIVE REVIEW

Subtract.

1.

   5 − 2 = ___
   - ○ 4
   - ○ 1
   - ○ 3

2.

   6 − 2 = ___
   - ○ 1
   - ○ 4
   - ○ 5

3.

   6 − 4 = ___
   - ○ 1
   - ○ 2
   - ○ 3

4.
   ```
     4
   − 0
   ```
   - ○ 4
   - ○ 3
   - ○ 0

Count on to add.

5. 4 + 2 = ___
   - ○ 7
   - ○ 6
   - ○ 5

6. 4¢ + 3¢ = ___
   - ○ 8¢
   - ○ 7¢
   - ○ 9¢

7.
   ```
     3
   + 0
   ```
   - ○ 4
   - ○ 0
   - ○ 3

8. Which is the turnaround fact for 2 + 6 = 8?
   - ○ 6 + 3 = 9
   - ○ 2 + 4 = 6
   - ○ 6 + 2 = 8

9. Choose the correct number sentence.

   - ○ 3 − 1 = 2
   - ○ 4 + 1 = 3
   - ○ 4 − 3 = 1

7
Measurement

Workmat

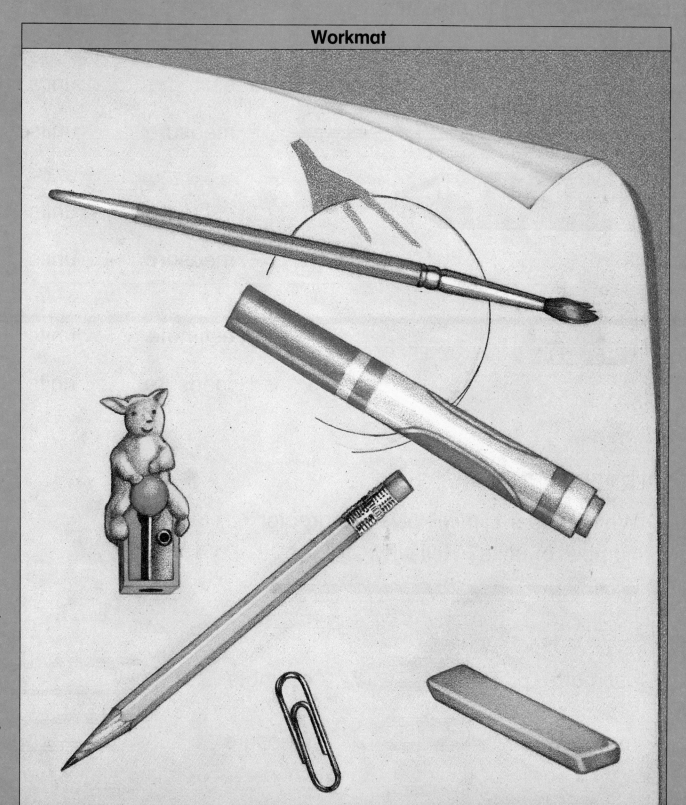

Estimating and Measuring Length
Nonstandard Units

Estimate how many units long.
Use  to measure.

1.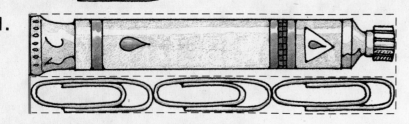

estimate ____ units

measure ____ units

2.

estimate ____ units

measure ____ units

3.

estimate ____ units

measure ____ units

TALK ABOUT IT

5. Which paper clip will give the greater
number of units? Tell why.

estimate ____    estimate ____

measure ____ 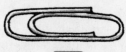   measure ____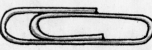

Estimating and Measuring Length
Inches

Cut out the [inch]. Estimate how many inches. Then measure.

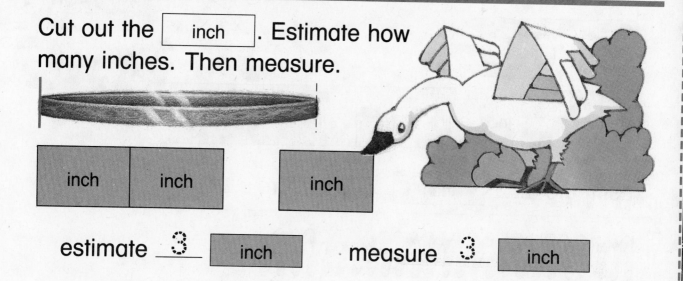

| inch | inch | | inch |

estimate ⫶3⫶ [inch]   measure ⫶3⫶ [inch]

1.

estimate ____ [inch]   measure ____ [inch]

2.

estimate ____ [inch]   measure ____ [inch]

3.

estimate ____ [inch]   measure ____ [inch]

4.

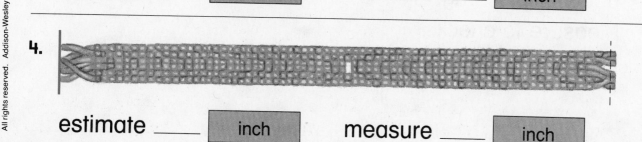

estimate ____ [inch]   measure ____ [inch]

Paste 5 | inch | on cardboard.
Estimate how many inches long.
Then measure with your inch strip.

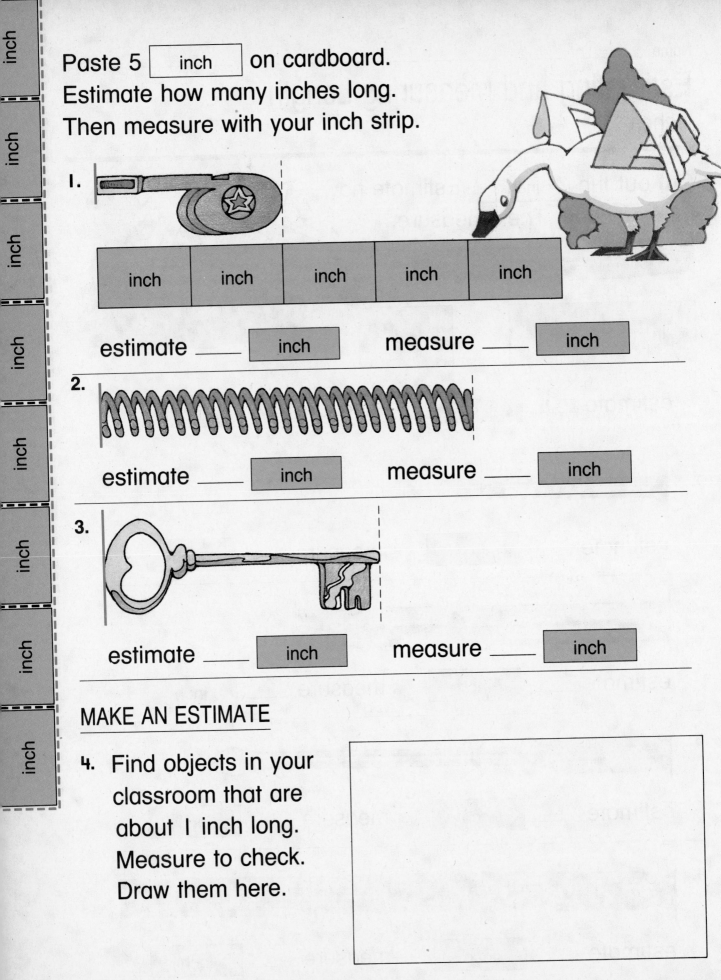

1.

| inch | inch | inch | inch | inch |

estimate _____ | inch | measure _____ | inch |

2.

estimate _____ | inch | measure _____ | inch |

3.

estimate _____ | inch | measure _____ | inch |

MAKE AN ESTIMATE

4. Find objects in your
   classroom that are
   about 1 inch long.
   Measure to check.
   Draw them here.

Name _____

Using a Ruler
Inches

Use your punchout inch (in.) ruler.
Measure. Write the length.

__3__ inches

inch ruler | 1 | 2 | 3

1.

Place ruler here.

_____ inches

2.

_____ inches

3.

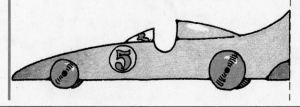

_____ inches

4.

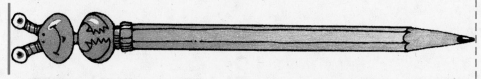

_____ inches

5.

_____ inches

Use your ruler. Measure.
Write the length or height.

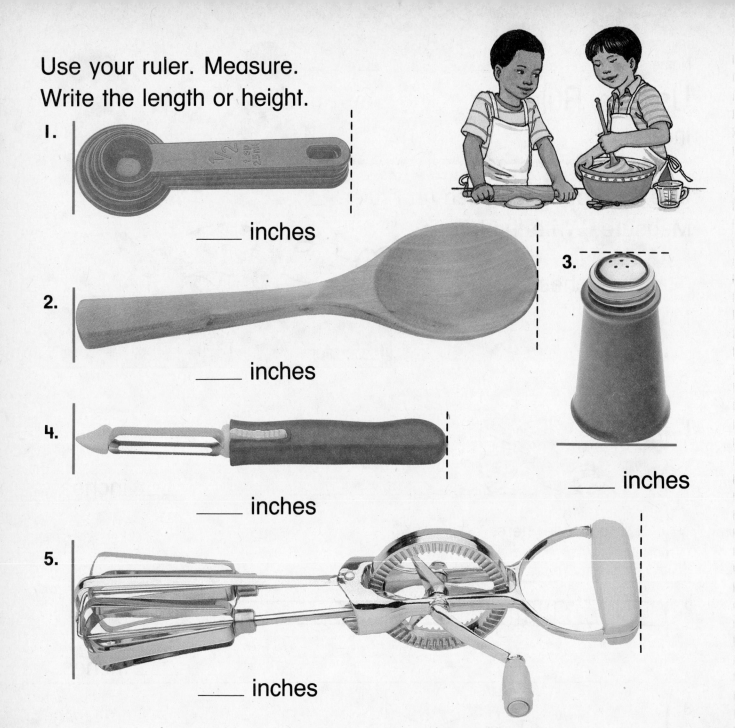

1. _____ inches

2. _____ inches

3. _____ inches

4. _____ inches

5. _____ inches

MIXED REVIEW

6. Count back.

8, 7, _____, _____   12, _____, _____, _____

7. Add.

4 + 4 = _____   6 + 6 = _____   5 + 5 = _____

Using a Ruler
Feet

A foot (ft) ruler is 12 inches long. Work in a group. Use a foot ruler. Cut pieces of yarn as long as those shown. Compare the yarn with the part of your body. Ring **longer** or **shorter**.

1.

The yarn is

longer.

shorter.

your height

2.

The yarn is

longer.

shorter.

elbow to fingertips

3.

The yarn is

longer.

shorter.

arm length

4.

The yarn is

longer.   shorter.

arm span

Work in a group. Use your foot ruler.
Measure. Ring the best answer.

1. your desk top

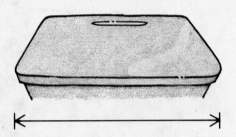

longer than 2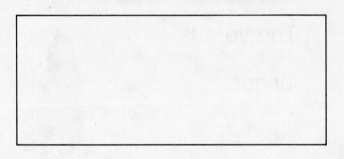
same as 2 ▭
shorter than 2 ▭

2. your teacher's desk top

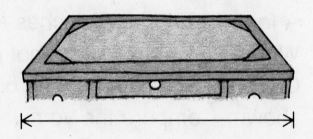

longer than 4 ▭
same as 4 ▭
shorter than 4 ▭

3. Draw something in your classroom. How many foot rulers long is it?

____

MIDCHAPTER REVIEW/QUIZ

1. Estimate how many ⬭ long.
Use ⬭ to measure.

estimate ____ units

measure ____ units

2. Estimate how many inches.
Then measure.

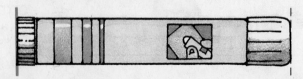

estimate ____ inch

measure ____ inch

Name _____

Ordering by Length and Height

Order from shortest to longest, too.

1. Order the ribbons from longest to shortest. Mark where each ends.

| Place ribbon here. Mark. | Place ribbon here. Mark. | Place ribbon here. Mark. | Place ribbon here. Mark. |

2. Which is longest? _____ 3. Which is shortest? _____

4. Which two are in between? _____

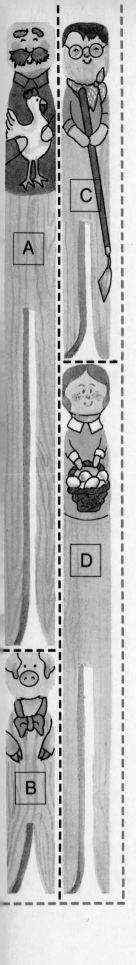

1. Order the clothespin dolls from tallest to shortest. Then paste.

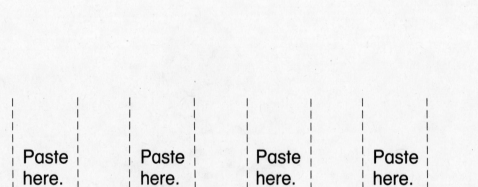

| Paste here. | Paste here. | Paste here. | Paste here. |

2. Which is tallest? ____

3. Which is shortest? ____

4. Which two are in between? _____

Problem Solving
Understanding the Operations

UNDERSTAND
FIND DATA
PLAN
ESTIMATE
SOLVE
CHECK

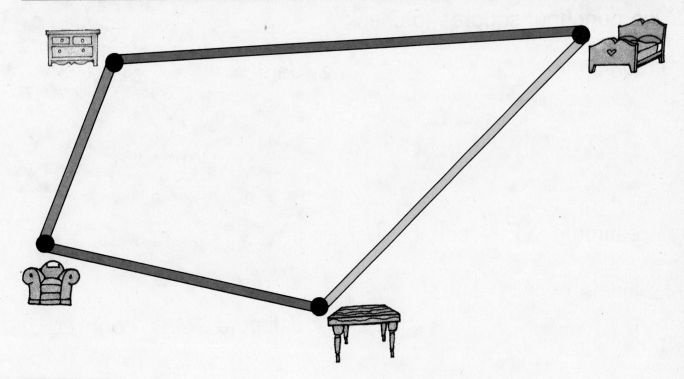

Measure.

1.  → 🛋️

_____ inches

2. 🪑 → 🛏️

_____ inches

3. 🗄️ → 🛋️ → 🪑

_____ inches

4. 🪑 → 🛏️ → 🗄️

_____ inches

Ring the longer path.
Write how much longer.

5. 🗄️ → 🛏️   or   🪑 → 🛏️   _____ inch longer

Estimating Area

How many tiles are needed to cover the
rooms in the doll house? Estimate.
Use punchout squares to check.

1. closet

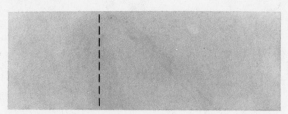

estimate __3__   count __3__

2. den

estimate _____   count _____

3. kitchen

estimate _____   count _____

4. baby's room

estimate _____   count _____

5. porch

estimate _____   count _____

Estimating and Measuring Length
Centimeters

Estimate in centimeters (cm).
Ring your estimate.
Use your punchout centimeter ruler to check.

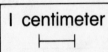

I centimeter

1 2 3 4 5 6 7 8 9 10 11 12 13 14 15

centimeter ruler

1. your pencil

more than 10 centimeters
10 centimeters
less than 10 centimeters

2. your eraser

more than 5 centimeters
5 centimeters
less than 5 centimeters

3. your shoe length

more than 20 centimeters
20 centimeters
less than 20 centimeters

4. the width of your hand

more than 10 centimeters
10 centimeters
less than 10 centimeters

5. Choose something to
measure. Draw it here.

about _____ centimeters

Use your punchout
centimeter ruler.
Estimate. Then measure.

centimeter ruler

estimate __6__ cm   measure __5__ cm

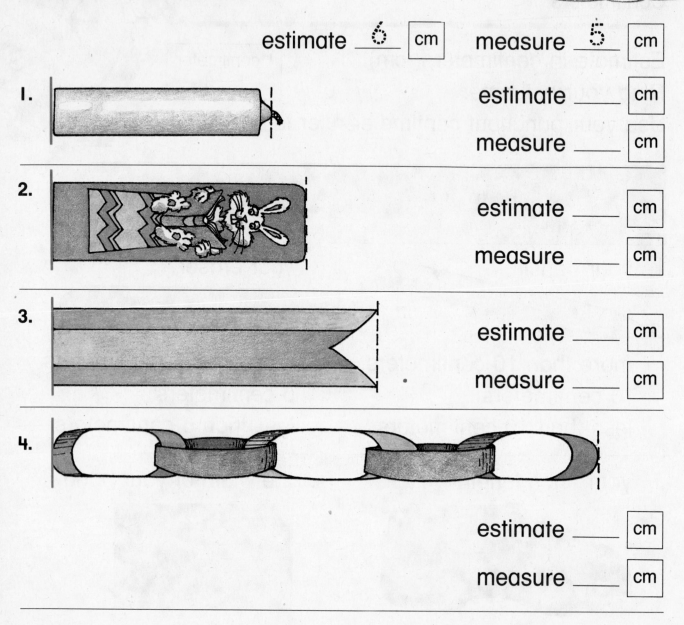

1.

estimate ____ cm

measure ____ cm

2.

estimate ____ cm

measure ____ cm

3.

estimate ____ cm

measure ____ cm

4.

estimate ____ cm

measure ____ cm

PROBLEM SOLVING

5. Megan's bow is 6 centimeters long.
Joan's bow is double the length.
How long is Joan's bow?

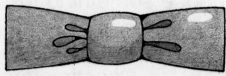

It is ____ centimeters long.

Estimating and Measuring Length
Decimeters

Make a decimeter (dm) paper strip unit.
Ring your estimate. Then use your
decimeter unit strip to check.

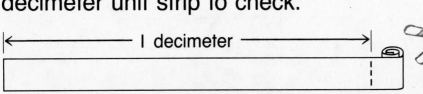

|←————— I decimeter —————→|

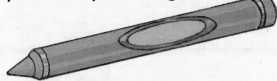

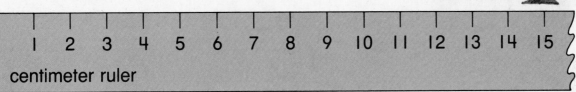

centimeter ruler

1. your crayon length

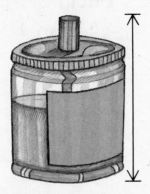

more than I decimeter
I decimeter
less than I decimeter

2. your paintbrush length

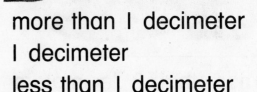

more than I decimeter
I decimeter
less than I decimeter

3. your paste
jar height

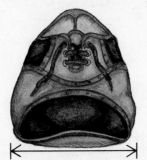

more than I decimeter
I decimeter
less than I decimeter

4. your shoe width

more than I decimeter
I decimeter
less than I decimeter

Tape 3 decimeter paper strip units together. Ring your estimate. Then use your decimeter unit train to check.

1. your book length

more than 3 decimeters
3 decimeters
less than 3 decimeters

2. your book width

more than 2 decimeters
2 decimeters
less than 2 decimeters

3. your shoe length

more than 2 decimeters
2 decimeters
less than 2 decimeters

4. height of a paper cup

more than 1 decimeter
1 decimeter
less than 1 decimeter

MAKE AN ESTIMATE

5. Find something that is about 1 decimeter long. Use your ruler to check. Then draw it.

Name _____

Estimating and Measuring Capacity

Work in a group. How many paper cups will each container fill? Estimate. Then pour to measure. Color to show your measure.

1.  I estimate it will fill _____ paper cups.

2.  I estimate it will fill _____ paper cups.

3.  I estimate it will fill _____ paper cups.

4.  Choose something to measure. Draw it.

I estimate it will fill _____ paper cups.

Chapter 7

Estimating and Measuring Weight

Work in a group. Use 12 cubes.
Estimate how many cubes will balance
each object. Then measure.
Color cubes to show your measure.

1. my pencil   I estimate that ____ cubes will balance it.

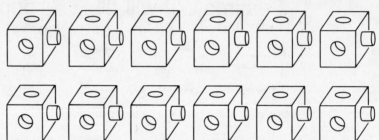

2. a comb   I estimate that ____ cubes will balance it.

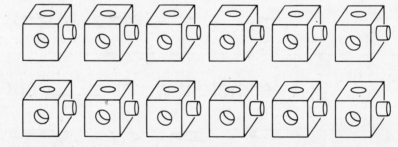

3. 3 nickels   I estimate that ____ cubes will balance them.

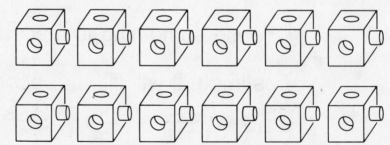

4. Order the objects above from
heaviest to lightest.   ____ , ____ , ____

Name _____

Problem Solving
Determining Reasonable Answers

UNDERSTAND
FIND DATA
PLAN
ESTIMATE
SOLVE
CHECK

Listen to the story. Ring the answer if it makes sense. Cross out if it does not make sense. Make an estimate that does make sense.

1. Bobby is 3 feet tall.

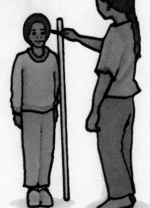

How many feet tall is Jill?

__2__ feet

_____ feet

2. This red pitcher fills 4 glasses.

How many glasses does this blue pitcher fill?

__8__ glasses

_____ glasses

3. This hamster and cage weigh 2 pounds.

How many pounds do these hamsters and cages weigh?

__3__ pounds   _____ pounds

Chapter 7   More Practice, page 418, set B   (one hundred fifty-one) 151

Problem Solving Strategy
Draw a Picture

Listen to the story. Draw pictures to help answer the question.

1.

_____ houses in all

2.

_____ flowers in all

Name _____

CHAPTER REVIEW/TEST

Estimate how many inches.
Then use your inch ruler to measure.

1.

estimate ____ inches

measure ____ inches

2. Use your foot ruler. Measure.
   Ring the best answer.

   longer than 3 [ruler 1 2 3 4 5 6 7 8 9 10 11 12]

   same as 3 [ruler 1 2 3 4 5 6 7 8 9 10 11 12]

   shorter than 3 [ruler 1 2 3 4 5 6 7 8 9 10 11 12]

3. Order from longest to shortest.

   A [nail]

   B [nail]

   C [nail]

   ____ , ____ , ____

4. Measure.

   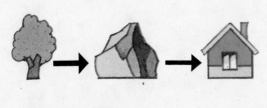

   ____ inches

   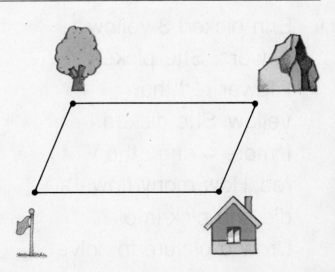

CHAPTER REVIEW/TEST

Estimate how many centimeters.
Then use your centimeter ruler to measure.

1.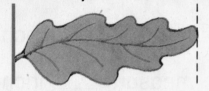
estimate ____ `cm`

measure ____ `cm`

2. Ring your estimate.

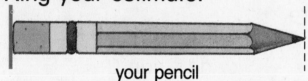

your pencil

more than 1 decimeter

1 decimeter

less than 1 decimeter

3. How many paper cups will the
container fill? Estimate. Then pour to
measure. Ring the number of cups to show
your measure.

 I estimate it will fill ____ paper cups.

4. Erin picked 3 yellow
flowers. She picked
1 fewer red than
yellow. She picked
1 more orange than
red. How many flowers
did she pick in all?
Draw a picture to solve.   ____ flowers in all

ENRICHMENT
Odd and Even Numbers

4 | Even numbers make pairs with none left over.

This is a pair.

5 | Odd numbers make pairs with one left over.

Work with a partner. Put counters in pairs.
Draw what you did. Ring **even** or **odd**.

1. ⊙ ⊙ ⊙ ⊙ ⊙ ⊙ ⊙

even

(odd)

7

2.

even

odd

6

3.

even

odd

12

4.

even

odd

9

5. Work with a partner. Put counters in pairs.
   Color 🖍 even numbers.
   Color 🖍 odd numbers.

1	2	3	4	5	6	7	8	9	10
11	12	13	14	15	16	17	18	19	20

CUMULATIVE REVIEW

Count on to add.

1.

    ○ 8
    ○ 7
    ○ 6

$5 + 2 =$ ___

2.

    ○ 10¢
    ○ 11¢
    ○ 12¢

Add.

3.
$$\begin{array}{r} 5 \\ +3 \\ \hline \end{array}$$

    ○ 5
    ○ 6
    ○ 8

4.
$$\begin{array}{r} 7 \\ +0 \\ \hline \end{array}$$

    ○ 6
    ○ 0
    ○ 7

Add.

5.

    ○ 10
    ○ 9
    ○ 8

$4 + 4 =$ ___

6. $6 + 5 =$ ___

    ○ 10
    ○ 9
    ○ 11

7.
$$\begin{array}{r} 8 \\ +4 \\ \hline \end{array}$$

    ○ 10
    ○ 12
    ○ 11

8.
$$\begin{array}{r} 6 \\ 2 \\ +4 \\ \hline \end{array}$$

    ○ 10
    ○ 11
    ○ 12

9. Sara spent 11¢.

What two things did she buy?

 5¢
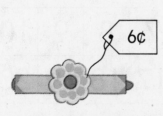 6¢
 4¢
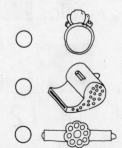
○
○
○

8
Subtraction Facts
Count Backs, Zeros, and Doubles

Workmat

Counting Back 1 or 2

Work with a partner. Use counters.
Lay out the number shown.
Take away 1 or 2 as you count
back. Finish the number sentence.

1. 9 ---- ___ ==== ___   2. 7 ---- ___ ==== ___

3. 6 ---- ___ ==== ___   4. 8 ---- ___ ==== ___

Subtract.

5.
$\begin{array}{r} 7 \\ -2 \\ \hline \end{array}$
$\begin{array}{r} 10 \\ -1 \\ \hline \end{array}$
$\begin{array}{r} 9 \\ -1 \\ \hline \end{array}$
$\begin{array}{r} 11 \\ -2 \\ \hline \end{array}$
$\begin{array}{r} 4 \\ -1 \\ \hline \end{array}$
$\begin{array}{r} 5 \\ -2 \\ \hline \end{array}$

6.
$\begin{array}{r} 8 \\ -2 \\ \hline \end{array}$
$\begin{array}{r} 6 \\ -1 \\ \hline \end{array}$
$\begin{array}{r} 3 \\ -1 \\ \hline \end{array}$
$\begin{array}{r} 4 \\ -2 \\ \hline \end{array}$
$\begin{array}{r} 6 \\ -2 \\ \hline \end{array}$
$\begin{array}{r} 7 \\ -1 \\ \hline \end{array}$

SHOW WITH COUNTERS

7. Count back to subtract.

8. Use counters to check one fact.

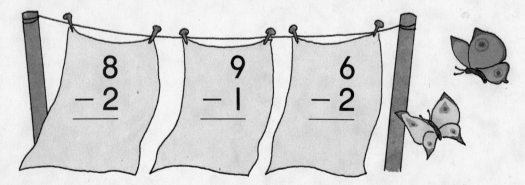

Chapter 8

Counting Back 3

Count back to subtract.

$$9 - 3 = 6$$

1.

7 6, 5, 4

$$7 - 3 = \underline{}$$

2.

5

$$5 - 3 = \underline{}$$

3.

11

$$11 - 3 = \underline{}$$

4.

4

$$4 - 3 = \underline{}$$

5.

9

$$9 - 3 = \underline{}$$

6.

12

$$12 - 3 = \underline{}$$

7.

10

$$10 - 3 = \underline{}$$

8.

8

$$8 - 3 = \underline{}$$

9.

6

$$6 - 3 = \underline{}$$

Subtract.

(7, 6, **5**)

1.

$$\begin{array}{r} 8 \\ -3 \\ \hline 5 \end{array}$$
$$\begin{array}{r} 10 \\ -3 \\ \hline \end{array}$$
$$\begin{array}{r} 7 \\ -2 \\ \hline \end{array}$$
$$\begin{array}{r} 11 \\ -3 \\ \hline \end{array}$$
$$\begin{array}{r} 10 \\ -1 \\ \hline \end{array}$$
$$\begin{array}{r} 6 \\ -3 \\ \hline \end{array}$$

2.

$$\begin{array}{r} 9 \\ -3 \\ \hline \end{array}$$
$$\begin{array}{r} 5 \\ -3 \\ \hline \end{array}$$
$$\begin{array}{r} 12 \\ -3 \\ \hline \end{array}$$
$$\begin{array}{r} 11 \\ -2 \\ \hline \end{array}$$
$$\begin{array}{r} 7 \\ -3 \\ \hline \end{array}$$
$$\begin{array}{r} 4 \\ -3 \\ \hline \end{array}$$

3.

$$\begin{array}{r} 11 \\ -1 \\ \hline \end{array}$$
$$\begin{array}{r} 10 \\ -2 \\ \hline \end{array}$$
$$\begin{array}{r} 12 \\ -3 \\ \hline \end{array}$$
$$\begin{array}{r} 6 \\ -3 \\ \hline \end{array}$$
$$\begin{array}{r} 9 \\ -2 \\ \hline \end{array}$$
$$\begin{array}{r} 8 \\ -3 \\ \hline \end{array}$$

4.

$$\begin{array}{r} 8 \\ -1 \\ \hline \end{array}$$
$$\begin{array}{r} 7 \\ -3 \\ \hline \end{array}$$
$$\begin{array}{r} 11 \\ -3 \\ \hline \end{array}$$
$$\begin{array}{r} 8 \\ -2 \\ \hline \end{array}$$
$$\begin{array}{r} 4 \\ -3 \\ \hline \end{array}$$
$$\begin{array}{r} 9 \\ -3 \\ \hline \end{array}$$

5.

$$\begin{array}{r} 7 \\ -1 \\ \hline \end{array}$$
$$\begin{array}{r} 6 \\ -2 \\ \hline \end{array}$$
$$\begin{array}{r} 5 \\ -3 \\ \hline \end{array}$$
$$\begin{array}{r} 10 \\ -3 \\ \hline \end{array}$$
$$\begin{array}{r} 7 \\ -2 \\ \hline \end{array}$$
$$\begin{array}{r} 5 \\ -2 \\ \hline \end{array}$$

USE CRITICAL THINKING

6. Write + or − in ◯.

$$\begin{array}{r} 5 \\ \bigcirc\, 2 \\ \hline 7 \end{array}$$
$$\begin{array}{r} 5 \\ \bigcirc\, 2 \\ \hline 3 \end{array}$$
$$\begin{array}{r} 9 \\ \bigcirc\, 1 \\ \hline 8 \end{array}$$
$$\begin{array}{r} 9 \\ \bigcirc\, 1 \\ \hline 10 \end{array}$$
$$\begin{array}{r} 8 \\ \bigcirc\, 2 \\ \hline 6 \end{array}$$
$$\begin{array}{r} 8 \\ \bigcirc\, 2 \\ \hline 10 \end{array}$$

Counting Back 1, 2, or 3

Work with a partner.

Use punchouts ⊟, ☑, and ⓷.
Take turns. Pick a card.
Write the number below.
Count back to subtract.

5, 4, 3

$$\begin{array}{r} 5 \\ -\ 2 \\ \hline 3 \end{array}$$

1. 4   7   9   3   10

  −   −   −   −   −

2. 5   10   3   6   7

  −   −   −   −   −

---

3. Match each fact to its answer.

9 − 1		7		12 − 3
11 − 2		8		9 − 2
10 − 3		9		10 − 2

Count back 1, 2, or 3
to subtract.

Are you subtracting
1, 2, or 3?
Count back.

1. $7 - 3 = \underline{4}$ $9 - 2 = \underline{}$

2. $7 - 1 = \underline{}$ $12 - 3 = \underline{}$ $8 - 3 = \underline{}$

3. $11 - 2 = \underline{}$ $10 - 1 = \underline{}$ $10 - 3 = \underline{}$

4. $9 - 2 = \underline{}$ $4 - 3 = \underline{}$ $5 - 2 = \underline{}$

5. $6 - 2 = \underline{}$ $4 - 2 = \underline{}$ $4 - 3 = \underline{}$

Midchapter Review/Quiz

Subtract.

1.
$$\begin{array}{r} 9 \\ -2 \\ \hline \end{array} \quad \begin{array}{r} 9 \\ -3 \\ \hline \end{array} \quad \begin{array}{r} 8 \\ -3 \\ \hline \end{array} \quad \begin{array}{r} 10 \\ -3 \\ \hline \end{array} \quad \begin{array}{r} 8 \\ -2 \\ \hline \end{array} \quad \begin{array}{r} 7 \\ -1 \\ \hline \end{array}$$

2.
$$\begin{array}{r} 11 \\ -2 \\ \hline \end{array} \quad \begin{array}{r} 9 \\ -1 \\ \hline \end{array} \quad \begin{array}{r} 12 \\ -3 \\ \hline \end{array} \quad \begin{array}{r} 11 \\ -3 \\ \hline \end{array} \quad \begin{array}{r} 10 \\ -1 \\ \hline \end{array} \quad \begin{array}{r} 6 \\ -2 \\ \hline \end{array}$$

Problem Solving
Understanding the Operations

UNDERSTAND
FIND DATA
PLAN
ESTIMATE
SOLVE
CHECK

Listen to the story. Use counters to
show it. Write the number sentence.

1. the 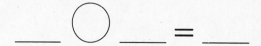 story

   ___ ◯ ___ = ___

   ___ butterflies

2. the story

   ___ ◯ ___ = ___

   ___ bluebirds

3. the story

   ___ ◯ ___ = ___

   ___ dragonflies

Calculator

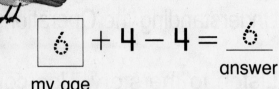

Write your age in each ☐.
Will the answer be your age?
Guess. Ring **yes** or **no**.
Calculate the answer.
Write it.

$$\boxed{6} + 4 - 4 = \underline{6}$$
my age   answer

My Guess

yes   no

Press. $\boxed{6}$ $\boxed{+}$ $\boxed{4}$ $\boxed{-}$ $\boxed{4}$ $\boxed{=}$

My Guess

1. $\boxed{} + 6 - 6 = \underline{}$
   my age   answer   yes   no

2. $\boxed{} + 8 - 8 = \underline{}$
   my age   answer   yes   no

3. $\boxed{} + 12 - 12 = \underline{}$
   my age   answer   yes   no

4. $\boxed{} + 8 - 7 = \underline{}$
   my age   answer   yes   no

5. $\boxed{} + 18 - 17 = \underline{}$
   my age   answer   yes   no

6. $\boxed{} + 19 - 19 = \underline{}$
   my age   answer   yes   no

Zero Subtraction Facts

9	All are
− 0	left.

9	0 is
− 9	left.

Subtract. Ring all zero facts.

1.

$$\begin{array}{r} 7 \\ -7 \\ \hline 0 \end{array} \qquad \begin{array}{r} 8 \\ -3 \\ \hline \end{array} \qquad \begin{array}{r} 7 \\ -2 \\ \hline \end{array} \qquad \begin{array}{r} 5 \\ -0 \\ \hline 5 \end{array} \qquad \begin{array}{r} 9 \\ -2 \\ \hline \end{array} \qquad \begin{array}{r} 4 \\ -4 \\ \hline \end{array}$$

2.

$$\begin{array}{r} 11 \\ -2 \\ \hline \end{array} \qquad \begin{array}{r} 4 \\ -0 \\ \hline \end{array} \qquad \begin{array}{r} 3 \\ -3 \\ \hline \end{array} \qquad \begin{array}{r} 0 \\ -0 \\ \hline \end{array} \qquad \begin{array}{r} 10 \\ -3 \\ \hline \end{array} \qquad \begin{array}{r} 2 \\ -2 \\ \hline \end{array}$$

3.

$$\begin{array}{r} 8 \\ -0 \\ \hline \end{array} \qquad \begin{array}{r} 9 \\ -3 \\ \hline \end{array} \qquad \begin{array}{r} 11 \\ -3 \\ \hline \end{array} \qquad \begin{array}{r} 6 \\ -0 \\ \hline \end{array} \qquad \begin{array}{r} 10 \\ -2 \\ \hline \end{array} \qquad \begin{array}{r} 7 \\ -1 \\ \hline \end{array}$$

4. Write and continue the number pattern in ☆3.

____, ____, ____, ____, ____, ____, ____, ____, ____

Subtract.

1.
$$1 - 1 =$$ $$9 - 3 =$$ $$8 - 2 =$$ $$3 - 0 =$$ $$11 - 2 =$$ $$7 - 1 =$$

2.
$$6 - 2 =$$ $$7 - 0 =$$ $$8 - 1 =$$ $$10 - 2 =$$ $$4 - 4 =$$ $$10 - 3 =$$

Be fast!

3. $4 - 3 =$ ___
    $6 - 0 =$ ___
    $12 - 3 =$ ___

4. $5 - 2 =$ ___
    $3 - 3 =$ ___
    $11 - 3 =$ ___
    $3 - 2 =$ ___

5. $9 - 2 =$ ___
    $7 - 3 =$ ___
    $4 - 2 =$ ___
    $5 - 5 =$ ___
    $6 - 3 =$ ___

PROBLEM SOLVING

[ ] owls

[ ] parrots

6. Count the owls and parrots.
    How many more owls than parrots are
    there? Ring and finish the number
    sentence that answers the question.

$4 + 2 =$ ___

$4 - 2 =$ ___

Adding to Check Subtraction

Addition checks the subtraction answer.

```
   7
 - 2        add-to-check
 ─────         fact          →
   5
```

```
   2
 + 5
 ─────
   7
```

Add-to-Check Facts

Add.

1.
```
  9        3        7        9        2        7
 +3       +8       +3       +2       +8       +2
 ──       ──       ──       ──       ──       ──
```

Subtract. Finish the add-to-check fact.

2.
12	3
− 3	+

10	3
− 3	+

11	2
− 2	+

3.
10	2
− 2	+

11	3
− 3	+

9	2
− 2	+

Subtract. Finish the add-to-check fact.
Cross out the other fact.

1.

$4 + 0 = \underline{4}$

$4 - 4 = \underline{0}$

$\cancel{4 + 2}$

$3 + 4 = \underline{}$

$6 - 3 = \underline{}$

$3 + 3 = \underline{}$

2.

$2 + 7 = \underline{}$

$9 - 2 = \underline{}$

$2 + 9 = \underline{}$

$2 + 8 = \underline{}$

$11 - 2 = \underline{}$

$2 + 9 = \underline{}$

3.

$3 + 5 = \underline{}$

$5 - 3 = \underline{}$

$3 + 2 = \underline{}$

$3 + 7 = \underline{}$

$10 - 3 = \underline{}$

$3 + 9 = \underline{}$

SHOW WITH COUNTERS

4. Subtract. Write the add-to-check fact.
Use counters to check.

$$\begin{array}{r} 8 \\ -\ 2 \\ \hline \end{array} \quad +$$

$$\begin{array}{r} 7 \\ -\ 3 \\ \hline \end{array} \quad +$$

$$\begin{array}{r} 5 \\ -\ 3 \\ \hline \end{array} \quad +$$

Subtraction Doubles

The add-to-check double fact helps you find the answer.

$$\begin{array}{r} 4 \\ + 4 \\ \hline 8 \end{array} \qquad \begin{array}{r} 5 \\ + 5 \\ \hline 10 \end{array} \qquad \begin{array}{r} 6 \\ + 6 \\ \hline 12 \end{array}$$

| $\begin{array}{r} 8 \\ - 4 \\ \hline 4 \end{array}$ | $\begin{array}{r} 4 \\ + 4 \\ \hline 8 \end{array}$ | $\begin{array}{r} 10 \\ - 5 \\ \hline 5 \end{array}$ | $\begin{array}{r} 5 \\ + 5 \\ \hline 10 \end{array}$ | $\begin{array}{r} 12 \\ - 6 \\ \hline 6 \end{array}$ | $\begin{array}{r} 6 \\ + 6 \\ \hline 12 \end{array}$ |

Subtract. Finish the add-to-check fact.

1.

| $\begin{array}{r} 8 \\ - 4 \\ \hline 4 \end{array}$ | $\begin{array}{r} 4 \\ + 4 \\ \hline 8 \end{array}$ | $\begin{array}{r} 12 \\ - 6 \\ \hline \end{array}$ | $\begin{array}{r} 6 \\ + \\ \hline \end{array}$ | $\begin{array}{r} 6 \\ - 3 \\ \hline \end{array}$ | $\begin{array}{r} 3 \\ + \\ \hline \end{array}$ |

2.

| $\begin{array}{r} 12 \\ - 6 \\ \hline \end{array}$ | $\begin{array}{r} 6 \\ + \\ \hline \end{array}$ | $\begin{array}{r} 10 \\ - 5 \\ \hline \end{array}$ | $\begin{array}{r} 5 \\ + \\ \hline \end{array}$ | $\begin{array}{r} 2 \\ - 1 \\ \hline \end{array}$ | $\begin{array}{r} 1 \\ + \\ \hline \end{array}$ |

3.

| $\begin{array}{r} 6 \\ - 3 \\ \hline \end{array}$ | $\begin{array}{r} 3 \\ + \\ \hline \end{array}$ | $\begin{array}{r} 8 \\ - 4 \\ \hline \end{array}$ | $\begin{array}{r} 4 \\ + \\ \hline \end{array}$ | $\begin{array}{r} 4 \\ - 2 \\ \hline \end{array}$ | $\begin{array}{r} 2 \\ + \\ \hline \end{array}$ |

Ring the subtraction double facts.
Then subtract all.

1.

$$\begin{array}{r} 10 \\ -\ 5 \\ \hline 5 \end{array}$$
$$\begin{array}{r} 9 \\ -3 \\ \hline \end{array}$$
$$\begin{array}{r} 6 \\ -2 \\ \hline \end{array}$$
$$\begin{array}{r} 9 \\ -2 \\ \hline \end{array}$$
$$\begin{array}{r} 12 \\ -\ 6 \\ \hline \end{array}$$

2.

$$\begin{array}{r} 10 \\ -\ 2 \\ \hline \end{array}$$
$$\begin{array}{r} 5 \\ -0 \\ \hline \end{array}$$
$$\begin{array}{r} 8 \\ -4 \\ \hline \end{array}$$
$$\begin{array}{r} 11 \\ -\ 2 \\ \hline \end{array}$$
$$\begin{array}{r} 9 \\ -1 \\ \hline \end{array}$$
$$\begin{array}{r} 10 \\ -\ 3 \\ \hline \end{array}$$

3.

$$\begin{array}{r} 3 \\ -2 \\ \hline \end{array}$$
$$\begin{array}{r} 8 \\ -2 \\ \hline \end{array}$$
$$\begin{array}{r} 12 \\ -\ 3 \\ \hline \end{array}$$
$$\begin{array}{r} 8 \\ -2 \\ \hline \end{array}$$
$$\begin{array}{r} 10 \\ -\ 5 \\ \hline \end{array}$$
$$\begin{array}{r} 7 \\ -3 \\ \hline \end{array}$$

4.

$$\begin{array}{r} 8 \\ -4 \\ \hline \end{array}$$
$$\begin{array}{r} 5 \\ -3 \\ \hline \end{array}$$
$$\begin{array}{r} 9 \\ -0 \\ \hline \end{array}$$
$$\begin{array}{r} 12 \\ -\ 6 \\ \hline \end{array}$$
$$\begin{array}{r} 8 \\ -3 \\ \hline \end{array}$$
$$\begin{array}{r} 4 \\ -3 \\ \hline \end{array}$$

5. Do these as fast as you can.

$$7 - 2 = \underline{\hspace{1cm}} \qquad 8 - 8 = \underline{\hspace{1cm}} \qquad 5 - 2 = \underline{\hspace{1cm}}$$

$$11 - 3 = \underline{\hspace{1cm}} \qquad 4 - 2 = \underline{\hspace{1cm}} \qquad 6 - 3 = \underline{\hspace{1cm}}$$

USE MENTAL MATH

6. Think about these facts.
Ring the one that has
the greater answer.

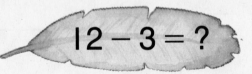

$$12 - 3 = ?$$

$$12 - 6 = ?$$

Fact Practice

What did the bee say
to the flower?

Secret Code

1 = u	4 = s	7 = h
2 = t	5 = y	8 = e
3 = w	6 = n	9 = o

To find out, first subtract.
Then write the letter code for
each answer in the box below.
Read the message.

$$\begin{array}{c} 9 \\ -2 \\ \hline 7 \end{array} \quad \begin{array}{c} 12 \\ -3 \\ \hline \end{array} \quad \begin{array}{c} 8 \\ -2 \\ \hline \end{array} \quad \begin{array}{c} 11 \\ -3 \\ \hline \end{array} \quad \begin{array}{c} 10 \\ -5 \\ \hline \end{array}$$

h _____ _____ _____ _____ , I'm

$$\begin{array}{c} 8 \\ -4 \\ \hline \end{array} \quad \begin{array}{c} 4 \\ -1 \\ \hline \end{array} \quad \begin{array}{c} 8 \\ -0 \\ \hline \end{array} \quad \begin{array}{c} 10 \\ -2 \\ \hline \end{array} \quad \begin{array}{c} 5 \\ -3 \\ \hline \end{array}$$

_____ _____ _____ _____ _____

$$\begin{array}{c} 11 \\ -2 \\ \hline \end{array} \quad \begin{array}{c} 12 \\ -6 \\ \hline \end{array} \qquad \begin{array}{c} 8 \\ -3 \\ \hline \end{array} \quad \begin{array}{c} 10 \\ -1 \\ \hline \end{array} \quad \begin{array}{c} 4 \\ -3 \\ \hline \end{array}$$

_____ _____ _____ _____ _____ .

Subtract. When each row is correct,
draw and color the bee's face.

1.
5¢	10¢	12¢	4¢	5¢
− 2¢	− 5¢	− 3¢	− 2¢	− 1¢
3¢				

2.
| 8¢ | 5¢ | 8¢ | 11¢ | 9¢ |
| − 4¢ | − 3¢ | − 8¢ | − 2¢ | − 3¢ |

3.
| 7¢ | 11¢ | 12¢ | 7¢ | 4¢ |
| − 3¢ | − 3¢ | − 6¢ | − 2¢ | − 0¢ |

MIXED REVIEW

4. Use your punchout centimeter
ruler. Estimate. Then measure.

estimate _____ cm

measure _____ cm

5. A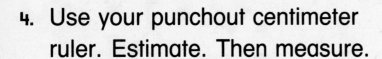

B

C

Which paintbrush is longest? _____

Which paintbrush is shortest? _____

Problem Solving
Asking the Question

Listen to the story.
Use counters to show it.
Ring the question you would ask.

1. the ✈ story

   Ring one.   How many hang gliders are there?

   How many hang gliders are left?

2. the 🎈 story

   Ring one.   How many in all are in the sky?

   How many balloons are left?

Problem Solving Strategy
Choose the Operation

UNDERSTAND
FIND DATA
PLAN
ESTIMATE
SOLVE
CHECK

Listen to the stories. Think about the action. Paste the pictures where they belong.

Addition	Subtraction
Put Together	Take Away Compare

Name _____

WRAP UP

MATH WORDS

Ring examples of each.

1.	counting back to subtract	8 − 1	10 − 5	9 − 9	10 − 2
2.	zero facts	7 − 2	5 − 0	6 − 3	4 − 4
3.	subtraction doubles	7 − 3	8 − 4	12 − 6	5 − 5

MATH REASONING

Ring the fact that has the smaller difference. Tell how you know.

4.

$\begin{array}{r} 9 \\ -3 \\ \hline \end{array}$
or

$\begin{array}{r} 9 \\ -1 \\ \hline \end{array}$

5.

$\begin{array}{r} 7 \\ -1 \\ \hline \end{array}$
or

$\begin{array}{r} 7 \\ -2 \\ \hline \end{array}$

6.

$\begin{array}{r} 10 \\ -2 \\ \hline \end{array}$
or
$\begin{array}{r} 8 \\ -2 \\ \hline \end{array}$

7.
$\begin{array}{r} 7 \\ -3 \\ \hline \end{array}$
or

$\begin{array}{r} 10 \\ -3 \\ \hline \end{array}$

8.

$\begin{array}{r} 12 \\ -6 \\ \hline \end{array}$
or
$\begin{array}{r} 8 \\ -4 \\ \hline \end{array}$

9.
$\begin{array}{r} 6 \\ -3 \\ \hline \end{array}$
or

$\begin{array}{r} 10 \\ -5 \\ \hline \end{array}$

Chapter Review/Test

Subtract.

1.

$$3 - 1 = \underline{}$$

2.

$$4 - 2 = \underline{}$$

3.
$$\begin{array}{r} 9 \\ -3 \\ \hline \end{array} \qquad \begin{array}{r} 4 \\ -2 \\ \hline \end{array} \qquad \begin{array}{r} 10 \\ -1 \\ \hline \end{array} \qquad \begin{array}{r} 12 \\ -6 \\ \hline \end{array} \qquad \begin{array}{r} 7 \\ -0 \\ \hline \end{array} \qquad \begin{array}{r} 11 \\ -5 \\ \hline \end{array}$$

4.
$$\begin{array}{r} 8 \\ -4 \\ \hline \end{array} \qquad \begin{array}{r} 6 \\ -0 \\ \hline \end{array} \qquad \begin{array}{r} 8 \\ -3 \\ \hline \end{array} \qquad \begin{array}{r} 10¢ \\ -5¢ \\ \hline \end{array} \qquad \begin{array}{r} 5¢ \\ -5¢ \\ \hline \end{array} \qquad \begin{array}{r} 6¢ \\ -3¢ \\ \hline \end{array}$$

5. Subtract. Write the add-to-check fact.

12	
− 3	+

8	
− 3	+

10	
− 4	+

6. Ring the question to finish the story.

3 and 4 are by the pond.

How many are left?

How many are there in all?

Name _____

ENRICHMENT
Finding 1-Foot Units

Work with a partner. Find objects in your classroom that are about 1 foot long. Draw them. Then check the length with your foot ruler.

Draw your object.	Is it 1 foot long? Ring one.
1.	yes no
2.	yes no
3.	yes no

CUMULATIVE REVIEW

Add.

1.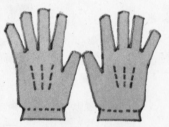

$5 + 5 = $ ___

- ○ 12
- ○ 10
- ○ 11

2. $8 + 2 = $ ___

- ○ 11
- ○ 10
- ○ 9

3.
$$\begin{array}{r} 6 \\ + 5 \\ \hline \end{array}$$

- ○ 11
- ○ 12
- ○ 9

4.
$$\begin{array}{r} 5 \\ 4 \\ + 3 \\ \hline \end{array}$$

- ○ 11
- ○ 12
- ○ 10

Use your inch ruler to measure each length.

5.

- ○ 1 inch
- ○ 2 inches
- ○ 3 inches

6.

- ○ 2 inches
- ○ 3 inches
- ○ 4 inches

7. Which is longest?

A
B
C

- ○ A
- ○ B
- ○ C

8. Which pencil above is shortest?

- ○ A
- ○ B
- ○ C

9. How much do 3 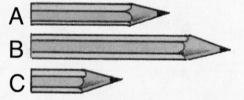 cost?

dinosaurs	🦕	🦕🦕	🦕🦕🦕
cost	2¢	4¢	___ ¢

- ○ 6¢
- ○ 5¢
- ○ 3¢

9
Geometry

Name _____

Sorting Solids

Use some solid figures like these.

 sphere  cone  cylinder  cube  box

1. Ring the one with no flat face.
2. Cross out the one with only one sharp tip.
3. Ring those that cannot roll

Cross out the solid that does not belong.

4.

5.

6.

TALK ABOUT IT

7. Mark the one that is not a cube.
   Tell why not.

Graphing Solids

Look for , ⬭, △, and ⬭ in the picture. Put an X on the graph for each solid you find. Cross out as you graph.

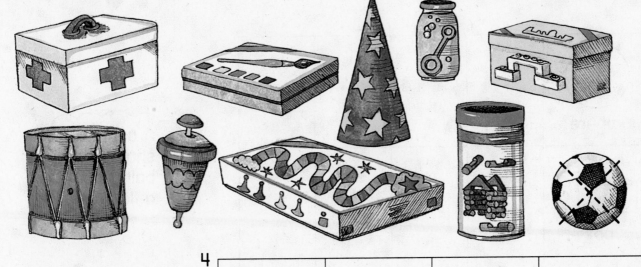

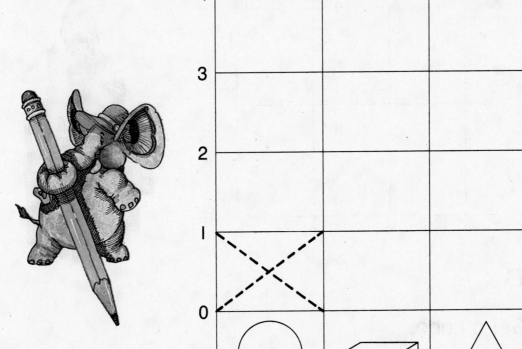

	sphere	box	cone	cylinder
4				
3				
2				
1				
0				

1. Put an X on the graph for each solid you find. Cross out as you graph.

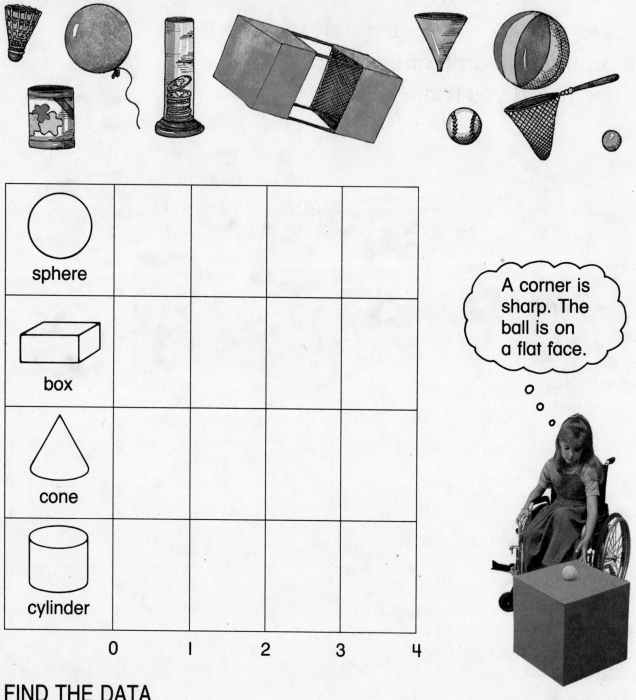

A corner is sharp. The ball is on a flat face.

FIND THE DATA

Data Hunt Get a cube.

2. How many flat faces does it have? _____ flat faces

3. How many corners does it have? _____ corners

Plane Figures and Solids

Use a solid. Draw around the flat
face shown. Match to the plane figure.

solid	flat face	plane figure

1.

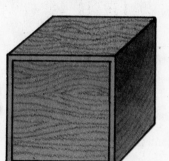

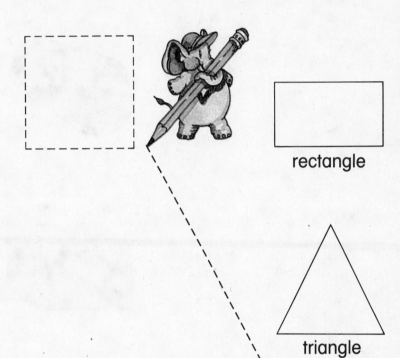

rectangle

triangle

square

circle

2.

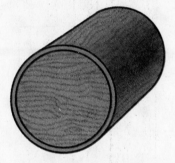

3.

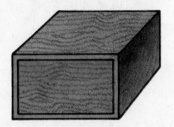

4.

1. **Match the plane figures to the solids.**

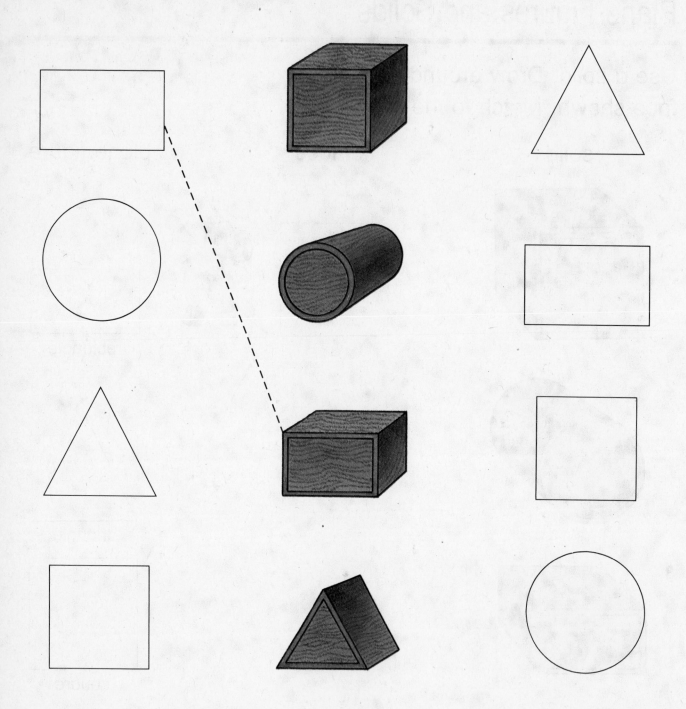

MAKE AN ESTIMATE

Ted

Ned

2. Who walks farther?
Ring one.
Tell why.

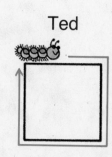

Sides and Corners

a side
a corner

Color 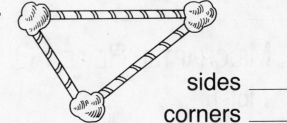 the straws. Color the clay.

Count the sides and corners. Write how many.

1.

sides _3_

corners _3_

2.

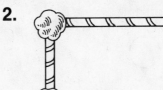

sides ____

corners ____

3.

sides ____

corners ____

4.

sides ____

corners ____

5.

sides ____

corners ____

6.

sides ____

corners ____

7. Which figure has the most sides? Ring
   with 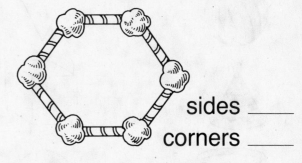.

8. Which two figures have the fewest sides? Ring
   with .

Draw the figure. Color sides .
Color corners . Write how many.

1.
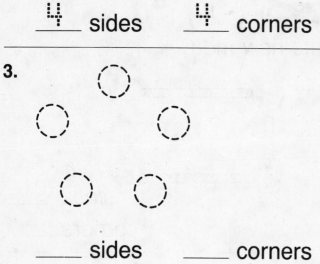

__4__ sides   __4__ corners

2.

____ sides   ____ corners

3.

____ sides   ____ corners

4. your choice

____ sides   ____ corners

MIDCHAPTER REVIEW/QUIZ

1. Match.

2. Match the plane figures
to the solids.

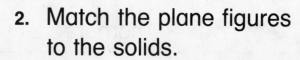

Name _____

My Geometry Book

Dear Family:
Ask your child
to read this book
to you.

Use your punchouts. Paste each picture next to the shape it matches. Write how many sides and corners the shape has.

rectangle

| Paste here. | | Paste here. |

_____ sides   _____ corners

square

| Paste here. | | Paste here. |

_____ sides

_____ corners

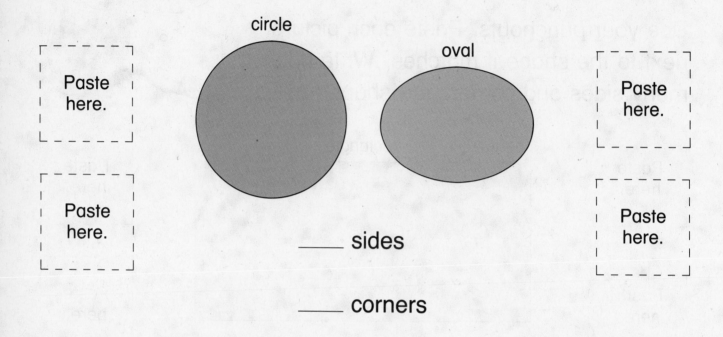

circle

oval

Paste here.

Paste here.

Paste here.

Paste here.

_____ sides

_____ corners

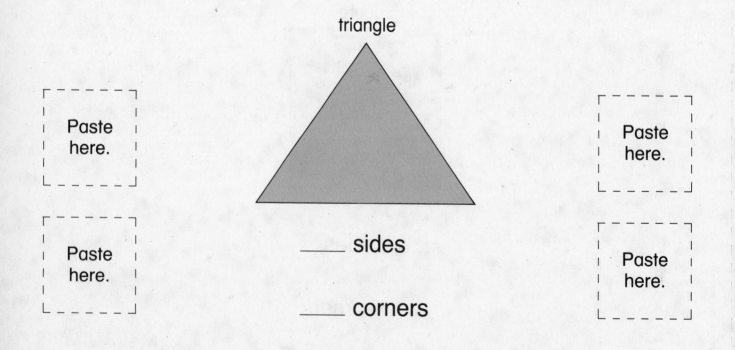

triangle

Paste here.

Paste here.

Paste here.

Paste here.

_____ sides

_____ corners

Name _____

Problem Solving
Understanding the Operations

Listen to the story. Use and draw coins to answer the question.

1. I have 4¢. How much more do I need?

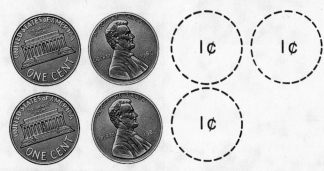 _____ ¢

ORK

2. I have 5¢. How much more do I need?

 _____ ¢

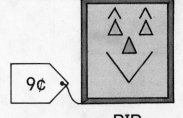

BIP

3. I have 6¢. How much more do I need?

 _____ ¢

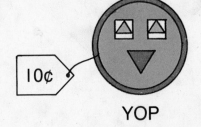

YOP

4. I have 6¢. How much more do I need?

 _____ ¢

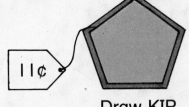

Draw KIP.

Using Critical Thinking

Draw a face on each figure.
Write its letter in the correct box.

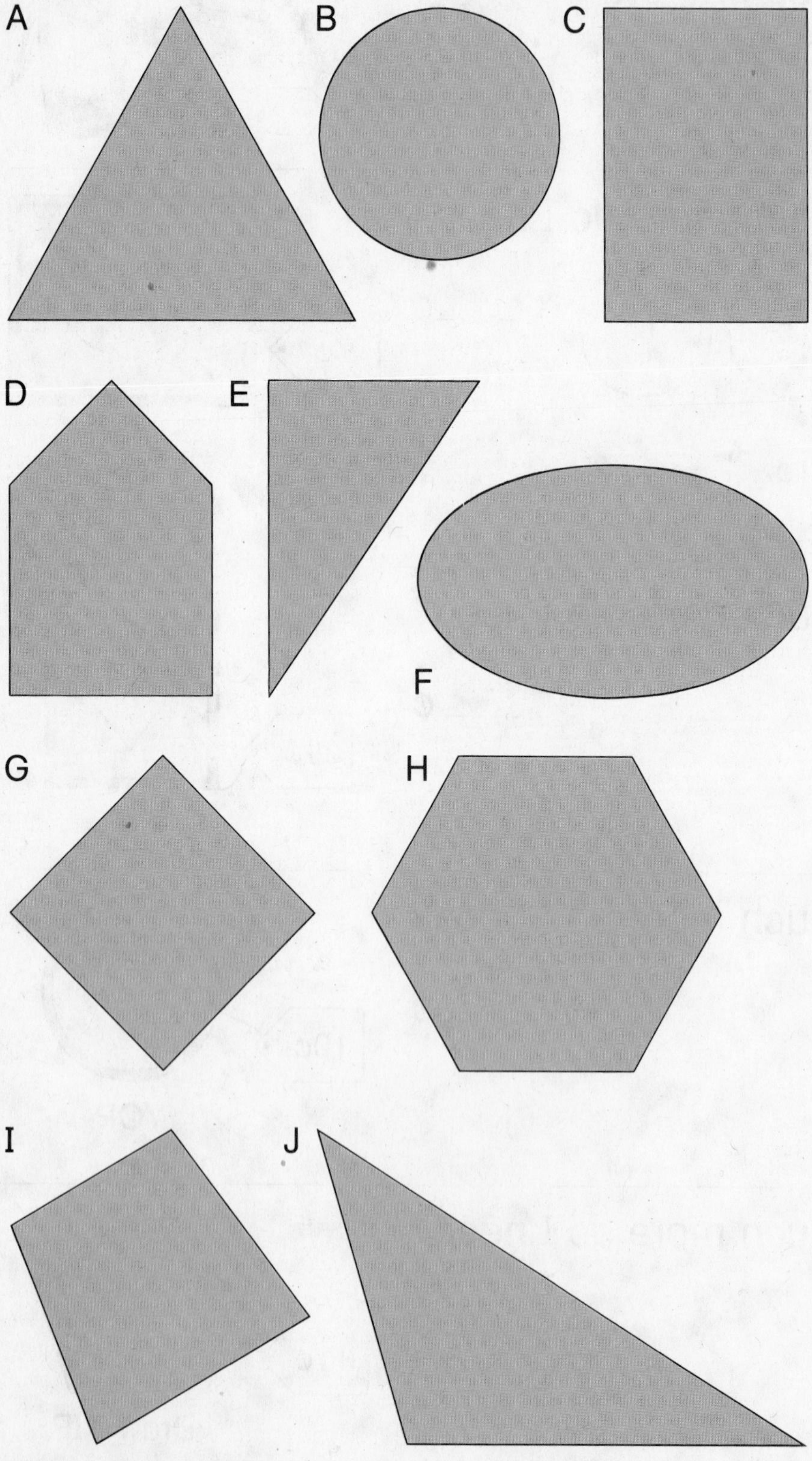

A

B

C

D

E

F

G

H

I

J

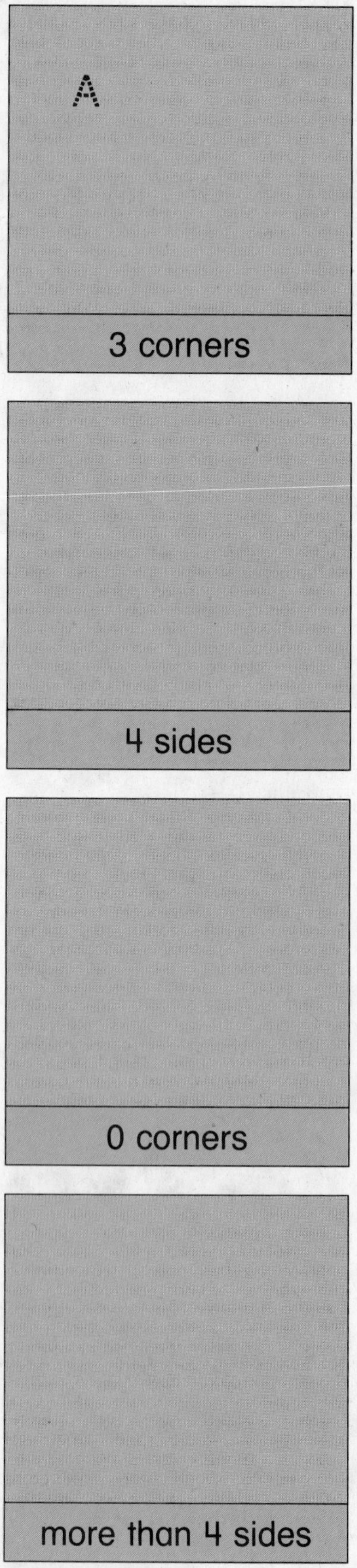

A

3 corners

4 sides

0 corners

more than 4 sides

Inside, Outside, and On

Work in a group. Make the figure on your geoboard. Write how many pegs inside, outside, and on.

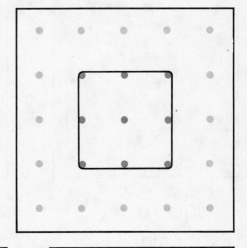

___1___ inside   • inside

___16___ outside   • outside

___8___ on   • on

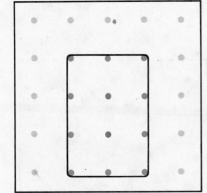
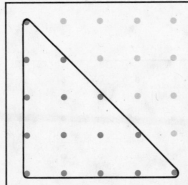
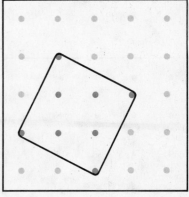

1. rectangle   **2.** triangle   **3.** square

____ inside   ____ inside   ____ inside

____ outside   ____ outside   ____ outside

____ on   ____ on   ____ on

4. Draw your own figure.

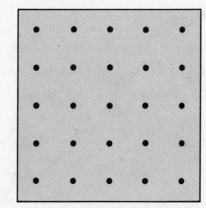

____ inside

____ outside

____ on

Work in a group. Make the shape on your geoboard.
Draw it here.

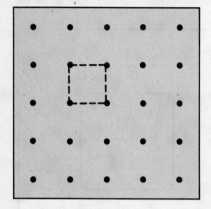

1. square
   0 inside

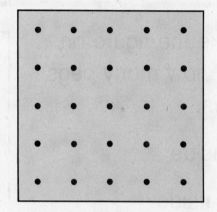

2. triangle
   0 inside

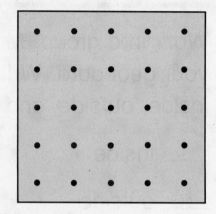

3. rectangle
   0 inside

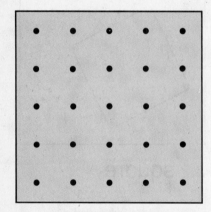

4. triangle
   1 inside

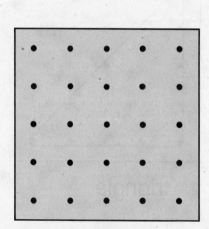

5. rectangle
   2 inside

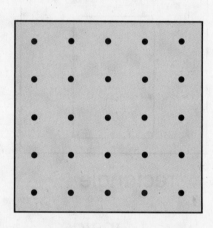

6. square
   4 inside

PROBLEM SOLVING

7. The inside pegs are covered.
   How many pegs are inside?

   _____ pegs

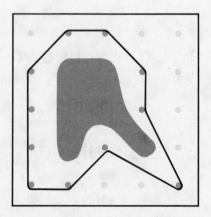

Symmetric Figures

Cut out the squares.
Paste to make
figures that match.

Both parts match.

1.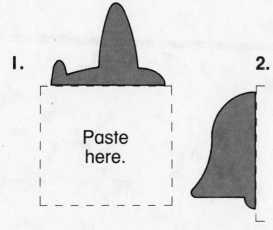

Paste here.

2.

Paste here.

3.

Paste here.

4.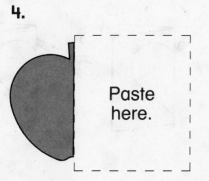

Paste here.

5.

Paste here.

6.

Paste here.

Chapter 9   (one hundred ninety-three)   193

Draw a line to make two matching parts. Color one part  and the other .

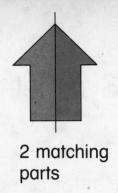

2 matching parts

1.

2.

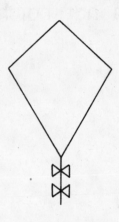

3.

4.

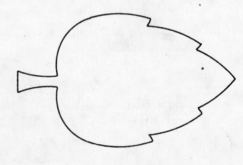

USE CRITICAL THINKING

5. Fold a piece of paper in half. Draw a figure. Start and end it at the fold. Say what it will look like when you unfold. Cut and unfold to check.

Congruent Figures

Work in a group. Take turns working in pairs. Make a figure on your geoboard. Draw it. Your partner makes one the same size and shape and draws it. Ring **yes** or **no** to answer the question.

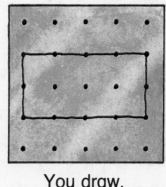
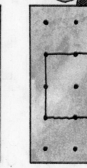

You draw.   Partner draws.

Same size and shape?   (yes)   no

1.

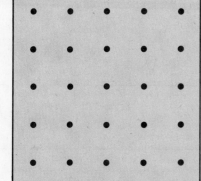

You draw.   Partner draws.

Same size and shape?

yes   no

2.

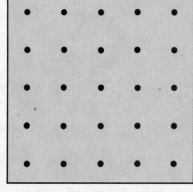
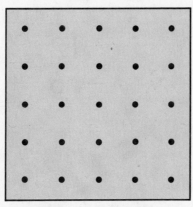

You draw.   Partner draws.

Same size and shape?

yes   no

Draw one the same size and shape.

1.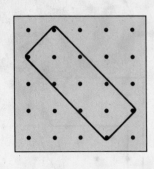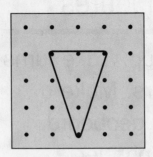

You draw.

2.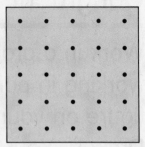

You draw.

Look at the first one. Ring ones
that are the same size and shape.

3.

4.

MIXED REVIEW

5. Subtract. Write the add-to-check fact.

$$\begin{array}{r} 11 \\ -\ 3 \end{array} +\ \underline{}$$

$$\begin{array}{r} 12 \\ -\ 6 \end{array} +\ \underline{}$$

$$\begin{array}{r} 9 \\ -\ 2 \end{array} +\ \underline{}$$

6. Add.

$6 + 3 = \underline{}$ $4 + 4 = \underline{}$ $5 + 6 = \underline{}$

More Practice, page 420, set C   Chapter 9

Problem Solving
Finding Data from a Map

UNDERSTAND
FIND DATA
PLAN
ESTIMATE
SOLVE
CHECK

Listen to the story. Use your inch ruler.
Write how many inches.

1. How far is it from home
to the store?

_____ inches

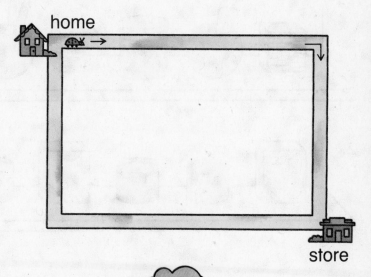

2. How far is it from home
past the pond to school?

_____ inches

3. How far is the shortest way
from school to home?

_____ inches

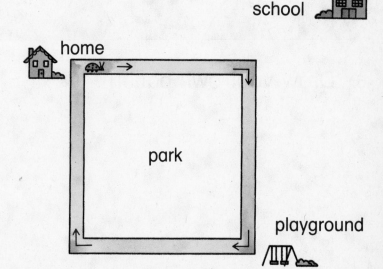

4. Start at home.
Go all the way around
the park. How far is it?

_____ inches

Problem Solving Strategy
Look for a Pattern

UNDERSTAND
FIND DATA
PLAN
ESTIMATE
SOLVE
CHECK

Listen to the story. Color the one that comes next. Talk about the patterns you see.

Things for school

1.

2.

3.

4.

5. Draw your own pattern.

Name _____

WRAP UP

MATH WORDS

Cross out words that do not
name the pictures.

1. triangle	2. cylinder	3. rectangle	4. circle 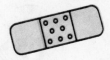
5. cube	6. square	7. circle 	8. cone
9. sphere	10. cone	11. cylinder	12. triangle

MATH REASONING

Look at the cutout lines. How many
sides and corners will the figure have?

13.    _____ sides

_____ corners

14.    _____ sides

_____ corners

15.    _____ sides

_____ corners

16. 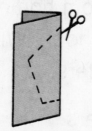   _____ sides

_____ corners

CHAPTER REVIEW/TEST

1. Match.

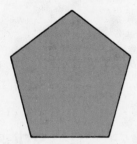

2. Match.

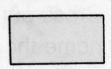

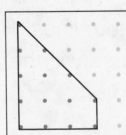

3. Write how many.

corners ____

sides ____

4. Write how many pegs.

inside ____

outside ____

on ____

5. Use your centimeter ruler.
How far is it from home past
the store to school? Write how
many centimeters.

____ centimeters

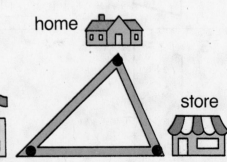

home

store

school

ENRICHMENT
Making Shapes

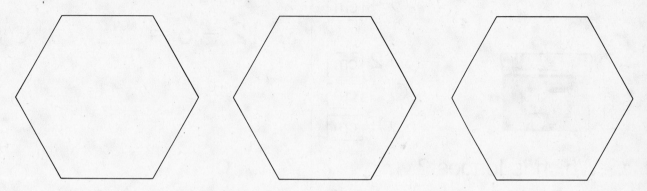

Use pattern blocks to make the
shapes. Draw what you did.

1. Try a different way for each 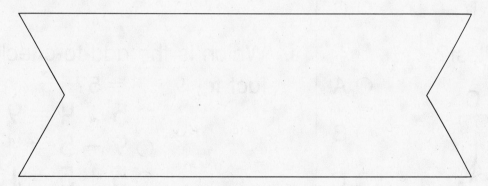.

2. Use all ▱.

3. Use some △ and some ◇.

CUMULATIVE REVIEW

Use your centimeter ruler to measure the length or height.

1.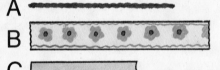
- ○ 2 cm
- ○ 3 cm
- ○ 4 cm

2.
- ○ 2 cm
- ○ 3 cm
- ○ 4 cm

3. Which is longest?

A
B
C

- ○ A
- ○ B
- ○ C

4. Which is tallest?

A B C

- ○ A
- ○ B
- ○ C

Subtract.

5.
9 − 3 = ____
- ○ 6
- ○ 8
- ○ 7

6. 12 − 6 = ____
- ○ 5
- ○ 6
- ○ 7

7.
  9
− 0
─────
- ○ 8
- ○ 0
- ○ 9

8. Which is the add-to-check fact for 9 − 4 = 5?
- ○ 5 + 4 = 9
- ○ 9 − 5 = 4
- ○ 5 + 5 = 10

9. Whose house is closest to Sal?

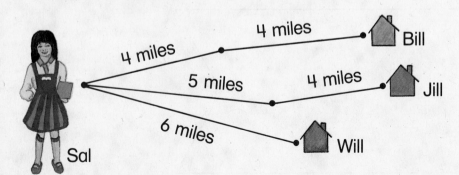

4 miles — Bill
4 miles
5 miles   4 miles — Jill
6 miles — Will

Sal

- ○ Bill's house
- ○ Jill's house
- ○ Will's house

10
Subtraction Facts
to 12

Workmat

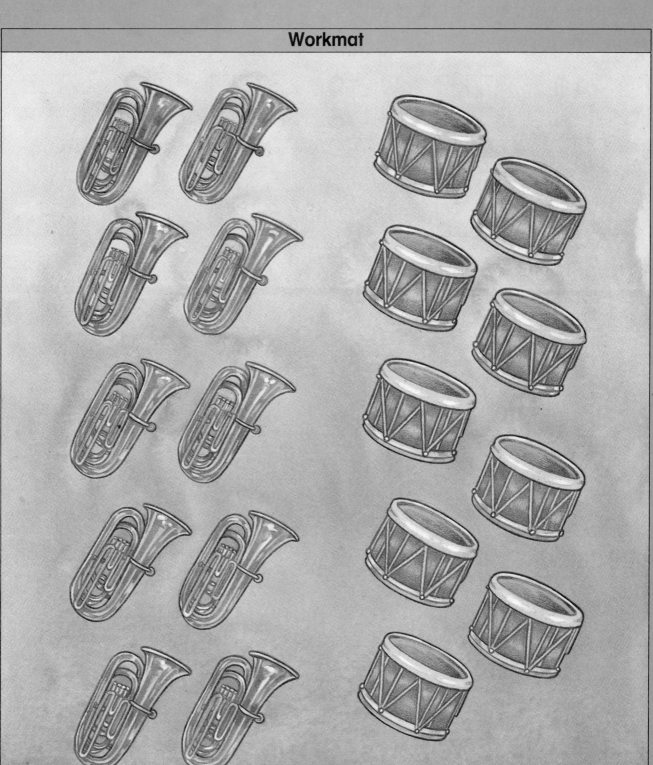

Name _____

Subtracting from 9 and 10

Use and counters.

Show each fact. Cross out
to show what you take away.
Write the answers.

1.
$$10 - 4 = $$

$$10 - 6 = $$

$$9 - 5 = $$

Subtract. Use ▦ and counters to help.

2.
$$10 - 3 = $$ $$9 - 5 = $$ $$7 - 3 = $$ $$10 - 8 = $$ $$9 - 2 = $$ $$10 - 4 = $$

3.
$$8 - 2 = $$ $$10 - 7 = $$ $$9 - 4 = $$ $$10 - 6 = $$ $$10 - 9 = $$ $$12 - 3 = $$

USE CRITICAL THINKING

4. Draw and color
   what is missing.

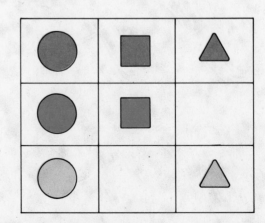

Fact Practice

Why are fish so smart?
To find out, first subtract. Then
write the letter code for each answer
below. Read the message.

Secret Code	
0 = w	7 = i
1 = h	8 = m
2 = t	9 = s
3 = l	10 = y
4 = e	11 = n
5 = c	12 = a
6 = o	

1.
$$\begin{array}{r} 10 \\ -\ 8 \\ \hline 2 \\ \hline t \end{array}$$
$$\begin{array}{r} 1 \\ -\ 0 \\ \hline \end{array}$$
$$\begin{array}{r} 10 \\ -\ 6 \\ \hline \end{array}$$
$$\begin{array}{r} 10 \\ -\ 0 \\ \hline \end{array}$$

2.
$$\begin{array}{r} 12 \\ -\ 3 \\ \hline \end{array}$$
$$\begin{array}{r} 6 \\ -\ 6 \\ \hline \end{array}$$
$$\begin{array}{r} 10 \\ -\ 3 \\ \hline \end{array}$$
$$\begin{array}{r} 11 \\ -\ 3 \\ \hline \end{array}$$

3.
$$\begin{array}{r} 9 \\ -\ 2 \\ \hline \end{array}$$
$$\begin{array}{r} 11 \\ -\ 0 \\ \hline \end{array}$$
$$\begin{array}{r} 12 \\ -\ 0 \\ \hline \end{array}$$

4.
$$\begin{array}{r} 11 \\ -\ 2 \\ \hline \end{array}$$
$$\begin{array}{r} 9 \\ -\ 4 \\ \hline \end{array}$$
$$\begin{array}{r} 4 \\ -\ 3 \\ \hline \end{array}$$
$$\begin{array}{r} 12 \\ -\ 6 \\ \hline \end{array}$$
$$\begin{array}{r} 10 \\ -\ 4 \\ \hline \end{array}$$
$$\begin{array}{r} 6 \\ -\ 3 \\ \hline \end{array}$$

Subtract.

1.
$$7 - 2 = 5 \qquad 10 - 6 \qquad 12 - 6 \qquad 8 - 0 \qquad 10 - 3 \qquad 9 - 6$$

2.
$$8¢ - 4¢ \qquad 10¢ - 1¢ \qquad 9¢ - 5¢ \qquad 10¢ - 2¢ \qquad 12¢ - 3¢ \qquad 9¢ - 2¢$$

3.

$3 - 1 = \underline{}$

$7 - 0 = \underline{}$

$5 - 5 = \underline{}$

$10 - 6 = \underline{}$

$9 - 5 = \underline{}$

$9 - 3 = \underline{}$

$10 - 2 = \underline{}$

$9 - 4 = \underline{}$

$10 - 7 = \underline{}$

4. Do these as fast as you can.

$8 - 3 = \underline{} \qquad 10 - 9 = \underline{} \qquad 11 - 2 = \underline{}$

$10 - 7 = \underline{} \qquad 9 - 4 = \underline{} \qquad 7 - 3 = \underline{}$

USE MENTAL MATH

5. Finish the number sentences.

$9 - 5 + 1 = \underline{}$

$9 - 4 + 2 = \underline{}$

Problem Solving
Understanding the Operations

Write the addition or subtraction
sentence for the story. Answer the question.

1. Taj saw 4 trumpet players in the
   parade. 1 trumpet player left. How
   many trumpet players are there now?

   ____ ◯ ____ = ____

   ____ trumpet
   players

2. 4 harps were big. 5 harps were
   small. How many harps were there
   in all?

   ____ ◯ ____ = ____

   ____ harps

3. Fumiko saw 4 red drums. Caitlin saw
   2 blue drums. How many more drums
   did Fumiko see than Caitlin?

   ____ ◯ ____ = ____

   ____ drums

Data Analysis

Take a survey. Find out what musical instruments your classmates like best.

1. Write **Music Survey** to name your graph.

2. Mark an x for each vote.

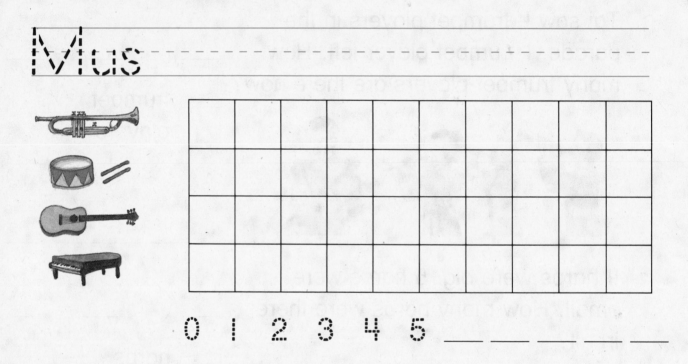

Mus _____

0 1 2 3 4 5 _____

3. Write the numbers across the bottom of your graph.

4. Ring what your classmates liked best.

Counting Up to Subtract

That is a count-up fact. The numbers are close to each other.

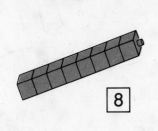

6

8

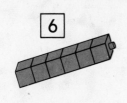

7, 8

$$\begin{array}{r} 8 \\ -\;\textcircled{6} \\ \hline 2 \end{array}$$

6, 7, 8

Subtract. Look for count-up facts.

1.
5, 6, 7, 8
$$\begin{array}{r} 8 \\ -\;\textcircled{5} \\ \hline 3 \end{array}$$

8, 9
$$\begin{array}{r} 9 \\ -\;\textcircled{8} \\ \hline \end{array}$$

9, 10, 11
$$\begin{array}{r} 11 \\ -\;\textcircled{9} \\ \hline \end{array}$$

6, 7, 8, 9
$$\begin{array}{r} 9 \\ -\;\textcircled{6} \\ \hline \end{array}$$

2.
$$\begin{array}{r} 6 \\ -\;1 \\ \hline \end{array}$$

$$\begin{array}{r} 12 \\ -\;9 \\ \hline \end{array}$$

$$\begin{array}{r} 7 \\ -\;7 \\ \hline \end{array}$$

$$\begin{array}{r} 11 \\ -\;2 \\ \hline \end{array}$$

$$\begin{array}{r} 8 \\ -\;6 \\ \hline \end{array}$$

3.
$$\begin{array}{r} 8 \\ -\;4 \\ \hline \end{array}$$

$$\begin{array}{r} 9 \\ -\;7 \\ \hline \end{array}$$

$$\begin{array}{r} 7 \\ -\;5 \\ \hline \end{array}$$

$$\begin{array}{r} 6 \\ -\;0 \\ \hline \end{array}$$

$$\begin{array}{r} 11 \\ -\;8 \\ \hline \end{array}$$

4. Write one count-up fact and its add-to-check fact.

−	+

Ring the count-up facts.
Then subtract all.

$$
\begin{array}{r} 9 \\ -\ 7 \\ \hline 2 \end{array}
$$
7, 8, 9

1.
$$
\begin{array}{r} 10 \\ -\ 2 \\ \hline \end{array}
$$
$$
\boxed{\begin{array}{r} 9 \\ -\ 7 \\ \hline \end{array}}
$$
$$
\begin{array}{r} 12 \\ -\ 6 \\ \hline \end{array}
$$
$$
\begin{array}{r} 7 \\ -\ 5 \\ \hline \end{array}
$$

2.
$$
\begin{array}{r} 8 \\ -\ 3 \\ \hline \end{array}
$$
$$
\begin{array}{r} 8 \\ -\ 6 \\ \hline \end{array}
$$
$$
\begin{array}{r} 10 \\ -\ 5 \\ \hline \end{array}
$$
$$
\begin{array}{r} 11 \\ -\ 9 \\ \hline \end{array}
$$
$$
\begin{array}{r} 9 \\ -\ 2 \\ \hline \end{array}
$$
$$
\begin{array}{r} 9 \\ -\ 6 \\ \hline \end{array}
$$

3.
$$
\begin{array}{r} 9 \\ -\ 8 \\ \hline \end{array}
$$
$$
\begin{array}{r} 11 \\ -\ 2 \\ \hline \end{array}
$$
$$
\begin{array}{r} 8 \\ -\ 2 \\ \hline \end{array}
$$
$$
\begin{array}{r} 9 \\ -\ 7 \\ \hline \end{array}
$$
$$
\begin{array}{r} 12 \\ -\ 3 \\ \hline \end{array}
$$
$$
\begin{array}{r} 8 \\ -\ 7 \\ \hline \end{array}
$$

4.
$$
\begin{array}{r} 8 \\ -\ 4 \\ \hline \end{array}
$$
$$
\begin{array}{r} 11 \\ -\ 8 \\ \hline \end{array}
$$
$$
\begin{array}{r} 10 \\ -\ 4 \\ \hline \end{array}
$$
$$
\begin{array}{r} 6 \\ -\ 4 \\ \hline \end{array}
$$
$$
\begin{array}{r} 10 \\ -\ 3 \\ \hline \end{array}
$$
$$
\begin{array}{r} 12 \\ -\ 9 \\ \hline \end{array}
$$

PROBLEM SOLVING

5. Tell one way to make the numbers the same. Use counters to help.

Ty has 6 rattles.   Rashunda has 2 rattles.

Ty gives _____ rattles to Rashunda.

Fact Practice

Subtract. Then color.

1 crayon 2 crayon 3 crayon
4 crayon
5 crayon

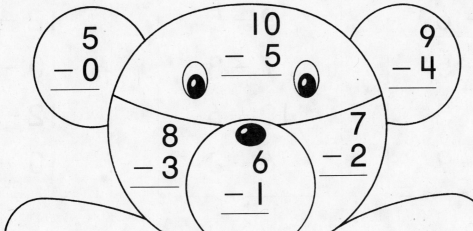

$$\begin{array}{r} 5 \\ -0 \\ \hline \end{array}$$

$$\begin{array}{r} 10 \\ -5 \\ \hline \end{array}$$

$$\begin{array}{r} 9 \\ -4 \\ \hline \end{array}$$

$$\begin{array}{r} 8 \\ -3 \\ \hline \end{array}$$

$$\begin{array}{r} 6 \\ -1 \\ \hline \end{array}$$

$$\begin{array}{r} 7 \\ -2 \\ \hline \end{array}$$

$9 - 7 = \underline{\hspace{1cm}}$ $5 - 3 = \underline{\hspace{1cm}}$ $8 - 6 = \underline{\hspace{1cm}}$

$9 - 8 = \underline{\hspace{1cm}}$

$12 - 9 = \underline{\hspace{1cm}}$

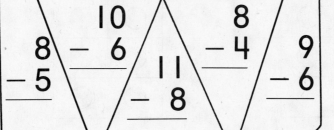

$$\begin{array}{r} 8 \\ -5 \\ \hline \end{array}$$

$$\begin{array}{r} 10 \\ -6 \\ \hline \end{array}$$

$$\begin{array}{r} 11 \\ -8 \\ \hline \end{array}$$

$$\begin{array}{r} 8 \\ -4 \\ \hline \end{array}$$

$$\begin{array}{r} 9 \\ -6 \\ \hline \end{array}$$

$3 - 2 = \underline{\hspace{1cm}}$ $6 - 5 = \underline{\hspace{1cm}}$

$6 - 1 = \underline{\hspace{1cm}}$ $5 - 0 = \underline{\hspace{1cm}}$

Ring the ways that make the answer.

1. **3**

$$11 - 8$$
$$9 - 6$$
$$8 - 5$$
$$9 - 5$$
$$12 - 9$$

(11 − 8 and 9 − 6 are ringed)

2. **4**

$$8 - 4$$
$$9 - 5$$
$$7 - 3$$
$$10 - 6$$
$$6 - 3$$

3. **9**

$$11 - 2$$
$$12 - 6$$
$$10 - 2$$
$$12 - 3$$
$$10 - 1$$

MIDCHAPTER REVIEW/QUIZ

Subtract. Cross out to show
what you take away.

1.

$$\begin{array}{r} 9 \\ -4 \\ \hline \end{array}$$

$$\begin{array}{r} 10 \\ -8 \\ \hline \end{array}$$

$$\begin{array}{r} 9 \\ -5 \\ \hline \end{array}$$
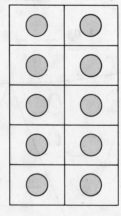

Ring the count-up facts.
Then subtract all.

2.

$$\begin{array}{r} 11 \\ -9 \\ \hline \end{array} \qquad \begin{array}{r} 10 \\ -4 \\ \hline \end{array} \qquad \begin{array}{r} 8 \\ -6 \\ \hline \end{array} \qquad \begin{array}{r} 9 \\ -2 \\ \hline \end{array} \qquad \begin{array}{r} 7 \\ -5 \\ \hline \end{array} \qquad \begin{array}{r} 10 \\ -3 \\ \hline \end{array}$$

Adding to Check Subtraction

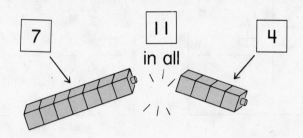

in all

add-to-check fact

$$\begin{array}{r} 7 \\ +4 \\ \hline 11 \end{array}$$ so $$\begin{array}{r} 11 \\ -4 \\ \hline 7 \end{array}$$ and $$\begin{array}{r} 11 \\ -7 \\ \hline 4 \end{array}$$

Finish the add-to-check fact.
Use cubes to help. Then subtract.

1. $$\begin{array}{r} 5 \\ +7 \\ \hline \end{array}$$ $$\begin{array}{r} 12 \\ -7 \\ \hline \end{array}$$ and $$\begin{array}{r} 12 \\ -5 \\ \hline \end{array}$$

2. $$\begin{array}{r} 6 \\ +5 \\ \hline \end{array}$$ $$\begin{array}{r} 11 \\ -5 \\ \hline \end{array}$$ and $$\begin{array}{r} 11 \\ -6 \\ \hline \end{array}$$

3. $$\begin{array}{r} 4 \\ +7 \\ \hline \end{array}$$ $$\begin{array}{r} 11 \\ -4 \\ \hline \end{array}$$ and $$\begin{array}{r} 11 \\ -7 \\ \hline \end{array}$$

4. $$\begin{array}{r} 9 \\ +3 \\ \hline \end{array}$$ $$\begin{array}{r} 12 \\ -3 \\ \hline \end{array}$$ and $$\begin{array}{r} 12 \\ -9 \\ \hline \end{array}$$

5. $$\begin{array}{r} 4 \\ +5 \\ \hline \end{array}$$ $$\begin{array}{r} 9 \\ -5 \\ \hline \end{array}$$ and $$\begin{array}{r} 9 \\ -4 \\ \hline \end{array}$$

6. $$\begin{array}{r} 8 \\ +4 \\ \hline \end{array}$$ $$\begin{array}{r} 12 \\ -4 \\ \hline \end{array}$$ and $$\begin{array}{r} 12 \\ -8 \\ \hline \end{array}$$

Subtract. Finish the add-to-check fact.

1.

12	4
− 4	+ 8
8	12

9	5
− 5	+

10	6
− 6	+

2.

11	5
− 5	+

12	9
− 9	+

11	7
− 7	+

3.

12	5
− 5	+

12	8
− 8	+

11	6
− 6	+

SHOW WITH CUBES

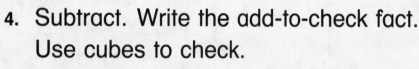

4. Subtract. Write the add-to-check fact.
Use cubes to check.

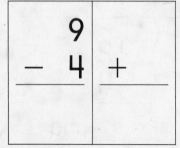

9	
− 4	+

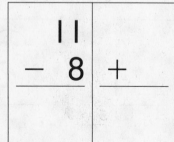

11	
− 8	+

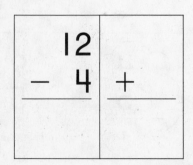

12	
− 4	+

Fact Families

Work in a group. Use 12 cubes
of one color and 12 cubes of
another color. Make a train.
Snap it. Finish the number
sentences.

1. Make a 12 train.

$7 + 5 =$

$5 + 7 =$

$12 - 5 =$

$12 - 7 =$

2. Make an 11 train.

$+ \quad =$

$+ \quad =$

$11 - \quad =$

$11 - \quad =$

3. Make a different 12 train.

$+ \quad =$

$+ \quad =$

$12 - \quad =$

$12 - \quad =$

4. Make a different 11 train.

$+ \quad =$

$+ \quad =$

$11 - \quad =$

$11 - \quad =$

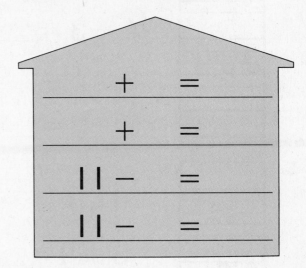

Make a fact family. Add or subtract.

1.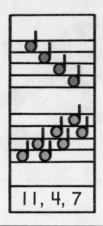

11, 4, 7

$4 + 7 = \underline{}$

$7 + 4 = \underline{}$

$11 - 7 = \underline{}$

$11 - 4 = \underline{}$

2.

11, 6, 5

$5 + 6 = \underline{}$

$6 + 5 = \underline{}$

$11 - 6 = \underline{}$

$11 - 5 = \underline{}$

3.

9, 6, 3

$3 + 6 = \underline{}$

$6 + 3 = \underline{}$

$9 - 6 = \underline{}$

$9 - 3 = \underline{}$

4.

12, 7, 5

$5 + 7 = \underline{}$

$7 + 5 = \underline{}$

$12 - 7 = \underline{}$

$12 - 5 = \underline{}$

5.

12, 8, 4

$4 + 8 = \underline{}$

$8 + 4 = \underline{}$

$12 - \underline{} = \underline{}$

$12 - \underline{} = \underline{}$

6.

9, 5, 4

$4 + 5 = \underline{}$

$5 + 4 = \underline{}$

$9 - \underline{} = \underline{}$

$9 - \underline{} = \underline{}$

WRITE ABOUT IT

7. Subtract. Finish the sentence.

$$\begin{array}{r} 3 \\ + 3 \\ \hline 6 \end{array} \quad \text{and} \quad \begin{array}{r} 6 \\ - 3 \\ \hline \end{array}$$

6, 3, 3

_____

- - - - - - - - - -

These two _____ make a family.

Name _____

Fact Practice

Help me if I'm wrong.

Check Percy Penguin's work.
If correct, write **C**. If not, cross out
and write the answer.

Start.
↓

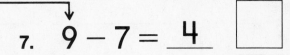

1. $3 - 3 = $ 6̸   [C]

2. $8 - 4 = $ 4   [C]

3. $11 - 9 = $ 2   [ ]

4. $8 - 3 = $ 6   [ ]

5. $9 - 6 = $ 3   [ ]

6. $12 - 9 = $ 3   [ ]

7. $9 - 7 = $ 4   [ ]

8. $11 - 8 = $ 3   [ ]

9. $9 - 5 = $ 4   [ ]

10. $10 - 8 = $ 3   [ ]

11. $8 - 6 = $ 2   [ ]

12. $10 - 3 = $ 7   [ ]

13.

$$\begin{array}{r} 9 \\ -4 \\ \hline 5 \end{array} \qquad \begin{array}{r} 8 \\ -5 \\ \hline 2̸ \end{array} \qquad \begin{array}{r} 9 \\ -2 \\ \hline 6 \end{array} \qquad \begin{array}{r} 2 \\ -2 \\ \hline 0 \end{array} \qquad \begin{array}{r} 9 \\ -3 \\ \hline 6 \end{array} \qquad \begin{array}{r} 6 \\ -1 \\ \hline 4 \end{array}$$

[C]   [3]   [ ]   [ ]   [ ]   [ ]

14. The smallest difference on the page is ____ .

Subtract. Finish the add-to-check fact.

1.

10	4
− 4	+ 6
6	10

11	8
− 8	+

9	6
− 6	+

2.

12	9
− 9	+

9	5
− 5	+

10	7
− 7	+

3.

8	6
− 6	+

10	2
− 2	+

7	4
− 4	+

MIXED REVIEW

Add.

4.

$$\begin{array}{r} 4 \\ 0 \\ +3 \\ \hline \end{array} \qquad \begin{array}{r} 5 \\ 1 \\ +5 \\ \hline \end{array} \qquad \begin{array}{r} 2 \\ 2 \\ +3 \\ \hline \end{array} \qquad \begin{array}{r} 6 \\ 6 \\ +0 \\ \hline \end{array} \qquad \begin{array}{r} 3 \\ 1 \\ +3 \\ \hline \end{array} \qquad \begin{array}{r} 4 \\ 4 \\ +1 \\ \hline \end{array}$$

5. $6 + 4 = \underline{}$ $\qquad$ $3 + 8 = \underline{}$ $\qquad$ $7 + 1 = \underline{}$

6. $0 + 8 = \underline{}$ $\qquad$ $5 + 5 = \underline{}$ $\qquad$ $9 + 2 = \underline{}$

Problem Solving
Telling a Story

UNDERSTAND
FIND DATA
PLAN
ESTIMATE
SOLVE
CHECK

Work with a partner. Tell an
addition or subtraction story.
Write the number sentence.

1.

____ boys   ____ went away.   ____ boys are left.

___ ◯ ___ = ___

2.

____ violins   ____ banjos   There are ____ in all.

___ ◯ ___ = ___

3.

____ girls   ____ stopped playing.   ____ girls are left.

___ ◯ ___ = ___

4.

____ records   ____ broke.   ____ records are left.

___ ◯ ___ = ___

Chapter 10   (two hundred nineteen)   219

Problem Solving Strategy
Use Logical Reasoning

UNDERSTAND
FIND DATA
PLAN
ESTIMATE
SOLVE
CHECK

Find Melia.

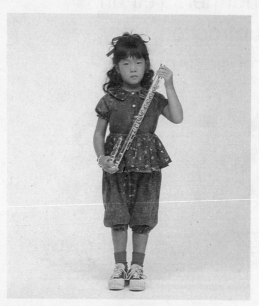

She has a .

She does not have ⬯.

She has a ◡.

Ring Melia.

Name _____

WRAP UP

MATH WORDS

1. Match.

| count-up fact |
| add-to-check fact |
| fact family |

$$3 + 6 = 9 \qquad 9 - 3 = 6$$
$$6 + 3 = 9 \qquad 9 - 6 = 3$$

$$12 - 9 = 3$$

$$11 - 6 = 5 \qquad 5 + 6 = 11$$

MATH REASONING

Fill in the blanks. Use the numbers and the ⊞ and ⊟. Use each as many times as you need to.

2.
$$\begin{array}{r} 7 \\ \underline{} \\ 12 \end{array} \qquad \begin{array}{r} 3 \\ \underline{} \\ 11 \end{array} \qquad \begin{array}{r} 5 \\ 8 \\ \underline{} \\ 12 \end{array} \qquad \begin{array}{r} 8 \\ \underline{} \\ 11 \end{array}$$

3.
$$\begin{array}{r} 8 \\ \underline{} \\ 3 \end{array} \qquad \begin{array}{r} 11 \\ 5 \\ \underline{} \\ 8 \end{array} \qquad \begin{array}{r} 5 \\ \underline{} \\ 7 \end{array} \qquad \begin{array}{r} 12 \\ \underline{} \\ 5 \end{array}$$

Name _____

CHAPTER REVIEW/TEST

Subtract. Cross out to show
what you take away.

1.
$$
\begin{array}{r} 10 \\ -7 \\ \hline \end{array}
$$

$$
\begin{array}{r} 9 \\ -5 \\ \hline \end{array}
$$

$$
\begin{array}{r} 9 \\ -4 \\ \hline \end{array}
$$

2. Ring the count-up facts.
   Then subtract all.

$$
\begin{array}{r} 7 \\ -3 \\ \hline \end{array}
\qquad
\begin{array}{r} 10 \\ -8 \\ \hline \end{array}
\qquad
\begin{array}{r} 9 \\ -7 \\ \hline \end{array}
\qquad
\begin{array}{r} 7 \\ -0 \\ \hline \end{array}
\qquad
\begin{array}{r} 11 \\ -9 \\ \hline \end{array}
\qquad
\begin{array}{r} 8 \\ -3 \\ \hline \end{array}
$$

Finish the fact family.
Add or subtract.

3. $4 + 8 =$ _____

   $8 + 4 =$ _____

   $12 -$ ___ $=$ ___

   $12 -$ ___ $=$ ___

4. $6 + 5 =$ _____

   $5 + 6 =$ _____

   $11 -$ ___ $=$ ___

   $11 -$ ___ $=$ ___

5. $7 + 4 =$ _____

   $4 + 7 =$ _____

   $11 -$ ___ $=$ ___

   $11 -$ ___ $=$ ___

6. Suki saw 7 clowns. 3 clowns
   ran away. How many clowns
   are there now?

   _____ clowns

Finish the number
sentence.

___ ◯ ___ $=$ ___

ENRICHMENT
Finding All Ways

Mrs. Chen used blue, yellow, and red paint
for art class. She asked Alex to put the paint
back on the shelf after class. Color to show
all the different ways Alex could put the
paint back. Use cubes to help.

1.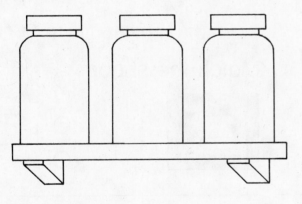

2.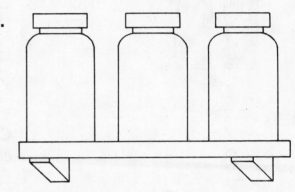

3.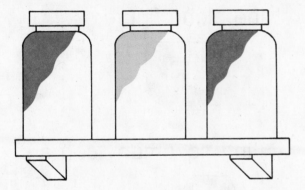

4.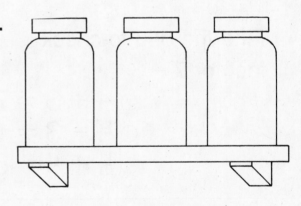

5.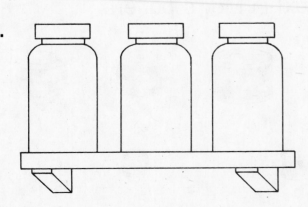

6.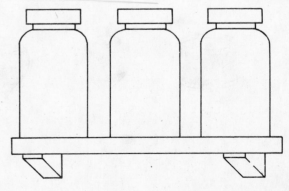

Name _____

CUMULATIVE REVIEW

Subtract.

1.

$$6$$
$$-\,2$$

○ 4
○ 5
○ 3

2.

$$10$$
$$-\,5$$

○ 6
○ 4
○ 5

3.
$$9$$
$$-\,0$$

○ 8
○ 9
○ 0

4. Find the add-to-check fact for $7 - 3 = 4$.

○ $4 + 3 = 7$
○ $4 - 3 = 1$
○ $4 + 4 = 8$

5. Match the shape.

○
○
○

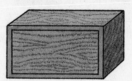

6. Match the flat face to the plane figure.

○ □
○ △
○ ▭

7. Find how many corners.

○ 5
○ 7
○ 6

8. Match the shape.

○ ◯
○ ◺
○ ⬭

9. Choose the toy that comes next in Meg's pattern.

○   ○   ○

Chapter 10 Cumulative Review

11

Place Value

Workmat

Name _____

Grouping by Tens

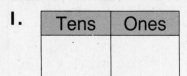

Take a pile of cubes.
Make trains of 10 cubes.
Write how many tens and extra ones.

1.

Tens	Ones

2.

Tens	Ones

3.

Tens	Ones

4.

Tens	Ones

5.

Tens	Ones

Ring groups of tens.
Write how many tens and ones.

6.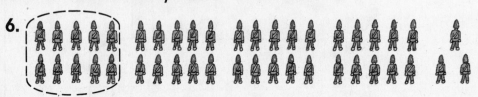

Tens	Ones
4	3

7.

Tens	Ones

USE MENTAL MATH

8. How many fingers do you have?

_____ fingers

9. How many fingers do friends have?

_____ fingers

10. How many fingers does this family have?

_____ fingers

Showing Tens and Ones

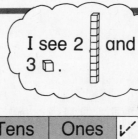

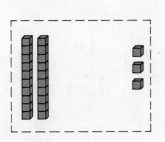

Paste.

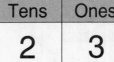

Use the tens and ones punchouts.

Place them to show the tens and ones.

✔ if correct. Then paste.

1.

Tens	Ones	
2	6	

Paste here.

2.

Tens	Ones	
1	3	

Paste here.

3.

Tens	Ones	
6	1	

Paste here.

4.

Tens	Ones	
3	2	

Paste here.

5.

Tens	Ones	
4	5	

Paste here.

6.

Tens	Ones	
5	4	

Paste here.

Color to show the tens and ones.
Count. Then 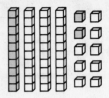 if correct.

Tens	Ones	
1	2	✓

1.

Tens	Ones	
3	5	

2.

Tens	Ones	
6	0	

3.

Tens	Ones	
2	3	

4.

Tens	Ones	
3	2	

5.

Tens	Ones	
4	1	

6.

Tens	Ones	
5	5	

FIND THE DATA

Data Bank (See page 398.)

7. How many ten-packs of soldiers are there? How many extras are there? Write the numbers in the box.

Tens	Ones

8. How many ten-packs of bowling pins are there? How many extras are there? Write the numbers in the box.

Tens	Ones

Name _____

Decade Numbers and Names

1. Cut out the number cards.
   Put a card in the box. Use
   blocks to show the number.

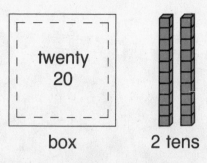

box   2 tens

First Card	Second Card	Third Card

2. Put all the cards in order on the
   train. Count. Then paste.

Paste here. | Paste here. | Paste here. | Paste here.

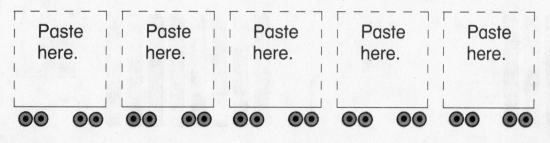

Paste here. | Paste here. | Paste here. | Paste here. | Paste here.

ten	10
twenty	20
thirty	30
forty	40
fifty	50
sixty	60
seventy	70
eighty	80
ninety	90

twenty
20

ten 10	

1. Write the tens.

twenty 20
thirty 30
forty 40
fifty 50
sixty 60
seventy 70
eighty 80
ninety 90

Write the number that tells how many.

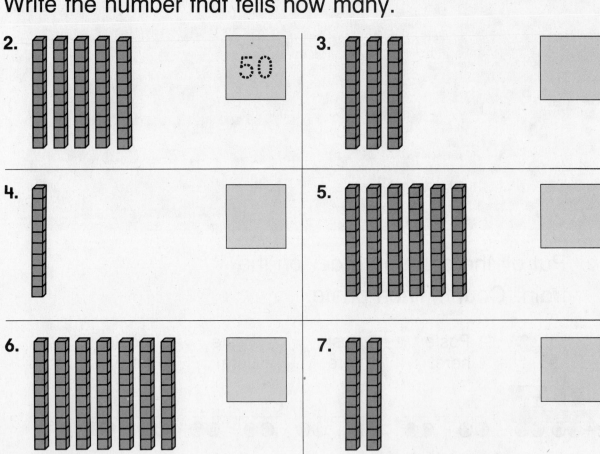

2. 50

3.

4.

5.

6.

7.

8.

9.

Showing and Writing 2-Digit Numbers

Write 43.

Count the tens and ones.
Use blocks to help. Write the number.

1.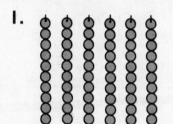

2.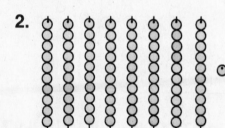

3.

4.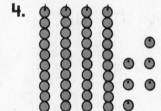

5.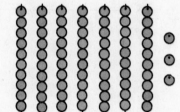

6.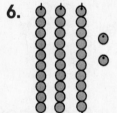

7. 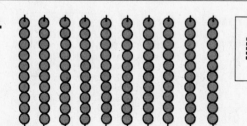 100

Color the tens and ones
to show how many. Count.
Then ✔ if correct.

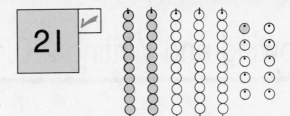

21 ✔

1.

49

2.

31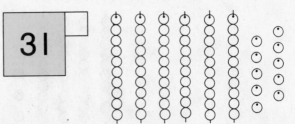

3.

26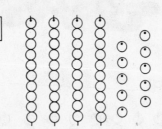

4.

65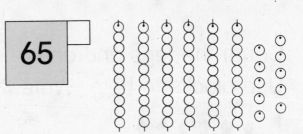

Midchapter Review/Quiz

1. Color to show the tens and ones.

Tens	Ones
3	4

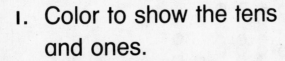

2. Ring groups of ten. Write how many tens and ones.

Tens	Ones

Write the number that tells how many.

3.

4.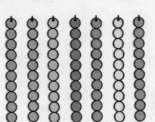

Tens and Ones

Work in a group. Use blocks.
Spin and show a number of tens.
Write it. Spin and show a number
of ones. Write it. Then ring
and write how many.

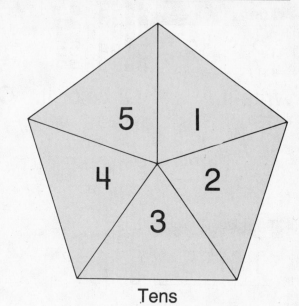

Tens

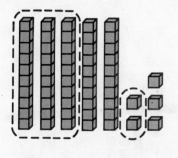 Ring it.

Tens	Ones
3	2

32

Write it.   Write how many.

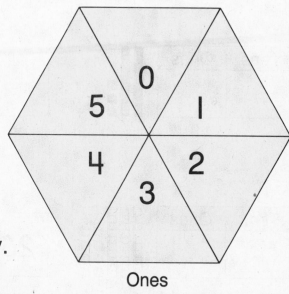

Ones

1.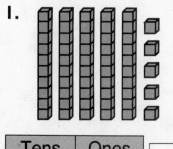

Tens	Ones

2.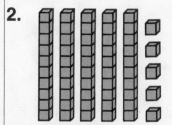

Tens	Ones

3.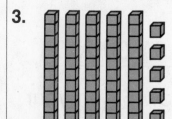

Tens	Ones

Fill in what is missing.

Tens	Ones
2	2

22

Write it.   Or color it.   Or write how many.

1.

Tens	Ones
1	5

2.

Tens	Ones
3	6

3.

Tens	Ones

4.

Tens	Ones

5.

Tens	Ones

26

6.

Tens	Ones

44

TRY A CALCULATOR

7. Show 57 on your .

Finish the sentence.

I can add _____ to change 57 to 67.

Check to see if you are right.

Problem Solving
Understanding the Operations

UNDERSTAND
FIND DATA
PLAN
ESTIMATE
SOLVE
CHECK

Listen to the story. Color the tens.
Finish the number sentence.
Then write the answer.

 10 red cars   10 blue cars   10 blue cars

Each pack is 1 ten.

1 ten ⊕ 2 tens = __3__ tens   __30__ cars

1. How many red and blue cars are there?

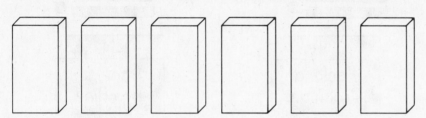

4 tens ◯ 2 tens = ____ tens   ____ cars

2. How many more red than blue cars are there?

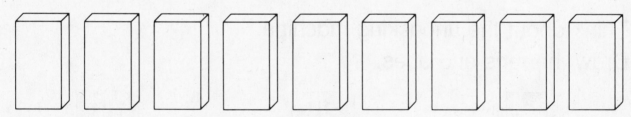

5 tens ◯ 4 tens = ____ ten   ____ cars

3. How many red and blue cars are there?

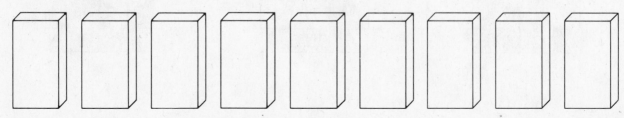

7 tens ◯ 2 tens = ____ tens   ____ cars

Informal Algebra

Think about the packing machine. Write how many in each box.

Put in 3 tens and 2 ones. Out comes a box of 32.

IN

Packing Machine

OUT

32 blocks

1.
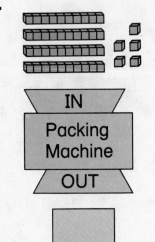

IN

Packing Machine

OUT

blocks

2.
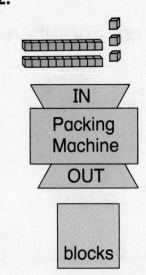

IN

Packing Machine

OUT

blocks

3.

IN

Packing Machine

OUT

blocks

Think about the unpacking machine.
Draw the tens and ones.

4.

13 blocks

IN

Unpacking Machine

OUT

5.

24 blocks

IN

Unpacking Machine

OUT

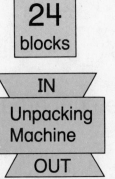

6.

43 blocks

IN

Unpacking Machine

OUT

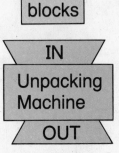

Trading Dimes and Pennies

Show 13 pennies.	Trade for a dime.	Write it.

Dimes	Pennies
1	3

Trade 10 pennies for 1 dime.

Work in a group. Use your penny
and dime punchouts. Show the pennies.
Trade for dimes. Write it.

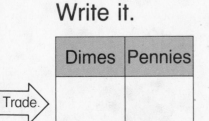

1. Show.   Write it.

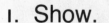

26 pennies	Trade.	Dimes	Pennies

2. Show.   Write it.

30 pennies	Trade.	Dimes	Pennies

3. Show.   Write it.

43 pennies	Trade.	Dimes	Pennies

4. Show.   Write it.

29 pennies	Trade.	Dimes	Pennies

Trade pennies for dimes.
Color enough dimes.
Color 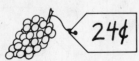 enough pennies.
Write how many.

I traded 70 pennies for 7 dimes. I had 3 pennies left over.

1. 73 pennies

Dimes	Pennies
7	3

2. 52 pennies

Dimes	Pennies

3. 25 pennies

Dimes	Pennies

4. 40 pennies

Dimes	Pennies

PROBLEM SOLVING

5. How much more money do I need?

I want  24¢ . I have . I need ____ ¢ .

Name _____

Dimes and Pennies

Work in a group. Use your coin punchouts. Spin and show a number of dimes. Write it. Spin and show a number of pennies. Write it. Then write how much money.

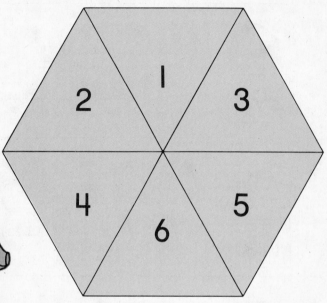

Dimes	Pennies
6	3

63¢

Write it.   Write how much money.

1.

Dimes	Pennies

___¢

2.

Dimes	Pennies

___¢

3.

Dimes	Pennies

___¢

4.

Dimes	Pennies

___¢

What did you spin?

5. Write the largest amount.

___¢

6. Write the smallest amount.

___¢

Show how much money.
Color ✏️ enough dimes.
Color ✏️ enough pennies.

21¢

1.

29¢

2.

12¢

3.

53¢

MIXED REVIEW

4. Add.

4	2	0	6	6	3
+5	+8	+5	+3	+6	+7

5. Subtract.

9	11	7	8	12	10
−5	−9	−5	−4	−3	−6

Problem Solving
Making Estimates

UNDERSTAND
FIND DATA
PLAN
ESTIMATE
SOLVE
CHECK

Listen to the story.
Without counting, tell about how many.
Ring your estimate.
Ring tens to check.

1.

About how many
strawberries are there?

10   30   70   100

2.

About how many pears
are there?

10   20   80   100

3.

About how many oranges
are there?

10   30   70   100

4.

About how many grapes
are there?

10   30   50   100

5.

About how many pieces of fruit are there?

10   50   100   200

Problem Solving Strategy
Make a List

UNDERSTAND
FIND DATA
PLAN
ESTIMATE
SOLVE
CHECK

Use 2 tens and 3 ones blocks. Draw and write to show the 2-digit numbers you can make.

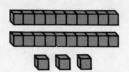

What 2-digit numbers can I show with these cubes?

Draw.	Write.	Draw.	Write.

Draw.	Write.	Draw.	Write.	Draw.	Write.

Draw.	Write.	Draw.	Write.	Draw.	Write.

WRAP UP

MATH WORDS

Ring what belongs. Tell why.

1.   seventeen   17

Tens	Ones
1	8

2. forty

Tens	Ones
4	0

3. 35

Tens	Ones
5	3

thirty-five

4.   6 tens   61   sixty

MATH REASONING

5. Use three dime and three penny punchouts. Take three coins at a time. Find different sums each time. Fill in the chart.

Number of Dimes	Number of Pennies	Money in All
0	3	
1		

CHAPTER REVIEW/TEST

Ring groups of ten. Write
how many tens and ones.

1.

Tens	Ones

2.

Tens	Ones

3. Color to show the
tens and ones.

Tens	Ones
2	7

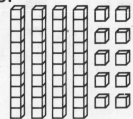

4. Write the number.

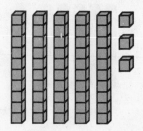

5. Trade pennies for dimes.
Write how much money.

58 pennies

Dimes	Pennies

6. Color enough dimes and
pennies to buy the toy.

34¢

7. Finish the number sentence.
How many more than are there?

5 tens $\bigcirc$ 3 tens = ____ tens

____

ENRICHMENT
Temperature

Cold Day

Warm Day

Hot Day

Match each picture to its temperature.

CUMULATIVE REVIEW

1. Match the shape.

○ ◯
○ △
○ ▢

2. Find how many sides.

○ 5
○ 6
○ 4

3. Find how many pegs are inside.

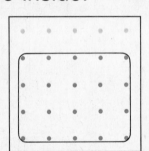

○ 5
○ 6
○ 14

4. Which shape is divided into two matching parts?

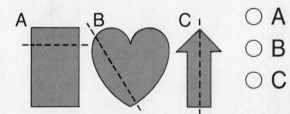

○ A
○ B
○ C

Subtract.

5. $9 - 3 = $ ___

○ 5
○ 6
○ 7

6.
$$\begin{array}{r} 11 \\ -\ 8 \\ \hline \end{array}$$

○ 2
○ 4
○ 3

7. Find a fact in the same family as $8 + 4 = 12$.

○ $7 + 5 = 12$
○ $8 - 4 = 4$
○ $12 - 8 = 4$

8. Find the add-to-check fact for $12 - 5 = 7$.

○ $7 + 5 = 12$
○ $12 - 7 = 5$
○ $7 + 4 = 11$

9. Choose the correct number sentence. Kris had 9 pens. She gave 5 away. How many pens are left?

○ $9 - 5 = 4$
○ $9 - 4 = 5$
○ $4 + 5 = 9$

Chapter 11 Cumulative Review

12
Number Relationships and Counting Patterns

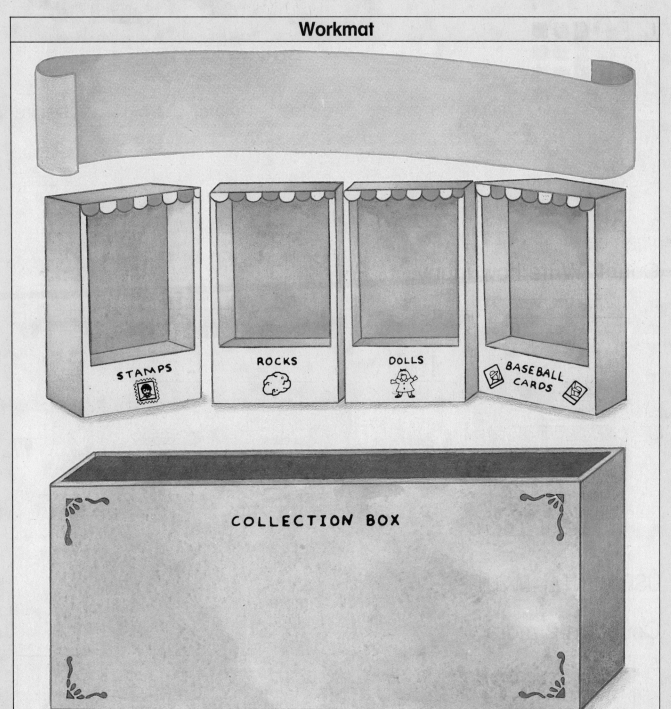

Workmat

STAMPS

ROCKS

DOLLS

BASEBALL CARDS

COLLECTION BOX

Counting to 50

One more than 19 makes another ten. That's 2 tens or 20.

Work in a group. Use blocks to show the number. Put in 1 more block. Write how many.

1. 19 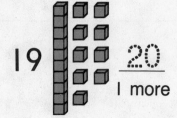 _20_   ____   ____   ____   ____   ____
        1 more   1 more   1 more   1 more   1 more   1 more

2. 27 _____ _____ _____ _____ _____ _____

3. 34 _____ _____ _____ _____ _____ _____

Count. Write how many.

4. 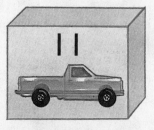 |11|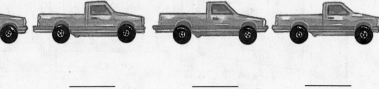

   _12_   ____   ____   ____

5.  |27|

   _____   _____   _____   _____

USE MENTAL MATH

Count on 2 more.

30, 2 more is 31, 32.

6. | Start 30 | →2 more | ☐ |

7. | Start 42 | →2 more | ☐ |

Name _____

Counting to 100

25 is 2 tens 5 ones.
I more makes
2 tens 6 ones.

Work with a partner. Use blocks to show each number in a yellow car. Put in I more ones block to show the next number. Write it.

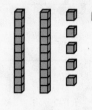

| 25 | 26 |

1.

| 1 | 2 | | | 5 | | | | | 10 |

2.

| 11 | 12 | | 14 | | 16 | | | | 20 |

3.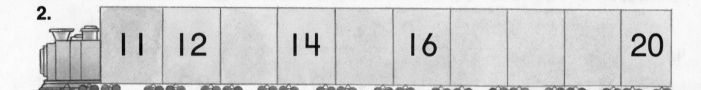

| 21 | | 23 | | 25 | | 27 | | 29 | |

4.

| | 32 | | 34 | | 36 | | 38 | | 40 |

5.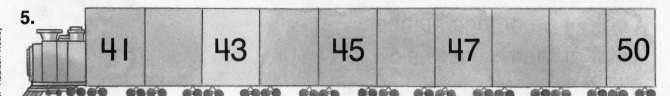

| 41 | | 43 | | 45 | | 47 | | | 50 |

6. Fill in the missing numbers above.

Write the missing numbers.

1. 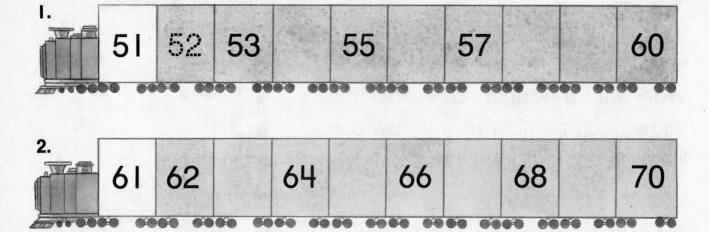 51 | 52 | 53 | | 55 | | 57 | | | 60

2. 61 | 62 | | 64 | | 66 | | 68 | | 70

3. 71 | | 73 | | 75 | | 77 | | | 80

4. 81 | 82 | | 84 | | 86 | | 88 | | 90

5. 91 | | 93 | | 95 | | 97 | | 99 | 100

TALK ABOUT IT

6. Color the first car in each row orange.
Look at an orange number.
Look at the number below it.
Tell what happens to the tens.
Tell what happens to the ones.

Name _____

Counting On and Back

Work in a group. Spin a tens number. Write it.
Spin a ones number. Write it.
Count on and back. Write the numbers.

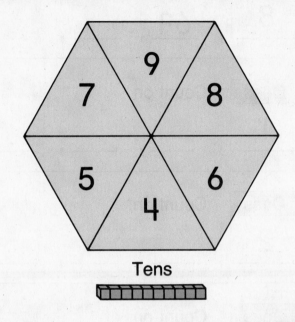

Tens

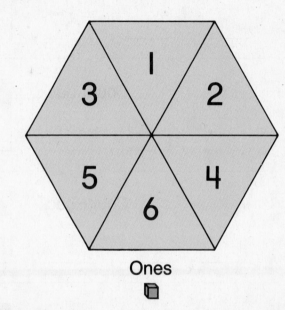

Ones

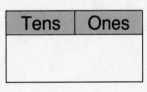

1. ←   Count back.

Tens	Ones
6	4

Count on. →

61 , 62 , 63 , | 6 | 4 | , 65 , 66 , 67

2. ←   Count back.

Tens	Ones

Count on. →

___ , ___ , ___ , | | | , ___ , ___ , ___

3. ←   Count back.

Tens	Ones

Count on. →

___ , ___ , ___ , | | | , ___ , ___ , ___

4. ←   Count back.

Tens	Ones

Count on. →

___ , ___ , ___ , | | | , ___ , ___ , ___

Count on and back. Write the numbers.

1. ⬅ Count back. | Tens | Ones | Count on. ➡

_____ , _____ , 67 , | **6** | **8** | , 69 , _____ , _____

2. ⬅ Count back. | Tens | Ones | Count on. ➡

_____ , _____ , _____ , | **5** | **1** | , _____ , _____ , _____

3. ⬅ Count back. | Tens | Ones | Count on. ➡

_____ , _____ , _____ , | **8** | **2** | , _____ , _____ , _____

4. ⬅ Count back. | Tens | Ones | Count on. ➡

_____ , _____ , _____ , | **2** | **4** | , _____ , _____ , _____

5. Check by counting. Start with the smallest number in each row.

PROBLEM SOLVING

6. I had   I bought   How many do I have in all?

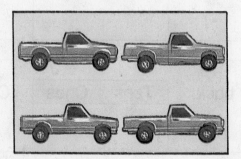

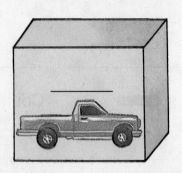

Numbers Before, After, Between

Work in a group. Use blocks. Show the red number. Put in 1 more ones block. Write the number. Show the blue number. Take away 1 ones block. Write the number. Then write the number between.

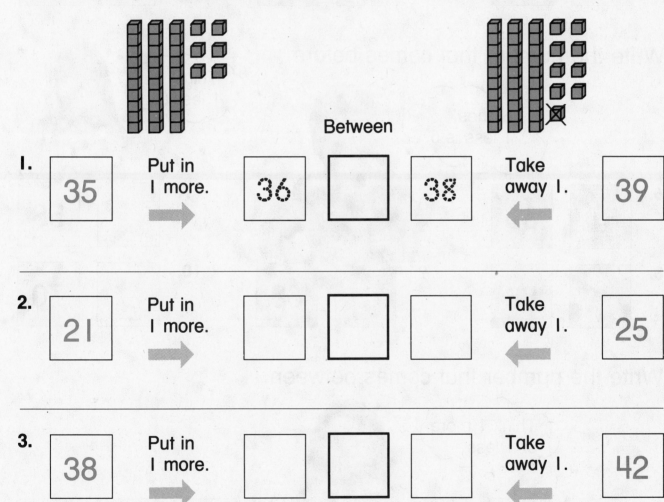

Between

1. | 35 | Put in 1 more. → | 36 | | 3̶8̶ | Take away 1. ← | 39 |

2. | 21 | Put in 1 more. → | | | | Take away 1. ← | 25 |

3. | 38 | Put in 1 more. → | | | | Take away 1. ← | 42 |

4. | 24 | Put in 1 more. → | | | | Take away 1. ← | 28 |

Write the number that comes after.

6 ones,
I more is 7.

Think
I more 🔲.

1. | 46 | 47 |

2. | 39 | |

3. | 96 | |

4. | 14 | |

5. | 59 | |

Write the number that comes before.

6 ones,
I less is 5.

Think
I less 🔲.

6. | 35 | 36 |

7. | | 58 |

8. | | 88 |

9. | | 63 |

10. | | 70 |

Write the number that comes between.

Think I more
or I less.

11. | 25 | | 27 |

12. | 96 | | 98 |

13. | 13 | | 15 |

14. | 78 | | 80 |

Name _____

Comparing Numbers

The one with more tens has more.

The tens are the same. Look at the ones.

Work with a partner. Use blocks to show the tens. ✔ if the tens are the same. Use blocks to show the ones. Color the box that has more. Take turns saying which has more.

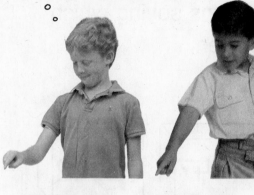

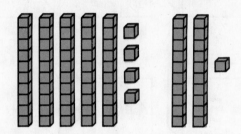

1. 54 21 ☐

2. 38 36 ✔

3. 51 50 ☐

4. 50 40 ☐

5. 33 53 ☐

6. 41 42 ☐

7. 31 35 ☐

8. 84 91 ☐

Work with a partner.

✔ if the tens are the same.

Color the box that has fewer.

Take turns saying which has fewer.

The tens are the same. Look at the ones. 2 ones is less than 4 ones.

 12   14   ☑

1.  47   42 ☐

2.  52   39 ☐

3. 12   21 ☐

4. 56   58 ☐

MIDCHAPTER REVIEW/QUIZ

1. Write the missing numbers.

| 41 | | 43 | 44 | | 46 | | 48 | 49 | |

2. Count on and back. Write the numbers.

← Count back.

Tens	Ones
2	2

Count on. →

____ , ____ , ____ , [2 2] , ____ , ____ , ____ ,

3. Write the number that comes before.

____ , 60

4. Write the number that comes between.

39 , ____ , 41

Problem Solving
Understanding the Operations

Ten cards in each pack.

UNDERSTAND
FIND DATA
PLAN
ESTIMATE
SOLVE
CHECK

Listen to the story.
Color the plant cards green.
Color the animal cards brown.
Finish the number sentence.

1. How many more animal than plant cards are there?

 5 tens $\bigcirc$ 1 ten = _____ tens

_____ more animal cards

2. How many more animal than plant cards are there?

4 tens $\bigcirc$ 2 tens = _____ tens

_____ more animal cards

3. How many more plant than animal cards are there?

 5 tens $\bigcirc$ 2 tens = _____ tens

_____ more plant cards

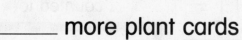

Calculator

Count with your calculator. Then write
the number. Press $\boxed{\text{ON/C}}$ to start each time.

1. Start with $\boxed{1}$. Press $\boxed{+}$ $\boxed{1}$ $\boxed{=}$. I counted to

   Then press $\boxed{=}$ $\boxed{=}$ $\boxed{=}$ Keep on going.

2. Start with $\boxed{10}$. Press $\boxed{+}$ $\boxed{10}$ $\boxed{=}$. I counted to

   Then press $\boxed{=}$ $\boxed{=}$ $\boxed{=}$ Keep on going.

3. Start with $\boxed{3}$. Press $\boxed{+}$ $\boxed{10}$ $\boxed{=}$. I counted to

   Then press $\boxed{=}$ $\boxed{=}$ $\boxed{=}$ Keep on going.

4. Pick a number. $\boxed{}$ Press $\boxed{+}$ $\boxed{10}$ $\boxed{=}$. I counted to

   Then press $\boxed{=}$ $\boxed{=}$ $\boxed{=}$ Keep on going.

Counting Patterns for 10s

1. Write the missing numbers.

2. Use blocks. Start with 10. Count by 10s.
   Color as you count aloud.

1	2	3	4		6	7		9	10
11	12		14	15	16		18	19	20
21		23	24	25		27	28	29	
31	32		34	35	36	37		39	40
41	42	43		45	46	47	48		50
	52	53	54		56	57	58	59	60
61		63	64	65	66		68	69	70
71	72	73		75	76	77	78	79	
81	82	83	84	85		87	88		90
91	92		94		96	97		99	100

3. Work with a partner.
   Use your ladder punchout.
   Put the ladder on some numbers in the chart.
   Count the numbers you see. Try again.

Start at the top of the ladder. Write as you count aloud ten more.

Add I more ten. The ones stay the same.

1. 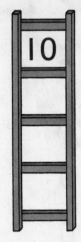 10

2. 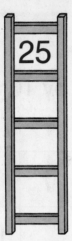 25

3. 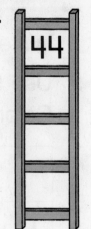 36

4. 44

5. 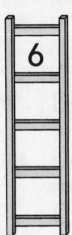 6

6.  43

7. 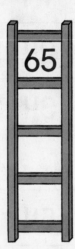 65

8.  59

MIXED REVIEW

9. Write how much.

 _____ ¢   _____ ¢   _____ ¢

10. Add. Ring sums of 10¢.

5¢	4¢	3¢	4¢	5¢	8¢
+ 5¢	+ 3¢	+ 9¢	+ 6¢	+ 6¢	+ 2¢

Counting Patterns for 2s and 5s

1. Work with a partner. Write the missing numbers.

2. Use cubes. Count by 2s. Color ▨ as you count aloud.

3. Use cubes. Count by 5s. Ring ▨ as you count aloud.

1	2				6	7	8		10
11	12	13	14		16	17	18	19	20
21		23	24		26	27		29	
31	32		34		36	37	38	39	40
	42	43	44	45		47		49	50
51	52	53	54	55	56	57	58		60
61	62		64	65	66		68	69	70
71		73	74		76	77	78	79	
	82		84	85	86		88		90
91		93	94		96	97		99	100

4. Count by 2s. Write the numbers.

2	4				

5. Count by 5s. Write the numbers.

5	10	0	0	0	0

Count by 2s or 5s. Write how many.

1. Ellen's shell collection

2 4 ___ ___ ___ ___ ___ ___ ___ ___

in all

2. Pamela's sock collection

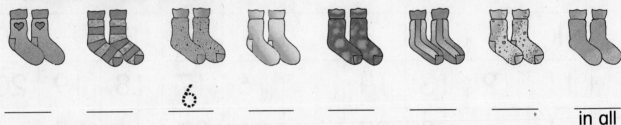

___ ___ 6 ___ ___ ___ ___ ___

in all

3. Lucy's nickel collection

5¢ ___¢ ___¢ ___¢ ___¢ ___¢ ___¢ ___¢

in all

4. Peter's marble collection

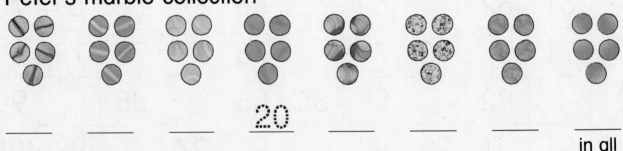

___ ___ ___ 20 ___ ___ ___ ___

in all

USE CRITICAL THINKING

5. Tip does not have
   enough money to buy the .
   Flip has more than he needs.
   How much is the ?

Tip's money

Flip's money

_____¢

Name _____

Ordinal Numbers

1. Cut out the number cards.
Put them in order on the train.
Check by counting. Then paste.

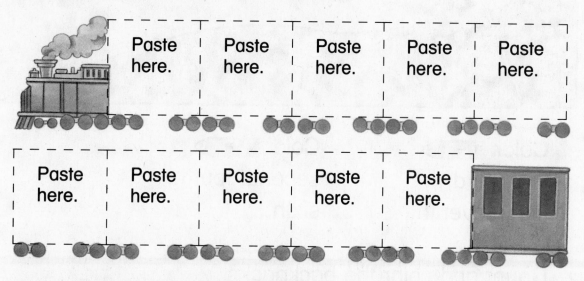

| Paste here. | Paste here. | Paste here. | Paste here. | Paste here. |

| Paste here. | Paste here. | Paste here. | Paste here. | Paste here. |

2. Count and color the trucks.

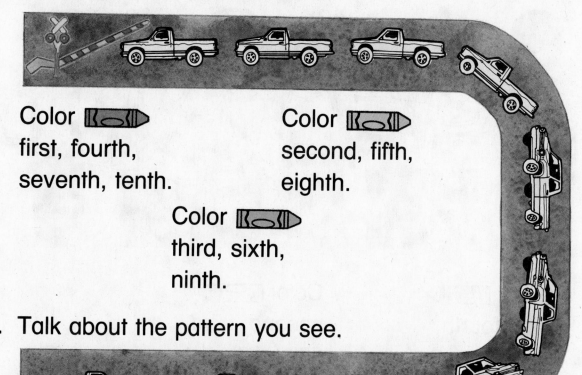

Color ▬▬▷
first, fourth,
seventh, tenth.

Color ▬▬▷
second, fifth,
eighth.

Color ▬▬▷
third, sixth,
ninth.

3. Talk about the pattern you see.

| first 1st |
| second 2nd |
| third 3rd |
| fourth 4th |
| fifth 5th |
| sixth 6th |
| seventh 7th |
| eighth 8th |
| ninth 9th |
| tenth 10th |

1. Count and color the race cars.

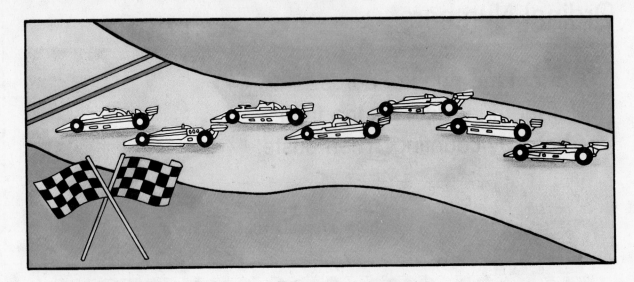

Color
first, third,
fifth, seventh.

Color
second, fourth,
sixth.

2. Count and color the backpacks.

Color
first, fourth,
seventh.

Color
second, third,
fifth, sixth.

3. Talk about the patterns you see.

More Practice, page 424, set C   Chapter 12

Problem Solving
Finding Extra Data

UNDERSTAND
FIND DATA
PLAN
ESTIMATE
SOLVE
CHECK

Write the number sentence.
Underline the extra data.

1. Lisa has 4 butterflies.
   2 are blue. 3 fly away.
   How many butterflies does she have now?

   ____ ◯ ____ = ____   She has ____ butterfly.

2. Peter won 8 marbles on Monday.
   He is 7 years old. He won 10 marbles on Friday.
   How many more did he win on Friday?

   ____ ◯ ____ = ____   He won ____ more.

3. Megan has 7 acorns.
   She gives 3 to a squirrel. The squirrel eats 1.
   How many acorns does Megan have now?

   ____ ◯ ____ = ____   She has ____ acorns.

4. Eric found 6 shells.
   He found 4 rocks. He found 3 more shells.
   He gave away 2 rocks.
   How many shells does he have now?

   ____ ◯ ____ = ____   He has ____ shells.

Problem Solving Strategy

Make a Table

Finish the tables. Use the tables to tell how much money.

					My Nickel Table				
Number of Nickels	1	2	3	4	5	6	7	8	9
Amount	5¢	10¢	15¢	20¢	25¢				

1. _____

2. _____

					My Dime Table				
Number of Dimes	1	2	3	4	5	6	7	8	9
Amount	10¢				50¢				

3. _____

4. _____

WRAP UP

MATH WORDS

1. Match. Then write the missing numbers.

   Count by 5s.   ▪   ▪ | 17 | 18 | 19 | 20 | |

   Count by 10s.   ▪   ▪ | 66 | 65 | 64 | | 62 |

   Count by 2s.   ▪   ▪ | 25 | 30 | | 40 | 45 |

   Count back.   ▪   ▪ | 42 | 44 | 46 | | 50 |

   Count on.   ▪   ▪ | 20 | | 40 | 50 | 60 |

MATH REASONING

Read the clues. Answer the riddle.

2. I am a number between 50 and 75.
   You say me when you count by 5s.
   My tens digit is 1 more than
   my ones digit. What am I?   _____

3.

   I am after the second car.
   I am not the fifth car.
   I am not blue. Ring me.

Name _____

CHAPTER REVIEW/TEST

1. Write the numbers.

64		66

between

	56	57

before

27	28	

after

Ring the number that is less.

2. 67   76 | 3. 85   93 | 4. 33   83

5. Count by 10s.

20						

6. Count by 5s.

10						

7. Color first, fifth, ninth.
   Color second, sixth, tenth.

8. Finish the number sentence.
   Underline the extra data.

   11 frogs sat on a rock.

   3 ducks swam on the pond.

   5 frogs hopped away.

   How many frogs are left?

   ____ ◯ ____ = ____

   ____ frogs are left.

Name _____

ENRICHMENT
Making and Reading a Pictograph

Write how much each person spent.

1. Amy bought 2  5¢ .   She spent _____ .

2. Lisa bought 4  5¢ .   She spent _____ .

3. Tony bought 3 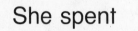 5¢ .   He spent _____ .

4. José bought 5 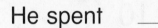 5¢ .   He spent _____ .

Money Spent

Amy

Lisa

Tony

José

Color the graph to show how much money each person spent. Then answer the questions.

5. Who spent the most? _____

6. Who spent the least? _____

CUMULATIVE REVIEW

Subtract.

1. $9 - 3 =$ _____

○ 5
○ 6
○ 7

2.
$$\begin{array}{r} 10 \\ -\ 8 \\ \hline \end{array}$$

○ 2
○ 3
○ 1

3.
$$\begin{array}{r} 12 \\ -\ 3 \\ \hline \end{array}$$

○ 9
○ 7
○ 8

4. Find the add-to-check fact for $8 - 3 = 5$.

○ $3 + 5 = 8$
○ $2 + 6 = 8$
○ $8 - 4 = 4$

How many are there?

5.

Tens	Ones
2	4

○

Tens	Ones
2	6

○

Tens	Ones
3	5

○

6.

○ 50
○ 40
○ 60

7.

○ 75
○ 57
○ 46

8. Trade pennies for dimes. How many dimes are there?

73 pennies

○ 8 dimes
○ 9 dimes
○ 7 dimes

9. Choose the best estimate. Benny wants to pack the fruit in tens. Without counting, estimate how many.

○ 30
○ 20
○ 40

13
Money

Counting Dimes and Pennies

Count dimes first, then pennies.

Work in a group. Spin for dimes. Then spin for pennies. Show with coin punchouts below. Write the amount on a price tag.

Dimes	Pennies

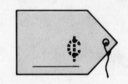

I. 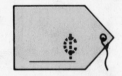　　2. 　　3. 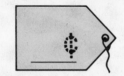　　4. 　　5.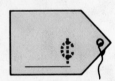

Use coin punchouts. Cover each coin as you count. Write the total amount.

6.  _____ ¢

7.  _____ ¢

PROBLEM SOLVING

8. Sid has 4 pennies. He has just as many dimes. How much money does he have? _____ ¢

Name _____

Counting Nickels and Pennies

Count the money. Write the price. Use money
cover-up punchouts on a counting board to check.

I.

$\underline{5}$, $\underline{10}$, $\underline{15}$, $\underline{16}$, $\underline{17}$ 17¢

2.

_____ , _____ , _____ , _____ ,   _____

3.

_____ , _____ , _____ , _____ , _____ ,   _____

4.

_____ , _____ , _____ , _____ , _____ ,   _____

Chapter 13

Use 6  and 4  punchouts.
Cover each coin as you count.
Write the amount.

Count nickels first, then pennies.

1.

Start here. →

2.

3.

4.

5.

6.

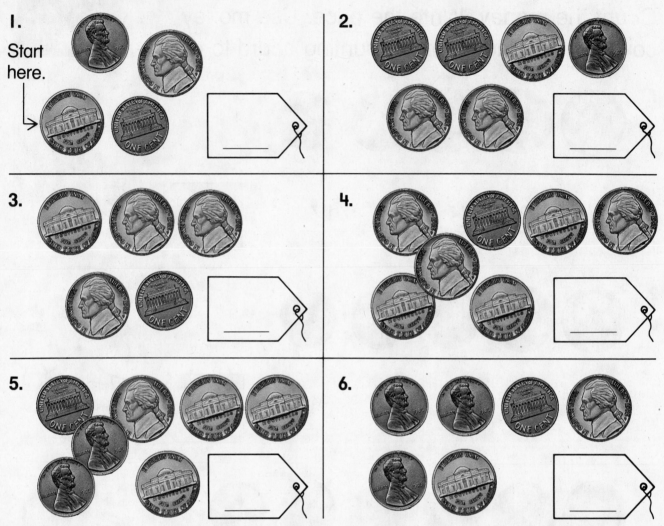

SHOW WITH COINS

7. Draw two ways to make 16¢.
Use money cover-up punchouts
on a counting board to check.

First Way

Second Way

 5¢ 5¢ 5¢   1¢

Counting Dimes and Nickels

Count the money. Write the price.
Use money cover-up punchouts
on a counting board to check.

1.

<u>10</u> , <u>20</u> , <u>25</u> , <u>30</u> , <u>35</u> , <u>40</u>   40¢

2.

____ , ____ , ____ , ____ ,

3.

____ , ____ , ____ , ____ ,

4.

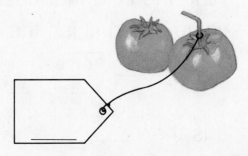

____ , ____ , ____ ,

Use 4 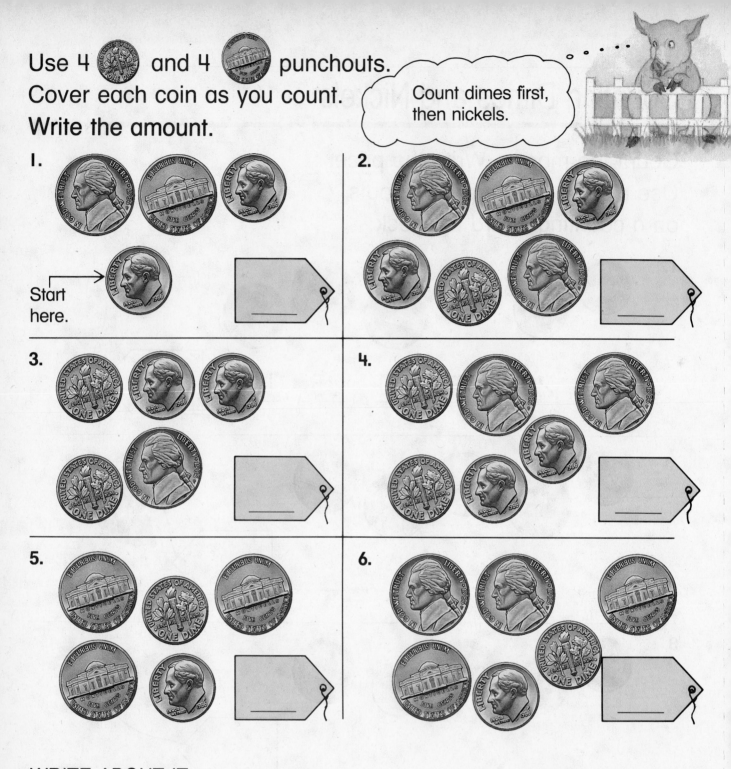 and 4 punchouts.
Cover each coin as you count.
Write the amount.

Count dimes first, then nickels.

1.

Start here.

___

2.

___

3.

___

4.

___

5.

___

6.

___

WRITE ABOUT IT

7. Ring the coin that has the greatest
   value. Then finish the sentence.

| penny | dime | nickel |

___

It is the _____.

276 (two hundred seventy-six)   More Practice, page 425, set B   Chapter 13

Counting Dimes, Nickels, and Pennies

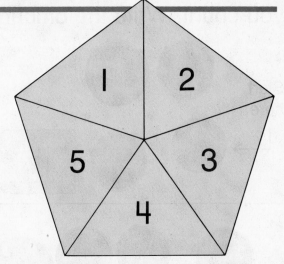

Work in a group. Use your
spinner and punchout coins.
Put coins in the coin box as you
count. Spin for dimes. Count.
Spin for nickels. Count on.
Spin for pennies. Count on.

Coin Box		
Dimes	Nickels	Pennies

Write how much in all.

1. first try _____ ¢   2. second try _____ ¢

3. third try _____ ¢   4. fourth try _____ ¢

5. fifth try _____ ¢   6. sixth try _____ ¢

Use 4 , and 4 , and 4 punchouts. Cover each coin as you count. Write the amount.

Count dimes first, then nickels, then pennies.

1.

Start here. →

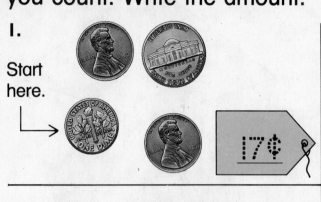

17¢

2.

_____

3.

_____

4.

_____

5.

_____

6.

_____

FIND THE DATA

DATA BANK

7. Data Bank

Mat has

He wants a toy .

Ring the answer. (See page 399.)

He can buy it.

He cannot buy it.

Counting and Comparing Money

Count dimes first, then nickels, then pennies.

Write the prices.
Ring the toy that costs less.

1.

10,   20,   25,   26,   27

27¢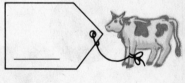

10,   20,   30,   31

2.

3.

Write the amounts.
Ring the one that is less.

Count dimes first, then nickels, then pennies.

1.

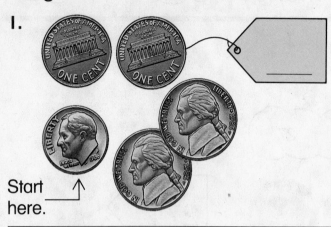

Start here. ↑

2.

MIDCHAPTER REVIEW/QUIZ

Count how much.

1.

_____

2.

_____

3. Count the money. Write the amount.

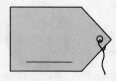

_____ , _____ , _____ , _____ , _____ ,

Chapter 13

Problem Solving
Understanding the Operations

Draw more or cross out some. Add
or subtract. Then write the answers.

1. Tim had 4 nickels.
   He spent 1 nickel.
   How many does he have now?

   Tim has ____ nickels.

$$\begin{array}{r} 4 \\ -\ 1 \\ \hline \end{array}$$

2. Shonie has 3 dimes. Flora has
   2 dimes. How many dimes
   are there in all?

   There are ____ dimes in all.

3. Ali has 4 nickels. Jan
   has 2 nickels. How many
   more does Ali have?

   Ali has ____ more nickels.

4. Megan had 5 dimes. She gave
   1 dime away. How many
   does she have now?

   Megan has ____ dimes.

Calculator

Work with a partner. 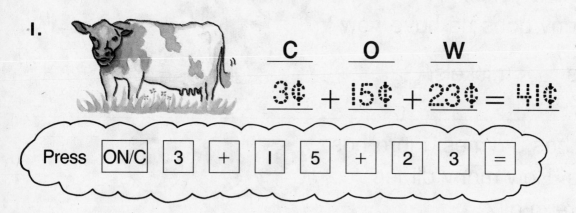 Use a 🖩. Look at the chart. Write the price of each letter. Add.

Letter Prices

A	B	C	D	E	F	G	H	I	J	K	L	M
1¢	2¢	3¢	4¢	5¢	6¢	7¢	8¢	9¢	10¢	11¢	12¢	13¢

N	O	P	Q	R	S	T	U	V	W	X	Y	Z
14¢	15¢	16¢	17¢	18¢	19¢	20¢	21¢	22¢	23¢	24¢	25¢	26¢

1. C   O   W

    3¢ + 15¢ + 23¢ = 41¢

    Press [ON/C] [3] [+] [1] [5] [+] [2] [3] [=]

2. p   i   g

    __ + __ + __ = __

3. c   a   t

    __ + __ + __ = __

4. Write your name. _____

    _____

    Find the total price. _____

Name ____

Counting Quarters and Other Coins

I can trade for a quarter.

I can trade this way, too.

I quarter

or

25¢
25 cents

Use I , 2 , 3 , and 3  punchouts. Cover each coin as you count. Write the price.

I.

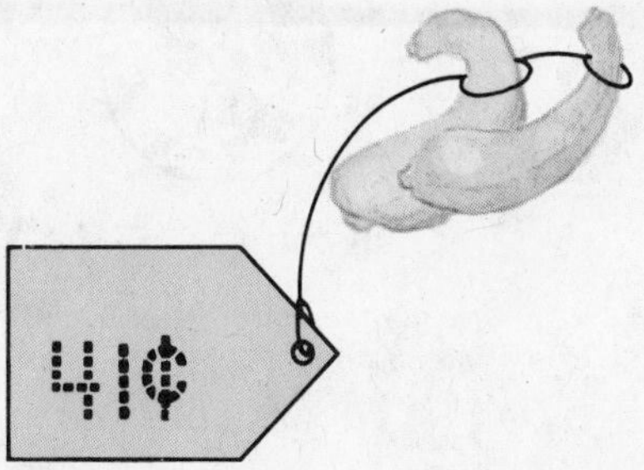

25, 35, ____, ____

2.

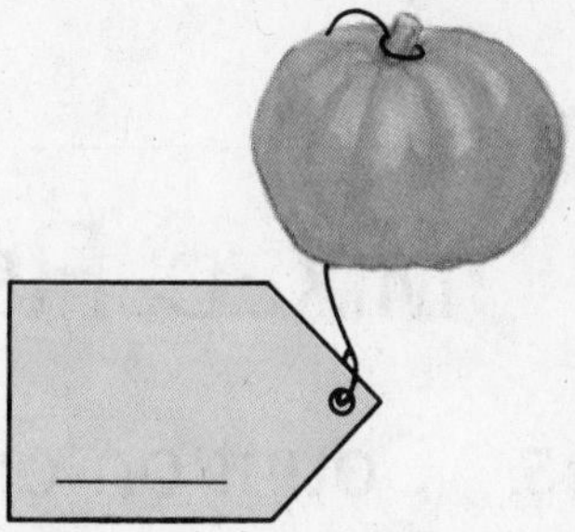

____, ____, ____, ____, ____

3.

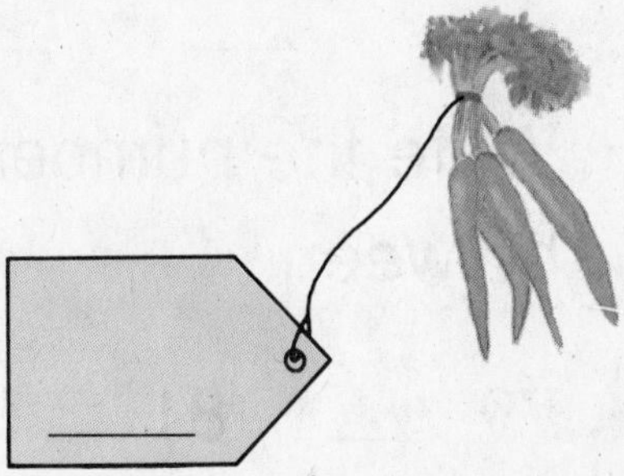

____, ____, ____, ____

Write how much is in each bank.

Count quarters first, then dimes, then nickels, then pennies.

1. ____

2. ____

3. ____

4. ____

MIXED REVIEW

5. Count on and back.

Tens	Ones
4	2

____ , ____ , ____ , ____ , | ____ , ____ , ____

6. Write the number between.

79, ____ , 81

7. Ring the number that is less.

82   36

Name _____

Problem Solving
Using Data from a Newspaper Ad

UNDERSTAND
FIND DATA
PLAN
ESTIMATE
SOLVE
CHECK

PRODUCE SALE

45¢   30¢   41¢   32¢   28¢   35¢

Count and write how much money each
person has. Is there enough to buy
what is wanted? Ring the answer.

1. Jake has _____.

He wants .

Jake can buy it.

Jake cannot buy it.

2. Kate has _____.

She wants .

Kate can buy it.

Kate cannot buy it.

3. Tom has _____.

He wants 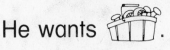 .

Tom can buy it.

Tom cannot buy it.

 10¢

 10¢

 10¢

 15¢

 15¢

 15¢

 20¢

 20¢

 25¢

 15¢

Problem Solving Strategy
Guess and Check

UNDERSTAND
FIND DATA
PLAN
ESTIMATE
SOLVE
CHECK

Work with a partner. Cut out the pictures. Listen to the story. Guess what each person bought. Use a 🖩 to check. Then paste.

1.

Mayumi

Mayumi spent ____.

[Paste here.] and [Paste here.] cost ____.

2.

Kay

Kay spent ____.

[Paste here.] and [Paste here.] cost ____.

3.

Max

Max spent ____.

[Paste here.] and [Paste here.] cost ____.

WRAP UP

MATH WORDS

Ring what belongs. Tell why.

1.

dime   20¢   10 pennies

2.

25 pennies   35¢   quarter

3.

5¢      nickel

MATH REASONING

4. How many of each coin do you need
    to buy the object? Use the fewest
    coins you can. Fill in the chart.

	Number of	Number of	Number of	Number of
41¢				
33¢				
45¢				

CHAPTER REVIEW/TEST

Count how much.

1.  _____

2.  _____

3.  _____

4.  _____

Write the prices. Ring the toy that costs less.

5.

6.

Write how much is in each bank.

7.  _____

8.  _____

9. Count and write how much money.

Emi has _____ ¢. She wants a

Ring one.

Emi can buy it.

Emi cannot buy it.

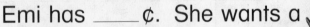

45¢

ENRICHMENT
Dollar Bill

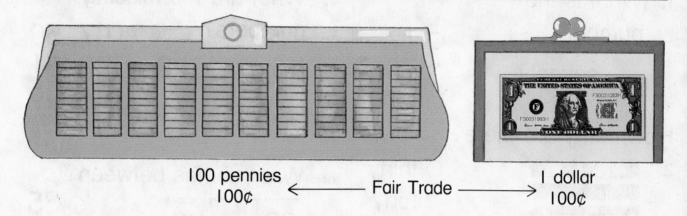

100 pennies
100¢

← Fair Trade →

1 dollar
100¢

Write how much money.
Is it a fair trade? Ring **yes** or **no**.

1.

_____   yes   no

2.

_____   yes   no

3.

_____   yes   no

Name _____

CUMULATIVE REVIEW

1. What is the number?

   seventy

   ○ 17
   ○ 70
   ○ 7

How many are there?

2.

   ○ thirty
   ○ forty
   ○ fifty

3.

   ○ 34
   ○ 23
   ○ 45

4. Count how much.

   ○ 70¢
   ○ 25¢
   ○ 52¢

5. What are the missing numbers?

   46, ____, 48,
   49, ____, 51

   ○ 47, 50
   ○ 49, 51
   ○ 46, 49

6. What comes between?

   | 32 | | 34 |

   ○ 35
   ○ 33
   ○ 31

7. Which is greater?

   ○ 35
   ○ 55
   ○ 50

8. Count by 5s.

   20, 25, 30, ____

   ○ 40
   ○ 33
   ○ 35

9. Choose the correct number sentence.
   How many more bird cards
   than cat cards are there?

   ○ 2 tens + 3 tens = 5 tens
   ○ 3 tens − 2 tens = 1 ten
   ○ 4 tens − 1 ten = 3 tens

14

Time

Workmat

Clock Parts

Work with a partner. Use your punchout clock. Write a number for the time. Your partner shows the time on the clock. Take turns.

1. __2__ o'clock   2. _____ o'clock   3. _____ o'clock

4. _____ o'clock   5. _____ o'clock   6. _____ o'clock

Where are the hands? Write the numbers.

7.

    hour   __7__

    minute   __12__

It is __7__ o'clock.

8.

    hour   _____

    minute   _____

It is _____ o'clock.

9.

    hour   _____

    minute   _____

It is _____ o'clock.

10.

    hour   _____

    minute   _____

It is _____ o'clock.

PROBLEM SOLVING

11. Ned went to school at ➡  He woke up 2 hours earlier. What time did he wake up?

Ned woke up at

_____ o'clock.

Time on the Hour

Write each time two ways.

1.

___ ___ o'clock

2.

_____ o'clock

3.

_____ o'clock

4.

_____ o'clock

5.

_____ o'clock

6.

_____ o'clock

7.

_____ o'clock

1. Show the time on each clock. Then write in ○ to number Eli's school day in order.

8 o'clock	First class

8:00

11 o'clock	Lunch

:   ○

3 o'clock	Go home

:   ○

10 o'clock	Recess

:   ○

MIXED REVIEW

2. Add.

$4 + 7 =$ ___ $8 + 4 =$ ___ $7 + 5 =$ ___

3. Subtract.

$8 - 0 =$ ___ $12 - 6 =$ ___ $10 - 4 =$ ___

$11 - 2 =$ ___ $9 - 5 =$ ___ $10 - 9 =$ ___

More Practice, page 426, set A   Chapter 14

Problem Solving
Understanding the Operations

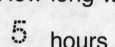

UNDERSTAND
FIND DATA
PLAN
ESTIMATE
SOLVE
CHECK

Add or subtract to answer the question.

1. Sue's family went to Grandma's house.
Mom drove 3 hours.
Dad drove 2 hours.
How long was the trip?

_5_ hours

2. Sue played with Grandma's dog for
5 minutes. She played with the
cat for 7 minutes. How much
longer did she play with the cat?

____ minutes

3. At Grandma's, Sue played ball for
2 hours. She played in the park
for 1 hour. How long did
Sue play?

____ hours

4. Sue and Grandpa dug up carrots from
the garden in 9 minutes. They
picked beans in 5 minutes. How much
longer did it take to dig up carrots?

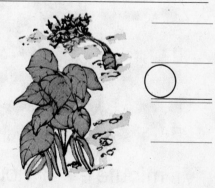

____ minutes

Estimation

About how long would it take?
Ring the better answer.

1. to make toast

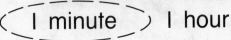

2. to watch a movie

2 minutes   2 hours

3. to get over a cold

1 hour   1 week

4. to eat a sandwich

10 minutes   10 hours

5. to wash your face

1 minute   1 hour

6. for your new tooth to come in all the way

2 days   2 months

Time on the Half Hour

Work with a partner. Use your punchout clocks. Make them show one half hour later than the blue clock. Then show the time on the red clocks below.

I.

2.

3.

4.

Use the chart. Write each name under the clock that shows the bedtime.

Cat Family Bedtimes

Mimi	10:30	Meg	8:30
Cam	7:30	Cal	11:30

1.
_____
- - - - - - - - - - - -

2.
_____
- - - - - - - - - - - -
_____

3.
- - - - - - - - - - - -
_____

4.
_____
- - - - - - - - - - - -
_____

MIDCHAPTER REVIEW/QUIZ

1. Draw hands on the clock to show the time.

6 o'clock

2. Where are the hands? Write the numbers.

hour  _____

minute _____

It is _____ o'clock.

Write each time two ways.

3.

 :

_____ o'clock

4.

:

_____ o'clock

  More Practice, page 426, set B   Chapter 14

The Mouse Family's Time Book

Show the times.

A Day
with the
Mouse Family

Max and Mort
get home at

3:30

At night, Mama
comes home at

5:00

The family
eats dinner at

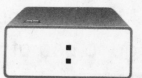

:

Mama and
Papa leave for
work at

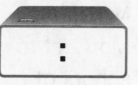

:

The sitter and
Baby go to
the park at

10:00

All rights reserved. Addison-Wesley

(two hundred ninety-nine) **299**

Max and Mort play ball at
 4:00

Baby wakes up at
 :

Max and Mort go to bed at
 7:30

The family watches the news at
 :
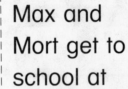

Sitter and Baby have lunch at
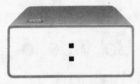 :

Max and Mort get to school at
 8:30

Name _____

Calendar

Make a calendar for this month.
Write the name and the dates.

Sunday	Monday	Tuesday	Wednesday	Thursday	Friday	Saturday

Use the calendar to answer
the questions.

1. What day is the first
   of this month? _____

2. How many days are in this month? _____ days

3. What is today's date? _____

4. What date is one week from today? _____

5. What date is the third Sunday? _____

6. How many school days are in this month? _____ days

May						
Sunday	Monday	Tuesday	Wednesday	Thursday	Friday	Saturday
				1	2	3
4	5	6	7	8	9	10
11	12	13	14	15	16	17
18	19	20	21	22	23	24
25	26	27	28	29	30	31

Ring one.

1. Mother's Day is the second Sunday, May ____.

   1   4

2. May 5 is a ____.

   Sunday   Monday

3. May 15 is a ____.

   Thursday   Friday

4. Memorial Day is the last Friday of this month, May ____.

   23   30   31

5. The last day of this month is Saturday, May ____.

   25   30   31

6. There will be a full moon on the fourth Saturday of this month, May ____.

   10   18   24

FIND THE DATA

7. **Data Bank** The last day of March in the year 2000 is ____. Ring your answer. (See page 399.)

   Thursday   Friday

Problem Solving
Using Data from a Chart

UNDERSTAND
FIND DATA
PLAN
ESTIMATE
SOLVE
CHECK

Use the chart. Write how long.
Then show the time.

Hours Spent

	Reading	Playing	Painting	Cleaning	Sleeping
Al	1	3	2	1	9
Sal	2	2	1	half hour	10

1. Sal read for __2__ hours.

Sal began to read at

She stopped at

2. Al painted for _____ hours.

Al went to paint class at

He stopped at

3. Sal cleaned _____ for a _____ hour.

Sal began to clean at

She stopped at

4. Al played for _____ hours.

Al began to play at

He stopped at

UNDERSTAND
FIND DATA
PLAN
ESTIMATE
SOLVE
CHECK

Problem Solving Strategy
Make a List

Answer the question.
Make a list to help.

Tim's grandmother has a cuckoo clock. The cuckoo comes out

  I time at I o'clock,

  2 times at 2 o'clock,

  3 times at 3 o'clock,

and so on.
The bird also comes out
I time each half hour.

How many times does the bird come out?

I. from 1:00 to 3:00

Clock Time	Number of times bird comes out
1:00	I
1:30	I
2:00	I I
2:30	
3:00	

The bird comes out

____ times.

2. from 2:30 to 5:00

Clock Time	Number of times bird comes out
2:30	I
3:00	I I I
3:30	
4:00	
4:30	
5:00	

The bird comes out

____ times.

Name _____

WRAP UP

MATH WORDS

1. Show the times on the clocks.
   Use  to draw the minute hand.
   Use  to draw the hour hand.

   3 o'clock   10:00   7:30   5 o'clock

2. Look at the calendar. Ring
    the first Monday
    the second Sunday
    the last week

APRIL						
Sunday	Monday	Tuesday	Wednesday	Thursday	Friday	Saturday
					1	2
3	4	5	6	7	8	9
10	11	12	13	14	15	16
17	18	19	20	21	22	23
24	25	26	27	28	29	30

MATH REASONING

3. Use the calendar above.
   The baseball game is today, April 9.

   _____

   What day of the week is it? _____

4. The game starts at 2:00.
   It takes us 1 hour to get
   there. It is now 1:30.
   We have not left yet.

   Will we be
   on time?
   Ring one.
   yes   no

Name _____

CHAPTER REVIEW/TEST

Write each time two ways.

1.  _____ o'clock
     :

2.  _____ o'clock
     :

Show the time on each clock.

3.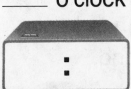
   3:30

4.
    :

5.
   12:30

Ring one.

6. The first day of May is _____.

   Friday   Tuesday   Sunday

May						
Sunday	Monday	Tuesday	Wednesday	Thursday	Friday	Saturday
		1	2	3	4	5
6	7	8	9	10	11	12

7. The second Friday of this month is May _____.

   4   18   11

Show or write the time.

8. Sam wakes up at .

9. Jo goes to bed at _____ o'clock.

	Sam	Jen	Jo
Bedtime	9:30	8:30	9:00
Wake-up Time	7:30	6:30	7:30

10. Who goes to bed first? Ring one.   Sam   Jen

ENRICHMENT
Finding Patterns on a Calendar

OCTOBER						
Sun.	Mon.	Tues.	Wed.	Thur.	Fri.	Sat.
			1	2	3	4
5	6	7	8	9	10	11
12	13	14	15	16	17	18
19	20	21	22	23	24	25
26	27	28	29	30	31	

Work with a partner. Use the calendar.

1. How many days are in a week? _____ days

2. Use ▣ to write the numbers for all the Tuesdays.
   Use ▣ to write the numbers for all the Thursdays.
   Talk about the patterns you see.

3. Color ▣ the squares with odd numbers.
   Color ▣ the squares with even numbers.
   Are there more odd or even days?
   Ring one.

   odd   even

4. Talk about any other patterns you see.

CUMULATIVE REVIEW

1. Count by 10s. Find the next number.

37
47

○ 57
○ 67
○ 75

2. How much money is there in all?

○ 25¢
○ 15¢
○ 20¢

3. Which car is second?

○
○
○

4. What number comes after?

66

○ 65
○ 60
○ 67

Count how much.

5.

○ 14¢
○ 24¢
○ 19¢

6.

○ 50¢
○ 52¢
○ 47¢

7.

○ 25¢
○ 30¢
○ 35¢

8. Which price is less?

56¢

43¢

○ 43¢
○ 56¢

9. Find the extra data.

Marci saw 5 rabbits. Then she saw 3 birds. She saw 4 more rabbits. How many rabbits did Marci see in all?

○ 5 rabbits

○ 3 birds

○ 4 more rabbits

Chapter 14 Cumulative Review

15
Addition Facts
Sums to 18

Workmat

Name _____

Adding 9

Start with 9.
Make 10,
add extra.

Work in a group.
Use 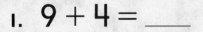 and counters.
To find each sum,
make 10 and add extra.

1. $9 + 4 =$ ___ $5 + 9 =$ ___ $9 + 3 =$ ___

2. $6 + 9 =$ ___ $9 + 8 =$ ___ $7 + 9 =$ ___

3. Write another fact with 9.
   Find the sum.   ___ + ___ = ___

Add. Look for 9. Use 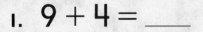 to help.

4.
$$\begin{array}{cccccc} 9 & 6 & 9 & 4 & 2 & 8 \\ +6 & +6 & +9 & +5 & +9 & +9 \end{array}$$

5.
$$\begin{array}{cccccc} 8 & 9 & 4 & 9 & 4 & 9 \\ +3 & +1 & +4 & +7 & +9 & +3 \end{array}$$

PROBLEM SOLVING

6. Bev has 9¢. Ben has 7¢.
   Together, can they buy the ball?
   Ring and finish the correct
   number sentence.

7. Ring one.

   They can buy.

   They cannot buy.

   $9¢ + 7¢ =$ ___ $9¢ - 7¢ =$ ___

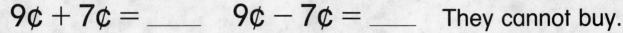

Doubles Through 9 + 9

See a double? Think of the picture to help.

Add.

1.
$$\begin{array}{r} 6 \\ + 6 \\ \hline 12 \end{array}$$

$$\begin{array}{r} 7 \\ + 7 \\ \hline \end{array}$$

February						
Sun	Mon	Tue	Wed	Thu	Fri	Sat
1	2	3	4	5	6	7
8	9	10	11	12	13	14
15	16	17	18	19	20	21
22	23	24	25	26	27	28

2.
$$\begin{array}{r} 8 \\ + 8 \\ \hline \end{array}$$

$$\begin{array}{r} 9 \\ + 9 \\ \hline \end{array}$$

Ring doubles. Then add all.

3.
$$\begin{array}{r} 8 \\ + 8 \\ \hline 16 \end{array}$$
$$\begin{array}{r} 5 \\ + 4 \\ \hline \end{array}$$
$$\begin{array}{r} 6 \\ + 6 \\ \hline \end{array}$$
$$\begin{array}{r} 9 \\ + 5 \\ \hline \end{array}$$
$$\begin{array}{r} 7 \\ + 7 \\ \hline \end{array}$$
$$\begin{array}{r} 9 \\ + 3 \\ \hline \end{array}$$

4.
$$\begin{array}{r} 9 \\ + 6 \\ \hline \end{array}$$
$$\begin{array}{r} 7 \\ + 7 \\ \hline \end{array}$$
$$\begin{array}{r} 8 \\ + 9 \\ \hline \end{array}$$
$$\begin{array}{r} 5 \\ + 5 \\ \hline \end{array}$$
$$\begin{array}{r} 6 \\ + 4 \\ \hline \end{array}$$
$$\begin{array}{r} 5 \\ + 6 \\ \hline \end{array}$$

5.
$$\begin{array}{r} 9 \\ + 9 \\ \hline \end{array}$$
$$\begin{array}{r} 9 \\ + 7 \\ \hline \end{array}$$
$$\begin{array}{r} 3 \\ + 7 \\ \hline \end{array}$$
$$\begin{array}{r} 8 \\ + 8 \\ \hline \end{array}$$
$$\begin{array}{r} 4 \\ + 9 \\ \hline \end{array}$$
$$\begin{array}{r} 2 \\ + 8 \\ \hline \end{array}$$

Add.

Look for doubles.

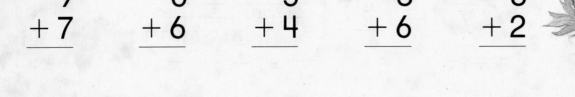

1.
$\begin{array}{r} 7 \\ +7 \\ \hline 14 \end{array}$
$\begin{array}{r} 2 \\ +6 \\ \hline \end{array}$
$\begin{array}{r} 8 \\ +8 \\ \hline \end{array}$
$\begin{array}{r} 4 \\ +6 \\ \hline \end{array}$
$\begin{array}{r} 1 \\ +7 \\ \hline \end{array}$

2.
$\begin{array}{r} 9 \\ +7 \\ \hline \end{array}$
$\begin{array}{r} 6 \\ +6 \\ \hline \end{array}$
$\begin{array}{r} 5 \\ +4 \\ \hline \end{array}$
$\begin{array}{r} 3 \\ +6 \\ \hline \end{array}$
$\begin{array}{r} 8 \\ +2 \\ \hline \end{array}$

3.
$\begin{array}{r} 9 \\ +9 \\ \hline \end{array}$
$\begin{array}{r} 9 \\ +4 \\ \hline \end{array}$
$\begin{array}{r} 2 \\ +7 \\ \hline \end{array}$
$\begin{array}{r} 6 \\ +9 \\ \hline \end{array}$
$\begin{array}{r} 7 \\ +7 \\ \hline \end{array}$
$\begin{array}{r} 9 \\ +8 \\ \hline \end{array}$

4.
$\begin{array}{r} 6 \\ +5 \\ \hline \end{array}$
$\begin{array}{r} 8 \\ +8 \\ \hline \end{array}$
$\begin{array}{r} 2 \\ +0 \\ \hline \end{array}$
$\begin{array}{r} 9 \\ +9 \\ \hline \end{array}$
$\begin{array}{r} 5 \\ +9 \\ \hline \end{array}$
$\begin{array}{r} 7 \\ +2 \\ \hline \end{array}$

PROBLEM SOLVING

5. Use and draw coins to help.

Kendra has 5 dimes.

Adam has 3 dimes.

How many more dimes does Kendra have than Adam? Ring and finish the number sentence that helps.

$5 + 3 =$ ___

Kendra has ___ more dimes.

$5 - 3 =$ ___

Fact Practice

Add the Across Facts. Fill in the puzzle.

Add the Down Facts to check.

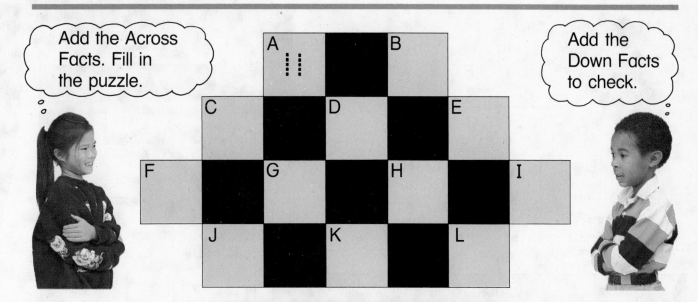

Across Facts

A	B	C	D	E	F
7 +4	4 +9	9 +3	4 +5	9 +9	4 +6

G	H	I	J	K	L
7 +9	9 +2	6 +9	2 +6	8 +9	9 +5

Down Facts

A	B	C	D	E	F
5 +6	9 +4	6 +6	2 +7	9 +9	5 +5

G	H	I	J	K	L
8 +8	8 +3	9 +6	4 +4	9 +8	7 +7

I. Add the Across Facts. Fill in the puzzle.
Add the Down Facts to check.

E

D F

C G

B H

A 12

I

Start.

Down Facts

A $5 + 7 = $ 12

B $7 + 2 = $ ___

C $5 + 2 = $ ___

D $7 + 7 = $ ___

E $8 + 2 = $ ___

F $4 + 4 = $ ___

G $9 + 9 = $ ___

H $9 + 6 = $ ___

I $7 + 9 = $ ___

Across Facts

A $6 + 6 = $ 12   B $6 + 3 = $ ___

C $4 + 3 = $ ___   D $9 + 5 = $ ___

E $6 + 4 = $ ___   F $5 + 3 = $ ___

G $9 + 9 = $ ___   H $6 + 9 = $ ___

I $8 + 8 = $ ___

MAKE AN ESTIMATE

About how many will fit across the
chalk tray in your classroom?

my guess   my count

2.   ___   ___

3. Your Math Book   ___   ___

Adding Three Numbers

Work with a partner. Each gets
punchouts ① to ⑤. Take turns. Pick
three cards. Put them in an order that
is easy to add. Write them. Add.

Do it the
easy way.
$5 + 5 = 10$
$10 + 2 = 12$

$$\begin{array}{r} 5 \\ 5 \\ + 2 \\ \hline 12 \end{array}$$

1.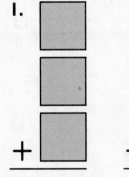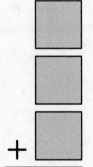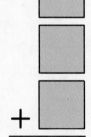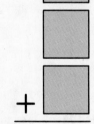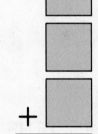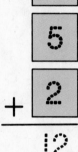

2.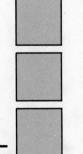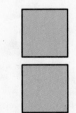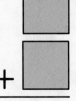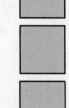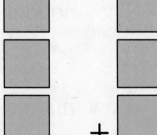

Add the easy way. Ring the two numbers to start. Look for sums of 10 or doubles to help.

1.

$$\begin{array}{r} 4 \\ 1 \\ +4 \\ \hline 9 \end{array}\ 8$$

$$\begin{array}{r} 7 \\ 1 \\ +7 \\ \hline \end{array}\ 14$$

$$\begin{array}{r} 2 \\ 3 \\ +7 \\ \hline \end{array}\ 10$$

$$\begin{array}{r} 4 \\ 6 \\ +3 \\ \hline \end{array}\ 10$$

$$\begin{array}{r} 3 \\ 2 \\ +3 \\ \hline \end{array}\ 6$$

2.

$$\begin{array}{r} 8 \\ 1 \\ +8 \\ \hline \end{array}$$

$$\begin{array}{r} 2 \\ 8 \\ +1 \\ \hline \end{array}$$

$$\begin{array}{r} 2 \\ 1 \\ +9 \\ \hline \end{array}$$

$$\begin{array}{r} 6 \\ 4 \\ +1 \\ \hline \end{array}$$

$$\begin{array}{r} 5 \\ 5 \\ +3 \\ \hline \end{array}$$

$$\begin{array}{r} 2 \\ 4 \\ +4 \\ \hline \end{array}$$

3.

$$\begin{array}{r} 8 \\ 2 \\ +3 \\ \hline \end{array}$$

$$\begin{array}{r} 1 \\ 7 \\ +3 \\ \hline \end{array}$$

$$\begin{array}{r} 4 \\ 6 \\ +2 \\ \hline \end{array}$$

$$\begin{array}{r} 1 \\ 9 \\ +5 \\ \hline \end{array}$$

$$\begin{array}{r} 9 \\ 9 \\ +2 \\ \hline \end{array}$$

$$\begin{array}{r} 5 \\ 2 \\ +5 \\ \hline \end{array}$$

FIND THE DATA

4. Data Bank Sil, Wil, and Dil went to a toy sale.

They bought a for 5¢,

a for 5¢, and a .

How much did the three toys cost?
(See page 400.)

_____ ¢

More Practice, page 427, set B   Chapter 15

Name _____

Problem Solving
Understanding the Operations

UNDERSTAND
FIND DATA
PLAN
ESTIMATE
SOLVE
CHECK

Listen to the story. Use counters to
show it. Write how many more are needed.

1.

Need
5 to play.

____ more must come.

2.

It takes 8
for the race.

____ more must come.

3.

Need 4 to
sing the song.

____ more must come.

Mentai Math

Work with a partner.
Use punchouts 9 to 18.
Show each clue.
Write the number.

1. Count by 5s. You said the number.
   It is greater than 6 + 6.

   The number is __15__.

2. It is a doubles sum. It is less than a
   dozen.

   The number is ____.

3. It is less than 9 + 9. It is greater
   than 16.

   The number is ____.

4. Count by 2s. You said the number.
   It is greater than 12. It is less than 15.

   The number is ____.

5. It is a doubles sum. It is greater than
   8 + 8.

   The number is ____.

Name _____

Doubles Plus One Through 8 + 9

Add.

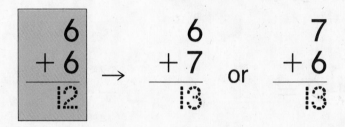

1.

| 6 |
| + 6 |
| 12 |

→

| I more |

| 6 |
| + 7 |
| 13 |

or

| 7 |
| + 6 |
| 13 |

2.

| 7 |
| + 7 |

→

| I more |

| 7 |
| + 8 |

or

| 8 |
| + 7 |

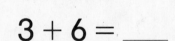

Ring the double-plus-one facts.
Then add all.

3. (8 + 9) = 17   7 + 7 = ___   3 + 6 = ___

4. 9 + 5 = ___   7 + 8 = ___   9 + 8 = ___

5. 8 + 7 = ___   7 + 6 = ___   4 + 4 = ___

6. 0 + 4 = ___   2 + 6 = ___   2 + 0 = ___

7. 8 + 9 = ___   5 + 5 = ___   6 + 4 = ___

8. 9 + 9 = ___   6 + 7 = ___   4 + 9 = ___

Write the double that helps. Add.

1.

$\begin{array}{r} 7 \\ +8 \\ \hline 15 \end{array}$ $\begin{array}{r} 7 \\ +7 \\ \hline 14 \end{array}$ $\begin{array}{r} 6 \\ +7 \\ \hline \end{array}$ $\begin{array}{r} \\ + \\ \hline \end{array}$ $\begin{array}{r} 8 \\ +7 \\ \hline \end{array}$ $\begin{array}{r} \\ + \\ \hline \end{array}$

Ring the double-plus-one facts.
Then add all.

2. $7 + 8 =$ ___ $8 + 2 =$ ___ $6 + 7 =$ ___

3. $3 + 7 =$ ___ $4 + 5 =$ ___ $8 + 7 =$ ___

4. $7 + 6 =$ ___ $2 + 9 =$ ___ $9 + 6 =$ ___

Midchapter Review/Quiz

1. Write the addition fact for each picture.

FEBRUARY

Sun	Mon	Tue	Wed	Thu	Fri	Sat
1	2	3	4	5	6	7
8	9	10	11	12	13	14
15	16	17	18	19	20	21
22	23	24	25	26	27	28

___ + ___ = ___   ___ + ___ = ___   ___ + ___ = ___

Add.

2. $4 + 9 =$ ___ $9 + 3 =$ ___ $5 + 9 =$ ___

3.
$\begin{array}{r} 6 \\ 3 \\ +6 \\ \hline \end{array}$ $\begin{array}{r} 4 \\ 4 \\ +2 \\ \hline \end{array}$ $\begin{array}{r} 3 \\ 4 \\ +3 \\ \hline \end{array}$ $\begin{array}{r} 3 \\ 5 \\ +5 \\ \hline \end{array}$ $\begin{array}{r} 9 \\ 2 \\ +7 \\ \hline \end{array}$ $\begin{array}{r} 1 \\ 5 \\ +9 \\ \hline \end{array}$

Sums to 18

Put in 8. Then put in as many of the 5 as you can.

You have 10 and 3 extra.
$8 + 5 = 13$

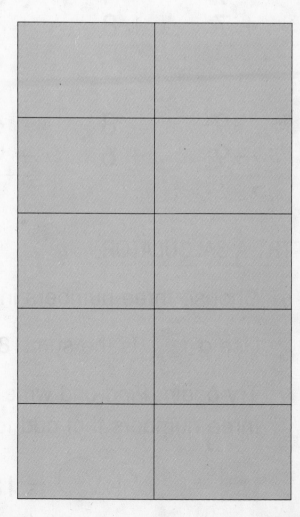

$$\begin{array}{r} 8 \\ + 5 \\ \hline 13 \end{array}$$

Work with a partner. Use counters and ▦. Put in counters for the greater number. Use the other number to make 10. Add the extras. Write the sum.

1. $\begin{array}{r} 8 \\ + 6 \\ \hline \end{array}$ 2. $\begin{array}{r} 4 \\ + 7 \\ \hline \end{array}$

3. $\begin{array}{r} 7 \\ + 5 \\ \hline \end{array}$ 4. $\begin{array}{r} 8 \\ + 4 \\ \hline \end{array}$

5. $\begin{array}{r} 5 \\ + 8 \\ \hline \end{array}$ 6. $\begin{array}{r} 6 \\ + 8 \\ \hline \end{array}$

Add. Use counters and  to help.

1.
$$\begin{array}{r} 9 \\ +1 \\ \hline \end{array}$$
$$\begin{array}{r} 8 \\ +7 \\ \hline \end{array}$$
$$\begin{array}{r} 7 \\ +4 \\ \hline \end{array}$$
$$\begin{array}{r} 6 \\ +7 \\ \hline \end{array}$$
$$\begin{array}{r} 8 \\ +4 \\ \hline \end{array}$$
$$\begin{array}{r} 5 \\ +7 \\ \hline \end{array}$$

2.
$$\begin{array}{r} 5 \\ +8 \\ \hline \end{array}$$
$$\begin{array}{r} 4 \\ +9 \\ \hline \end{array}$$
$$\begin{array}{r} 4 \\ +7 \\ \hline \end{array}$$
$$\begin{array}{r} 9 \\ +3 \\ \hline \end{array}$$
$$\begin{array}{r} 6 \\ +8 \\ \hline \end{array}$$
$$\begin{array}{r} 7 \\ +7 \\ \hline \end{array}$$

3.
$$\begin{array}{r} 9 \\ +7 \\ \hline \end{array}$$
$$\begin{array}{r} 4 \\ +8 \\ \hline \end{array}$$
$$\begin{array}{r} 8 \\ +8 \\ \hline \end{array}$$
$$\begin{array}{r} 8 \\ +5 \\ \hline \end{array}$$
$$\begin{array}{r} 9 \\ +5 \\ \hline \end{array}$$
$$\begin{array}{r} 8 \\ +3 \\ \hline \end{array}$$

4.
$$\begin{array}{r} 9 \\ +9 \\ \hline \end{array}$$
$$\begin{array}{r} 8 \\ +6 \\ \hline \end{array}$$
$$\begin{array}{r} 6 \\ +9 \\ \hline \end{array}$$
$$\begin{array}{r} 2 \\ +9 \\ \hline \end{array}$$
$$\begin{array}{r} 7 \\ +5 \\ \hline \end{array}$$
$$\begin{array}{r} 8 \\ +9 \\ \hline \end{array}$$

TRY A CALCULATOR

5. Choose three numbers in a row.

Use a . Is the sum 18?

Try again. Find and write the three numbers that add to 18.

I'll try 3, 4, and 5.

$$\blacksquare + \triangle + \bigcirc = 18$$

| 2 | 3 | 4 | 5 | 6 | 7 | 8 | 9 |

Fact Practice

Kara Kangaroo, do you eat with your tail?

To find out, first add. Then write the code letters in the boxes below.

O 5 + 4 = ___   F 3 + 4 = ___
T 8 + 9 = ___   R 8 + 8 = ___
I 8 + 5 = 13   V 6 + 9 = ___   V 7 + 8 = ___
A 2 + 8 = ___   F 2 + 5 = ___   N 7 + 7 = ___
K 3 + 5 = ___   I 4 + 9 = ___   S 6 + 6 = ___
O 2 + 7 = ___   A 5 + 5 = ___   Y 9 + 9 = ___
V 9 + 6 = ___   K 6 + 2 = ___   E 5 + 6 = ___

Read the message.

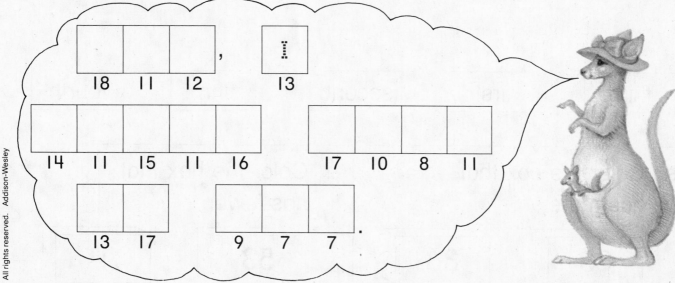

			,		:
18	11	12		13	

14	11	15	11	16

17	10	8	11

13	17

			.
9	7	7	

Add. Cross out each sum in the box to check.

1.
$$\begin{array}{r} 6 \\ +7 \\ \hline 13 \end{array}$$
$$\begin{array}{r} 9 \\ +9 \\ \hline \end{array}$$
$$\begin{array}{r} 5 \\ +6 \\ \hline \end{array}$$
$$\begin{array}{r} 8 \\ +8 \\ \hline \end{array}$$

Check Box	
7	~~13~~
8	14
9	15
10	16
11	17
12	18

2.
$$\begin{array}{r} 9 \\ +5 \\ \hline \end{array}$$
$$\begin{array}{r} 6 \\ +2 \\ \hline \end{array}$$
$$\begin{array}{r} 5 \\ +5 \\ \hline \end{array}$$
$$\begin{array}{r} 6 \\ +9 \\ \hline \end{array}$$

3.
$$\begin{array}{r} 8 \\ +4 \\ \hline \end{array}$$
$$\begin{array}{r} 3 \\ +6 \\ \hline \end{array}$$
$$\begin{array}{r} 8 \\ +9 \\ \hline \end{array}$$
$$\begin{array}{r} 5 \\ +2 \\ \hline \end{array}$$

MIXED REVIEW

4. Match.

| third | first | second | fifth | fourth |

5. Color the box that has more.

| 33 | 36 |

6. Color the box that has fewer.

| 53 | 41 |

Chapter 15

Problem Solving
Determining Reasonable Answers

UNDERSTAND
FIND DATA
PLAN
ESTIMATE
SOLVE
CHECK

Ring if the number is correct. Cross out if it is wrong. Write the correct number sentence.

1. There are 6 gum trees.
   2 are Snow Gum trees.
   How many are not?

   ✗̶8̶ are not Snow Gum trees.

   6 ⟨−⟩ 2 ▣ 4

2. 3 kangaroos each had a joey.
   I did not. How many more had joeys than did not?

   __2__ more had joeys.

   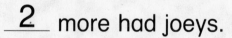

3. 8 koalas are eating.
   2 are sleeping.
   How many more are eating?

   __10__ more koalas are eating.

4. 5 parrots are in the tree.
   2 more come.
   How many are in the tree now?

   __3__ parrots are in the tree.

Problem Solving Strategy
Use Objects

UNDERSTAND
FIND DATA
PLAN
ESTIMATE
SOLVE
CHECK

Cut out the boats. Listen to the stories.
Use the boats to act them out.
Paste to match the second story.

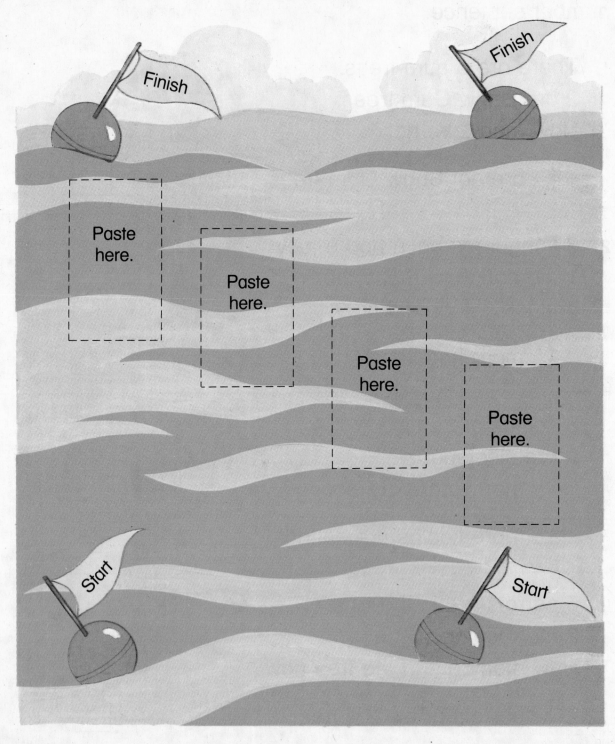

Chapter 15

Name _____

WRAP UP

MATH WORDS

Use 🖍 to ring the double facts.
Use 🖍 to ring the double-plus-one facts. Then add all.

1.
$$7 + 7 \qquad 7 + 6 \qquad 9 + 9 \qquad 6 + 7 \qquad 7 + 9 \qquad 8 + 3$$

2.
$$9 + 8 \qquad 8 + 8 \qquad 6 + 9 \qquad 8 + 7 \qquad 7 + 8 \qquad 6 + 6$$

MATH REASONING

Look at the figure.

3. How many triangles are there in all? ____ triangles

4. Write a number in each circle so that each triangle has a sum of 18.

Try the numbers 5, 6, and 7.

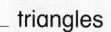

CHAPTER REVIEW/TEST

1. Write the double fact for each picture.

___ + ___ = ___   ___ + ___ = ___   ___ + ___ = ___

Add.

2.

8	9	9	4	7	9
+8	+6	+9	+9	+7	+3

3. 4 + 5 = ___   7 + 6 = ___   7 + 8 = ___

4.

9	5	4	2	8	8
1	5	6	3	8	2
+6	+4	+5	+7	+1	+3

5.

5	7	8	6	5	8
+8	+4	+4	+8	+7	+6

6. Write how many more are needed. There are 3 children. It takes 6 children to play the game. How many more children must come to play the game?

___ more must come.

ENRICHMENT
Exploring Addition

$3 + 4 + 5 =$ ___12___ $3 + 4 + 5 =$ ___12___

Work with a partner. Use cubes.
Add the red numbers to start.
Add the first way. Then add
the second way. Did you get
the same answer? Ring **yes** or **no**.

$7 + 5$ $3 + 9$

I got the same answer.

	First Way	Second Way	Same Answer?
1.	$2 + 4 + 3 =$ ___	$2 + 4 + 3 =$ ___	yes no
2.	$9 + 0 + 9 =$ ___	$9 + 0 + 9 =$ ___	yes no
3.	$8 + 1 + 3 =$ ___	$8 + 1 + 3 =$ ___	yes no
4.	$6 + 2 + 5 =$ ___	$6 + 2 + 5 =$ ___	yes no
5.	$7 + 2 + 7 =$ ___	$7 + 2 + 7 =$ ___	yes no

6. Write different ways you could
   add to find the sum of $4 + 2 + 5$.

First Add	Then Add
___ + ___	___ + ___ = ___
___ + ___	___ + ___ = ___
___ + ___	___ + ___ = ___

7. Does it matter in which
   order you add? Ring one.   yes   no

CUMULATIVE REVIEW

Count how much.

1.
   - ○ 11¢
   - ○ 12¢
   - ○ 21¢

2.
   - ○ 21¢
   - ○ 26¢
   - ○ 31¢

3.
   - ○ 39¢
   - ○ 42¢
   - ○ 47¢

4. **Which is less?**
   - ○ A
   - ○ B

   A

   B

What time is it?

5.
   - ○ 8 o'clock
   - ○ 7 o'clock
   - ○ 9 o'clock

6.
   - ○ 1:00
   - ○ 11:00
   - ○ 12:00

7. **What is the time one half hour later?**

   - ○ 10:30
   - ○ 10:00
   - ○ 9:30

8. **How many days are in one week?**
   - ○ 9 days
   - ○ 7 days
   - ○ 8 days

9. Raj had    He bought a 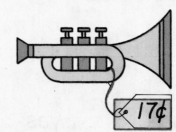   How much money does he have now?
   - ○ 18¢
   - ○ 16¢
   - ○ 17¢

16
Addition and Subtraction Facts to 18

Workmat

Subtraction Doubles to 18

Work with a partner. Use counters.
Lay out your counters like the
picture. Write a doubles fact.
Take away the counters on one
side. Write a subtraction fact.

1.

____ + ____ = ____

____ − ____ = ____

2.

____ + ____ = ____

____ − ____ = ____

3.

____ + ____ = ____

____ − ____ = ____

4.

____ + ____ = ____

____ − ____ = ____

Ring the subtraction doubles.
Then subtract all.

5.

$$14 - 7 \qquad 10 - 4 \qquad 18 - 9 \qquad 12 - 9 \qquad 9 - 5 \qquad 16 - 8$$

TALK ABOUT IT

6. Write the answer. $4 + 5 + 2 - 2 - 5 = \underline{\quad}$

Guess what the answer will be if you
start with 6. Guess what the answer
will be if you start with 8. Tell why.

Subtracting 9

Take out 9.
Write what
is left.

You have I
in the frame
and 6 extra.
7 are left.

$$\begin{array}{r} 16 \\ -\ 9 \\ \hline 7 \end{array}$$

Work with a partner.
Use counters and .
Show the first number
with ten and extras.
Take 9 from the ▤.
Write what is left.

1. $\begin{array}{r} 13 \\ -\ 9 \\ \hline \end{array}$ 2. $\begin{array}{r} 17 \\ -\ 9 \\ \hline \end{array}$

3. $\begin{array}{r} 16 \\ -\ 9 \\ \hline \end{array}$ 4. $\begin{array}{r} 15 \\ -\ 9 \\ \hline \end{array}$

5. $\begin{array}{r} 12 \\ -\ 9 \\ \hline \end{array}$ 6. $\begin{array}{r} 14 \\ -\ 9 \\ \hline \end{array}$

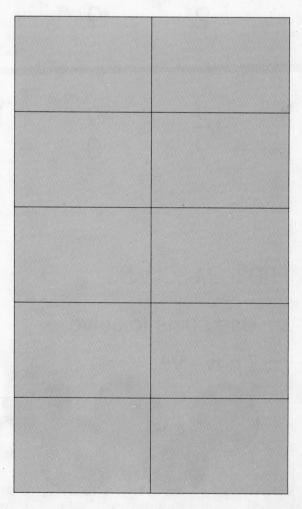

Ring where you subtract 9.
Then subtract all.
Use counters and  to help.

When I subtract 9, my answer is the extras and 1 more.

1.
(13 − 9)   4 − 3   16 − 9   7 − 3   8 − 5   15 − 9

2.
4 − 2   9 − 3   7 − 0   14 − 9   6 − 2   8 − 2

3.
7 − 2   17 − 9   6 − 4   9 − 4   18 − 9   6 − 5

4.
12 − 9   9 − 0   10 − 7   15 − 9   14 − 7   11 − 9

PROBLEM SOLVING

5. Use coins to solve.

I have 9¢.

How much more do I need to buy the ball?

I need ____ ¢.

13¢

Fact Practice

Subtract the Across Facts.
Fill in the puzzle. Subtract
the Down Facts to check.

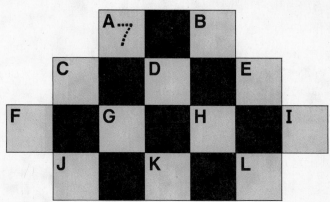

Across Facts

A $\begin{array}{r} 14 \\ -\ 7 \\ \hline 7 \end{array}$	**B** $\begin{array}{r} 17 \\ -\ 9 \\ \hline \end{array}$	**C** $\begin{array}{r} 14 \\ -\ 9 \\ \hline \end{array}$	**D** $\begin{array}{r} 12 \\ -\ 9 \\ \hline \end{array}$	**E** $\begin{array}{r} 12 \\ -\ 6 \\ \hline \end{array}$	**F** $\begin{array}{r} 10 \\ -\ 6 \\ \hline \end{array}$
G $\begin{array}{r} 10 \\ -\ 8 \\ \hline \end{array}$	**H** $\begin{array}{r} 16 \\ -\ 8 \\ \hline \end{array}$	**I** $\begin{array}{r} 10 \\ -\ 3 \\ \hline \end{array}$	**J** $\begin{array}{r} 10 \\ -\ 5 \\ \hline \end{array}$	**K** $\begin{array}{r} 18 \\ -\ 9 \\ \hline \end{array}$	**L** $\begin{array}{r} 13 \\ -\ 9 \\ \hline \end{array}$

Down Facts

A $\begin{array}{r} 16 \\ -\ 9 \\ \hline \end{array}$	**B** $\begin{array}{r} 11 \\ -\ 3 \\ \hline \end{array}$	**C** $\begin{array}{r} 9 \\ -\ 4 \\ \hline \end{array}$	**D** $\begin{array}{r} 11 \\ -\ 8 \\ \hline \end{array}$	**E** $\begin{array}{r} 15 \\ -\ 9 \\ \hline \end{array}$	**F** $\begin{array}{r} 8 \\ -\ 4 \\ \hline \end{array}$
G $\begin{array}{r} 11 \\ -\ 9 \\ \hline \end{array}$	**H** $\begin{array}{r} 10 \\ -\ 2 \\ \hline \end{array}$	**I** $\begin{array}{r} 9 \\ -\ 2 \\ \hline \end{array}$	**J** $\begin{array}{r} 8 \\ -\ 3 \\ \hline \end{array}$	**K** $\begin{array}{r} 9 \\ -\ 0 \\ \hline \end{array}$	**L** $\begin{array}{r} 7 \\ -\ 3 \\ \hline \end{array}$

1. **Subtract the Across Facts. Fill in the puzzle. Subtract the Down Facts to check.**

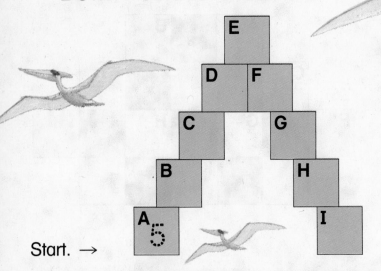

Start. →

Down Facts	
A	$14 - 9 =$ ___
B	$8 - 6 =$ ___
C	$8 - 4 =$ ___
D	$5 - 2 =$ ___
E	$15 - 9 =$ ___
F	$10 - 1 =$ ___
G	$17 - 9 =$ ___
H	$16 - 9 =$ ___
I	$10 - 8 =$ ___

Across Facts

A $10 - 5 = 5$ B $9 - 7 =$ ___

C $13 - 9 =$ ___   D $10 - 7 =$ ___

E $10 - 4 =$ ___   F $18 - 9 =$ ___

G $16 - 8 =$ ___   H $14 - 7 =$ ___

I $11 - 9 =$ ___

USE CRITICAL THINKING

2. Here are three square numbers. Show the next square number with dots. Then write the number.

```
          . .        . . .
  .       . .        . . .
                     . . .

  I        4          9        ___
```

Chapter 16

Problem Solving
Understanding the Operations

UNDERSTAND
FIND DATA
PLAN
ESTIMATE
SOLVE
CHECK

Use counters to show the story.
Finish the subtraction sentence.

1. There are 7 dinosaurs by the swamp.

   3 are . The rest are .

   How many 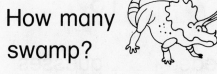 are by the
   swamp?

   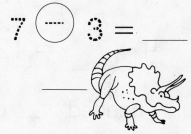

   7 ⊝ 3 = ____
   ____

2. There are 5 dinosaurs on
   the grass. 4 eat plants.
   The others eat meat.
   How many eat meat?

   5 ⊝ ____ = ____

   ____ dinosaur

3. 8 dinosaurs wake up.

   3 are . The rest are 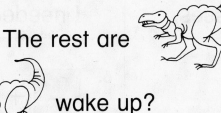.

   How many 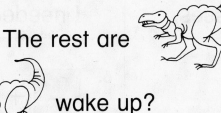 wake up?

   8 ◯ ____ = ____

   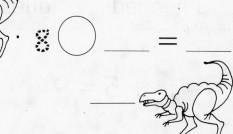
   ____

4. There are 6 dinosaurs by the tree.
   2 have plates on their back.
   The rest do not.
   How many do not have plates?

   ____ ◯ ____ = ____

   ____ dinosaurs

Informal Algebra

Use these numbers.
Guess which number goes
in the . Write it. Check.
Try again if you need to.

1.

$4 + \boxed{} = 12$

$4 + \boxed{} = 12$

$4 + \boxed{} = 12$

I needed _____ guesses.

2.

$6 + \boxed{} = 13$

$6 + \boxed{} = 13$

$6 + \boxed{} = 13$

I needed _____ guesses.

3.

$9 + \boxed{} = 12$

$9 + \boxed{} = 12$

$9 + \boxed{} = 12$

I needed _____ guesses.

4.

$7 + \boxed{} = 13$

$7 + \boxed{} = 13$

$7 + \boxed{} = 13$

I needed _____ guesses.

5.

$\boxed{} + 5 = 9$

$\boxed{} + 5 = 9$

$\boxed{} + 5 = 9$

I needed _____ guesses.

6.

$\boxed{} + 8 = 13$

$\boxed{} + 8 = 13$

$\boxed{} + 8 = 13$

I needed _____ guesses.

Chapter 16

Using Addition to Subtract 4, 5, and 6

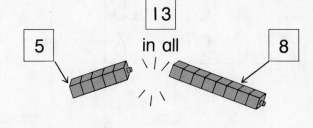

add-to-check fact

$$\begin{array}{r} 8 \\ + 5 \\ \hline 13 \end{array} \rightarrow \text{so} \begin{array}{r} 13 \\ - 5 \\ \hline 8 \end{array}$$

Work with a partner. Use the add-to-check fact to help subtract. Show with cubes.

1.

$$\begin{array}{r} 9 \\ + 5 \\ \hline 14 \end{array} \qquad \begin{array}{r} 14 \\ - 5 \\ \hline 9 \end{array}$$

2.

$$\begin{array}{r} 9 \\ + 4 \\ \hline 13 \end{array} \qquad \begin{array}{r} 13 \\ - 4 \\ \hline \end{array}$$

3.

$$\begin{array}{r} 9 \\ + 6 \\ \hline 15 \end{array} \qquad \begin{array}{r} 15 \\ - 6 \\ \hline \end{array}$$

4.

$$\begin{array}{r} 8 \\ + 6 \\ \hline 14 \end{array} \qquad \begin{array}{r} 14 \\ - 6 \\ \hline \end{array}$$

5.

$$\begin{array}{r} 8 \\ + 4 \\ \hline 12 \end{array} \qquad \begin{array}{r} 12 \\ - 4 \\ \hline \end{array}$$

6.

$$\begin{array}{r} 7 \\ + 6 \\ \hline 13 \end{array} \qquad \begin{array}{r} 13 \\ - 6 \\ \hline \end{array}$$

Subtract. Use the add-to-check fact to help.

If it helps, use cubes to show.

1.

| 6
 + 9
 ———
 15 | 15
 − 6
 ———
 9 | | 4
 + 5
 ———
 9 | 9
 − 4
 ——— |

2.

| 2
 + 5
 ———
 7 | 7
 − 2
 ——— | | 6
 + 7
 ———
 13 | 13
 − 6
 ——— | | 2
 + 2
 ———
 4 | 4
 − 2
 ——— |

3.

| 5
 + 9
 ———
 14 | 14
 − 5
 ——— | | 3
 + 7
 ———
 10 | 10
 − 3
 ——— | | 4
 + 9
 ———
 13 | 13
 − 4
 ——— |

MIDCHAPTER REVIEW/QUIZ

1. Ring the subtraction doubles.
Then subtract all.

| 14
 − 7 | 11
 − 2 | 12
 − 6 | 18
 − 9 | 12
 − 3 | 16
 − 8 |

2. Subtract.

| 10
 − 9 | 10
 − 5 | 13
 − 9 | 15
 − 9 | 18
 − 9 | 12
 − 6 |

Using Addition to Subtract 7 and 8

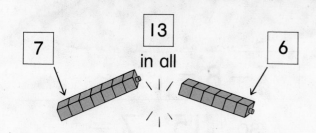

13
in all

7   6

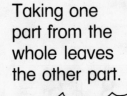

Taking one part from the whole leaves the other part.

$$\begin{array}{r} 7 \\ +6 \\ \hline 13 \end{array} \rightarrow \begin{array}{r} 13 \\ -7 \\ \hline 6 \end{array}$$
so

Work with a partner. Use the add-to-check fact to help subtract. Show with cubes.

1. $7 + 8 = 15$

$15 - 8 = \underline{7}$

2. $5 + 8 = 13$

$13 - 8 = \underline{}$

3. $9 + 8 = 17$

$17 - 8 = \underline{}$

4. $8 + 7 = 15$

$15 - 7 = \underline{}$

5. $9 + 7 = 16$

$16 - 7 = \underline{}$

6. $6 + 8 = 14$

$14 - 8 = \underline{}$

Subtract. Use the add-to-check fact to help.

If it helps, use cubes to show.

1. $8 + 5 = 13$

so $13 - 8 = 5$

2. $7 + 8 = 15$

so $15 - 7 = \underline{}$

3. $8 + 8 = 16$

so $16 - 8 = \underline{}$

4. $8 + 6 = 14$

so $14 - 8 = \underline{}$

5. $8 + 9 = 17$

so $17 - 8 = \underline{}$

6. $9 + 9 = 18$

so $18 - 9 = \underline{}$

7. $7 + 7 = 14$

so $14 - 7 = \underline{}$

8. $8 + 7 = 15$

so $15 - 8 = \underline{}$

9. $7 + 9 = 16$

so $16 - 7 = \underline{}$

10. $6 + 6 = 12$

so $12 - 6 = \underline{}$

MAKE AN ESTIMATE

11. Look at the picture. About how many of the first graders would it take to be as tall as the dinosaur?

_____ first graders

Talk about how to check.

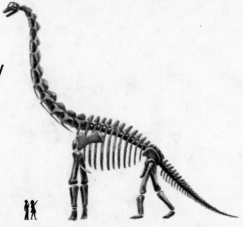

Related Subtraction Facts

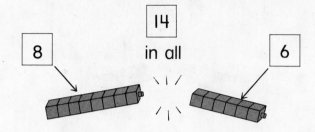

14
in all

8 → ▭▭▭▭▭▭▭▭   ▭▭▭▭▭▭ ← 6

$$\begin{array}{r} 14 \\ -\ 8 \\ \hline 6 \end{array}$$ ← and → $$\begin{array}{r} 14 \\ -\ 6 \\ \hline 8 \end{array}$$

Work with a partner. Use cubes. Start with the greater number. Take away one of the parts. Write the other part.

1. $$\begin{array}{r} 13 \\ -\ 6 \\ \hline \end{array}$$ and $$\begin{array}{r} 13 \\ -\ 7 \\ \hline \end{array}$$

2. $$\begin{array}{r} 15 \\ -\ 6 \\ \hline \end{array}$$ and $$\begin{array}{r} 15 \\ -\ 9 \\ \hline \end{array}$$

3. $$\begin{array}{r} 14 \\ -\ 5 \\ \hline \end{array}$$ and $$\begin{array}{r} 14 \\ -\ 9 \\ \hline \end{array}$$

4. $$\begin{array}{r} 15 \\ -\ 7 \\ \hline \end{array}$$ and $$\begin{array}{r} 15 \\ -\ 8 \\ \hline \end{array}$$

5. $$\begin{array}{r} 13 \\ -\ 5 \\ \hline \end{array}$$ and $$\begin{array}{r} 13 \\ -\ 8 \\ \hline \end{array}$$

6. $$\begin{array}{r} 13 \\ -\ 4 \\ \hline \end{array}$$ and $$\begin{array}{r} 13 \\ -\ 9 \\ \hline \end{array}$$

Finish the subtraction facts.

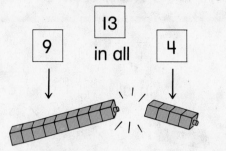

1.

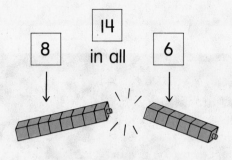

| 8 | 14 in all | 6 |

$14 - 8 = $ _____ and

$14 - 6 = $ _____

2.

| 9 | 13 in all | 4 |

$13 - 9 = $ _____ and

$13 - 4 = $ _____

3.

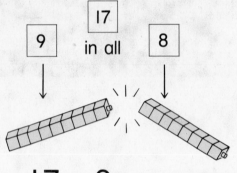

| 9 | 17 in all | 8 |

$17 - 9 = $ _____ and

$17 - 8 = $ _____

4.

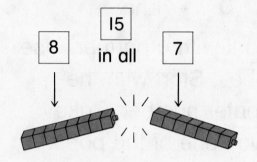

| 8 | 15 in all | 7 |

$15 - 8 = $ _____ and

$15 - 7 = $ _____

FIND THE DATA

DATA BANK

5. Data Bank How much longer is

the _____ than the _____ ?

(See page 400.) Ring the number
sentence that helps. Count by
tens. Write the answer.

$40 + 30 = $ _____

$40 - 30 = $ _____

_____ feet

Fact Families

Fact Family

$$\begin{array}{r} 4 \\ +7 \\ \hline 11 \end{array} \qquad \begin{array}{r} 7 \\ +4 \\ \hline 11 \end{array} \qquad \begin{array}{r} 11 \\ -4 \\ \hline 7 \end{array} \qquad \begin{array}{r} 11 \\ -7 \\ \hline 4 \end{array}$$

When you know one fact, you know them all.

Work in a group. Use cubes. Show each fact family. Write to finish.

1. [7] [13] [6]

$$\begin{array}{r} 7 \\ +6 \\ \hline 13 \end{array} \qquad \begin{array}{r} 6 \\ +7 \\ \hline \end{array} \qquad \begin{array}{r} 13 \\ -7 \\ \hline \end{array} \qquad \begin{array}{r} 13 \\ -6 \\ \hline \end{array}$$

2. [9] [16] [7]

$$\begin{array}{r} 9 \\ +7 \\ \hline \end{array} \qquad \begin{array}{r} 7 \\ +9 \\ \hline \end{array} \qquad \begin{array}{r} 16 \\ -9 \\ \hline \end{array} \qquad \begin{array}{r} 16 \\ -7 \\ \hline \end{array}$$

3. [7] [12] [5]

$$\begin{array}{r} 7 \\ +5 \\ \hline \end{array} \qquad \begin{array}{r} 5 \\ +7 \\ \hline \end{array} \qquad \begin{array}{r} 12 \\ -7 \\ \hline \end{array} \qquad \begin{array}{r} 12 \\ -5 \\ \hline \end{array}$$

4. [6] [11] [5]

$$\begin{array}{r} 6 \\ +5 \\ \hline \end{array} \qquad \begin{array}{r} 5 \\ +6 \\ \hline \end{array} \qquad \begin{array}{r} 11 \\ -6 \\ \hline \end{array} \qquad \begin{array}{r} 11 \\ -5 \\ \hline \end{array}$$

5. [7] [15] [8]

$$\begin{array}{r} 7 \\ +8 \\ \hline \end{array} \qquad \begin{array}{r} 8 \\ +7 \\ \hline \end{array} \qquad \begin{array}{r} 15 \\ -7 \\ \hline \end{array} \qquad \begin{array}{r} 15 \\ -8 \\ \hline \end{array}$$

6. [8] [12] [4]

$$\begin{array}{r} 8 \\ +4 \\ \hline \end{array} \qquad \begin{array}{r} 4 \\ +8 \\ \hline \end{array} \qquad \begin{array}{r} 12 \\ -8 \\ \hline \end{array} \qquad \begin{array}{r} 12 \\ -4 \\ \hline \end{array}$$

Cross out the one that is not in the
fact family. Finish the others.
Use counters and to help.

1. $8 + 9 = \underline{17}$ $9 + 8 = \underline{17}$ $17 - 9 = \underline{}$

~~$9 + 7 =$~~ $17 - 8 = \underline{}$

2. $9 + 4 = \underline{}$ $13 - 4 = \underline{}$

$4 + 9 = \underline{}$ $13 - 5 = \underline{}$ $13 - 9 = \underline{}$

3. $5 + 8 = \underline{}$ $13 - 5 = \underline{}$

$8 + 5 = \underline{}$ $13 - 9 = \underline{}$ $13 - 8 = \underline{}$

MIXED REVIEW

4. Count how many.
   Write the number.

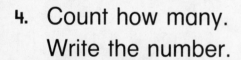 $\underline{}$

5. Color to show the tens
   and ones.

Tens	Ones
2	4

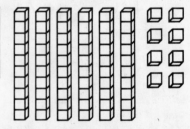

6. Add. Can you trade for a dime?   Ring **yes** or **no.**

yes

no

$4¢ + 5¢ = \underline{}¢$

Problem Solving
Using a Number Sentence

Write the number sentence for the story.
Write the answer. Ring to finish the story.

1. 5 dinosaurs were eating
plants. 3 ran away.
How many stayed?

$\underset{5}{\dotuline{}}$ ⊖ $\underset{3}{\dotuline{}}$ = ____

____ dinosaurs ran away.
____ dinosaurs are still there.

2.

3 [stegosaurus] and 5 [apatosaurus]
are looking for food. How
many are looking for food? ____

____ ◯ ____ = ____

____ dinosaurs in all.
____ dinosaurs are left.

3.

3 big [dinosaur] are joined
by 2 little ones.
How many more big ones
than little ones are there? ____

____ ◯ ____ = ____

____ dinosaurs in all.
____ more big than little.

UNDERSTAND
FIND DATA
PLAN
ESTIMATE
SOLVE
CHECK

Problem Solving Strategy
Use Objects

Cut out the dinosaurs. Listen to the story. Find and write the ways the dinosaurs can line up.

A then T then S ____   ____ then ____ then ____

____ then ____ then ____   ____ then ____ then ____

____ then ____ then ____   ____ then ____ then ____

____ ways in all

 A for Apatosaurus

 T for Tyrannosaurus

 S for Stegosaurus

WRAP UP

MATH WORDS

1. Use  to ring subtraction doubles.
   Use to ring where you subtract 9.
   Then subtract all.

$$\begin{array}{cccccc} 14 & 13 & 16 & 16 & 17 & 15 \\ -7 & -9 & -8 & -9 & -9 & -7 \\ \hline \end{array}$$

2. Subtract. $13 - 7 = \underline{\quad}$

   Write the add-to-check fact. $\underline{\quad} + \underline{\quad} = \underline{\quad}$

   Finish the fact family.

   $\underline{\quad} \bigcirc \underline{\quad} = \underline{\quad}$ $\underline{\quad} \bigcirc \underline{\quad} = \underline{\quad}$

MATH REASONING

Write + or − in each $\bigcirc$.

3. $16 \bigcirc 7 = 18 \bigcirc 9$

4. $6 \bigcirc 2 = 14 \bigcirc 6$

5. $9 \bigcirc 4 = 8 \bigcirc 5$

6. $17 \bigcirc 9 = 4 \bigcirc 4$

7. $9 \bigcirc 9 = 6 \bigcirc 6$

CHAPTER REVIEW/TEST

Ring the subtraction doubles. Then subtract all.

1. $\begin{array}{r} 18 \\ -\,9 \\ \hline \end{array}$
    $\begin{array}{r} 15 \\ -\,7 \\ \hline \end{array}$
    $\begin{array}{r} 10 \\ -\,5 \\ \hline \end{array}$
    $\begin{array}{r} 13 \\ -\,9 \\ \hline \end{array}$
    $\begin{array}{r} 11 \\ -\,9 \\ \hline \end{array}$
    $\begin{array}{r} 10 \\ -\,7 \\ \hline \end{array}$

2. $\begin{array}{r} 14 \\ -\,9 \\ \hline \end{array}$
    $\begin{array}{r} 12 \\ -\,6 \\ \hline \end{array}$
    $\begin{array}{r} 16 \\ -\,8 \\ \hline \end{array}$
    $\begin{array}{r} 13 \\ -\,4 \\ \hline \end{array}$
    $\begin{array}{r} 15 \\ -\,9 \\ \hline \end{array}$
    $\begin{array}{r} 14 \\ -\,7 \\ \hline \end{array}$

Subtract. Use the add-to-check fact to help.

3. | $\begin{array}{r} 9 \\ +\,5 \\ \hline \end{array}$ | $\begin{array}{r} 14 \\ -\,5 \\ \hline \end{array}$ |

4. | $\begin{array}{r} 5 \\ +\,6 \\ \hline \end{array}$ | $\begin{array}{r} 11 \\ -\,6 \\ \hline \end{array}$ |

5. | $\begin{array}{r} 8 \\ +\,7 \\ \hline \end{array}$ | $\begin{array}{r} 15 \\ -\,7 \\ \hline \end{array}$ |

Finish each fact family.

6. $5 + 8 = \underline{\hspace{1cm}}$
    $8 + 5 = \underline{\hspace{1cm}}$
    $13 - \underline{\hspace{1cm}} = \underline{\hspace{1cm}}$
    $13 - \underline{\hspace{1cm}} = \underline{\hspace{1cm}}$

7. $8 + 9 = \underline{\hspace{1cm}}$
    $9 + 8 = \underline{\hspace{1cm}}$
    $17 - \underline{\hspace{1cm}} = \underline{\hspace{1cm}}$
    $17 - \underline{\hspace{1cm}} = \underline{\hspace{1cm}}$

8. 3 big tigers come to play with
    5 little tigers. How many more
    little ones are there?

    $\underline{\hspace{1cm}} \bigcirc \underline{\hspace{1cm}} = \underline{\hspace{1cm}}$

    Ring to finish the story.

    _____ tigers in all.

    _____ more little ones.

Name _____

ENRICHMENT
Using a Number Line to Add or Subtract

$$8 - 2 = \underline{6}$$ $$11 + 3 = \underline{14}$$

Add or subtract.
Use the number line.

1. $6 + 2 = \underline{\quad}$ $16 - 5 = \underline{\quad}$ $8 + 3 = \underline{\quad}$

2. $5 + 5 = \underline{\quad}$ $8 + 8 = \underline{\quad}$ $12 - 6 = \underline{\quad}$

3. $18 - 9 = \underline{\quad}$ $17 - 8 = \underline{\quad}$ $9 + 5 = \underline{\quad}$

4. $9 + 4 = \underline{\quad}$ $13 - 4 = \underline{\quad}$ $8 + 6 = \underline{\quad}$

5. $3 + 7 = \underline{\quad}$ $10 - 3 = \underline{\quad}$ $13 - 7 = \underline{\quad}$

6. $15 - 7 = \underline{\quad}$ $17 - 7 = \underline{\quad}$ $9 + 8 = \underline{\quad}$

Name _____

CUMULATIVE REVIEW

1. Where is the hour hand?

- ○ 9
- ○ 12
- ○ 10

2. Where is the minute hand?

- ○ 4
- ○ 12
- ○ 1

3. What is the time?

- ○ 4:30
- ○ 2:30
- ○ 3:30

4. Which class comes first?

math class 11:00

reading class 10:30

art class 9:30

- ○ math
- ○ art
- ○ reading

Add.

5. $9 + 9 =$ ____

- ○ 17
- ○ 18
- ○ 19

6.
$$\begin{array}{r} 4 \\ + 9 \\ \hline \end{array}$$

- ○ 12
- ○ 13
- ○ 14

7.
$$\begin{array}{r} 6 \\ 6 \\ + 1 \\ \hline \end{array}$$

- ○ 12
- ○ 13
- ○ 14

8. Find the double-plus-one fact for $7 + 7 = 14$.

- ○ $6 + 7 = 13$
- ○ $8 + 9 = 17$
- ○ $8 + 7 = 15$

9. Choose the correct number sentence.

There are 9 .

We need 15 to play.

How many more do we need?

- ○ $15 - 8 = 7$
- ○ $15 - 7 = 8$
- ○ $15 - 9 = 6$

17
Understanding 2-Digit Addition and Subtraction

Workmat

Name _____

Counting On by Ones

Work with a partner. Use blocks. Lay out blocks for the blue number. Count on as you lay out blocks for the yellow number. Write the sum.

1. [31] + [2] = ____

2. [16] + [3] = ____

3. [28] + [3] = ____

4. [39] + [1] = ____

Write the numbers as you count on. Write the sum.

5.

40, ____, ____

40 + 2 = ____

6.

22, ____, ____, ____

22 + 3 = ____

Add.

7. 63 + 3 = ____

8. 49 + 1 = ____

USE MENTAL MATH

Count on to find the sum.

41, 42, 43, 44

9. 41 + 3 = ____

10. 54 + 3 = ____

Name _____

Making a Ten

Work in a group. Use  and counters.
Put counters in the to show the first
number. Put counters outside the
to show the second number. Then
make a ten. Write how many in all.

17 is I ten, 7 ones.
3 more makes a ten.
That is 2 tens and
3 extra, 23 in all.

$$\begin{array}{r} 17 \\ +\ 6 \\ \hline 23 \end{array}$$

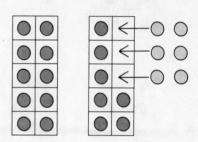

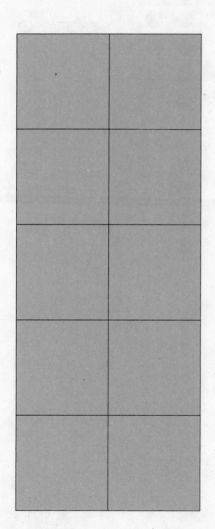
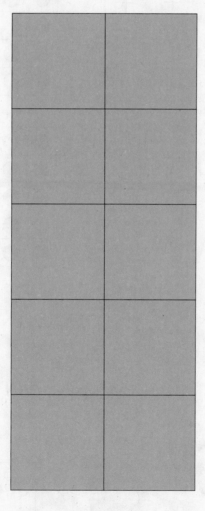

$$\begin{array}{r} 18 \\ +\ 4 \\ \hline \end{array} \qquad \begin{array}{r} 19 \\ +\ 5 \\ \hline \end{array} \qquad \begin{array}{r} 16 \\ +\ 6 \\ \hline \end{array} \qquad \begin{array}{r} 15 \\ +\ 8 \\ \hline \end{array} \qquad \begin{array}{r} 14 \\ +\ 4 \\ \hline \end{array} \qquad \begin{array}{r} 17 \\ +\ 7 \\ \hline \end{array}$$

Draw lines to make a ten.
Write how many in all.

1. 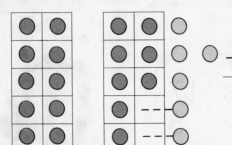 $\begin{array}{r} 18 \\ +\ 6 \\ \hline 24 \end{array}$

2. 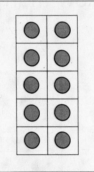 $\begin{array}{r} 15 \\ +\ 7 \\ \hline \end{array}$

3.  $\begin{array}{r} 16 \\ +\ 4 \\ \hline \end{array}$

4. $\begin{array}{r} 19 \\ +\ 3 \\ \hline \end{array}$

5. $\begin{array}{r} 17 \\ +\ 4 \\ \hline \end{array}$

6. $\begin{array}{r} 14 \\ +\ 5 \\ \hline \end{array}$

PROBLEM SOLVING

7. I have  The pear costs 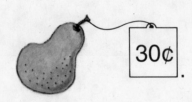 How much more do I need?

_____ ¢

Problem Solving
Understanding the Operations

UNDERSTAND
FIND DATA
PLAN
ESTIMATE
SOLVE
CHECK

Count on or use a ▊ to solve.
Write the answer.

1.
Lucy jumped 18 times.
She jumped 3 more times.
How many times did she
jump in all?

_____ times

$\begin{array}{r} 18 \\ + 3 \\ \hline \end{array}$

2.
Ruth bounced the ball 23 times.
She bounced it 3 more times.
How many times did she bounce
the ball in all?

_____ times

3.
Sylvia hopped 5 times.
She hopped 16 more times.
How many times did she
hop in all?

_____ times

4.
Peter did 26 toe touches.
He did 5 more.
How many toe touches
did he do in all?

_____ toe touches

Data Analysis

Which sports do your classmates like best? Take a survey to find out.

1. Make a tally mark for each vote.

biking _____ total

softball _____ total

soccer _____ total

roller skating _____ total

2. Mark X on the graph for each tally.

3. Write **Sports Survey** to name the graph.

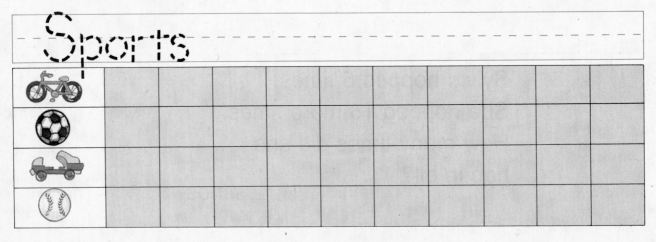

Sports

0   1 __ 3 __ 5   6 __ 8 __ 10

4. Write the missing numbers on the graph.

5. Ring what your classmates liked best. Cross out what they liked least.

Name ______________________________

Counting On By Tens

33, 43.
2 more tens, no more ones.
23
33
43

Use your punchout.
Put the top of the ladder on the first number. Count on by tens to add the second number.
Write the sum.

$$\begin{array}{r} 23 \\ +\ 20 \\ \hline 43 \end{array}$$

1	2	3	4	5	6	7	8	9	10
11	12	13	14	15	16	17	18	19	20
21	22	23	24	25	26	27	28	29	30
31	32	33	34	35	36	37	38	39	40
41	42	43	44	45	46	47	48	49	50

1. $\begin{array}{r} 21 \\ +\ 10 \\ \hline \end{array}$ $\begin{array}{r} 15 \\ +\ 30 \\ \hline \end{array}$ $\begin{array}{r} 28 \\ +\ 20 \\ \hline \end{array}$ $\begin{array}{r} 36 \\ +\ 10 \\ \hline \end{array}$ $\begin{array}{r} 17 \\ +\ 20 \\ \hline \end{array}$

2. $\begin{array}{r} 33 \\ +\ 10 \\ \hline \end{array}$ $\begin{array}{r} 29 \\ +\ 10 \\ \hline \end{array}$ $\begin{array}{r} 13 \\ +\ 30 \\ \hline \end{array}$ $\begin{array}{r} 21 \\ +\ 20 \\ \hline \end{array}$ $\begin{array}{r} 16 \\ +\ 20 \\ \hline \end{array}$

Write the first number in the ladder.
Count on by tens. Write the
numbers. Write how many in all.
Use blocks to help.

Count on by tens. The ones stay the same.

1.
$$\begin{array}{r} 32 \\ +10 \\ \hline 42 \end{array}$$

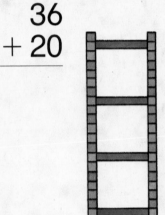
32
42

2.
$$\begin{array}{r} 28 \\ +20 \\ \hline \end{array}$$

28

3.
$$\begin{array}{r} 17 \\ +10 \\ \hline \end{array}$$

17

4.
$$\begin{array}{r} 36 \\ +20 \\ \hline \end{array}$$

5.
$$\begin{array}{r} 42 \\ +30 \\ \hline \end{array}$$

6.
$$\begin{array}{r} 24 \\ +30 \\ \hline \end{array}$$

TRY A CALCULATOR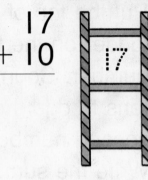

7. A can help you count.

Start at 16. To count by tens,

press | ON/C | | 16 | | + | | 10 | | = | | = | | = | | = | | = | .

Write the numbers
you see. Try it with
a different number.

16, _____, _____, _____, _____, _____

_____, _____, _____, _____, _____, _____

Adding Tens and Ones

Work in a group. Cut out
the score cards. Place cards
on the squares. Show each
number with blocks. Write
the numbers. Then add.

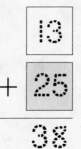

$$\begin{array}{r} 13 \\ + 25 \\ \hline 38 \end{array}$$

Jump-a-Thon
Score Box

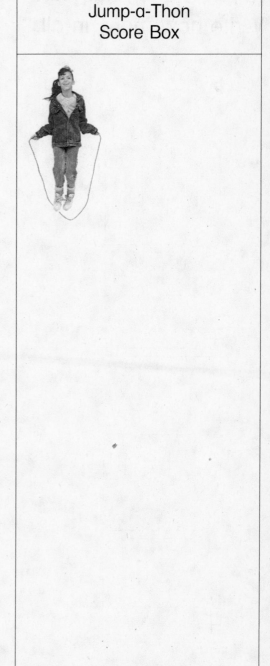

1.

2.

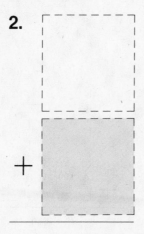

3.

4.

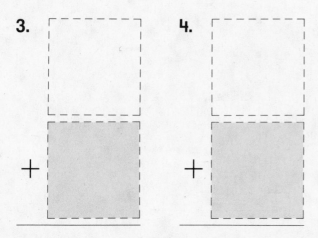

 31   13   24   32   20   15   25   14

Paste the score cards
on the squares below.
Draw tens and ones
to show each number.
Write how many in all.

$$\begin{array}{r} \boxed{23} \\ +\ \boxed{11} \\ \hline 34 \end{array}$$

That is 3 tens
and 4 ones,
34.

1.

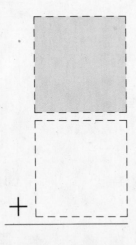

+ _____

2.

+ _____

3.

+ _____

4.

+ _____

| 35 | 11 | 21 | 34 | 23 | 12 | 22 | 33 |

Counting Back By Ones

24
Soccer
Balls

18
Balls

36
Cones

23
Jump
Ropes

Listen to the story. Use blocks. Write
the numbers as you count back.

1.

<u>23</u> , _____ , _____

How many are left?

$24 - 3 =$ _____

2.

_____ , _____

How many are left?

$18 - 2 =$ _____

3.

_____ , _____ , _____

How many are left?

$36 - 3 =$ _____

4.

_____ , _____

How many are left?

$23 - 2 =$ _____

Chapter 17

Use blocks. Count back to
find the difference.

1.

35

——— , ———

$35 - 2 =$ ___

2.

26

——— , ——— , ———

$26 - 3 =$ ___

1. Draw lines to make a ten.
   Write how many in all.

$$\begin{array}{r} 18 \\ + 4 \\ \hline \end{array}$$

2. Count on by tens. Write
   the numbers. Then
   write how many in all.

$$\begin{array}{r} 33 \\ + 20 \\ \hline \end{array}$$

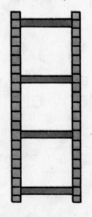

Write the numbers as you count on.
Write the sum.

3.

 31, ___ , ___ , ___

$31 + 3 =$ ___

4.

 23, ___ , ___

$23 + 2 =$ ___

364   (three hundred sixty-four)   Chapter 17

Counting Back By Tens

Use your  punchout. Put the bottom of the ladder on the first number. Count back by tens to take away the second number. Write the answer.

$$\begin{array}{r} 43 \\ -\ 20 \\ \hline 23 \end{array}$$

1	2	3	4	5	6	7	8	9	10
11	12	13	14	15	16	17	18	19	20
21	22	23	24	25	26	27	28	29	30
31	32	33	34	35	36	37	38	39	40
41	42	43	44	45	46	47	48	49	50

1.
$$\begin{array}{r} 34 \\ -10 \\ \hline \end{array} \qquad \begin{array}{r} 47 \\ -30 \\ \hline \end{array} \qquad \begin{array}{r} 42 \\ -20 \\ \hline \end{array} \qquad \begin{array}{r} 38 \\ -10 \\ \hline \end{array} \qquad \begin{array}{r} 26 \\ -10 \\ \hline \end{array}$$

2.
$$\begin{array}{r} 33 \\ -20 \\ \hline \end{array} \qquad \begin{array}{r} 46 \\ -10 \\ \hline \end{array} \qquad \begin{array}{r} 23 \\ -20 \\ \hline \end{array} \qquad \begin{array}{r} 37 \\ -30 \\ \hline \end{array} \qquad \begin{array}{r} 48 \\ -20 \\ \hline \end{array}$$

Write the first number in the ladder.
Count back by tens. Write the
numbers. Write the answer. Use
blocks to help.

Count back by
tens. The ones
stay the same.

1.
42
− 10
‾‾‾‾
32

32
42

2.
56
− 20

56

3.
32
− 10

32

4.
54
− 30

5.
33
− 20

6.
47
− 30

MAKE AN ESTIMATE

7. How many times can
you hop on one foot?

Try it!

Was your estimate close?

Ring one.   yes   no

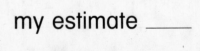

my estimate ____

I hopped ____ times.

Subtracting Tens and Ones

Work in a group. Use blocks.
Show the goal number.
Take away the number
done. Write how
many are left to do.

goal   **33**
done   **− 21**
to do   **12**

Score Box

1.

skip

goal   **36**
done   **− 23**

to do

2.

hop

goal   **28**
done   **− 12**

to do

3.

gallop

goal   **45**
done   **− 32**

to do

4.

side-step

goal   **35**
done   **− 21**

to do

Find the difference. Cross out
tens and ones to show it.

1.
$$\begin{array}{r} 47 \\ -24 \\ \hline 23 \end{array}$$
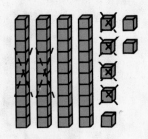

2.
$$\begin{array}{r} 35 \\ -21 \\ \hline \end{array}$$
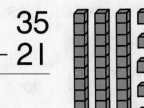

3.
$$\begin{array}{r} 37 \\ -16 \\ \hline \end{array}$$
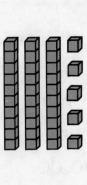

4.
$$\begin{array}{r} 23 \\ -13 \\ \hline \end{array}$$
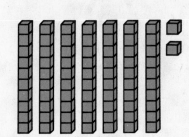

5.
$$\begin{array}{r} 54 \\ -33 \\ \hline \end{array}$$

6.
$$\begin{array}{r} 72 \\ -41 \\ \hline \end{array}$$

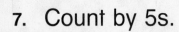

Mixed Review

7. Count by 5s.

   5, ____ , ____ , ____

8. Count by 2s.

   2, ____ , ____ , ____

9. Draw a line to make two
   matching parts.

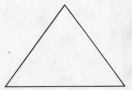

Problem Solving
Choosing a Calculation Method

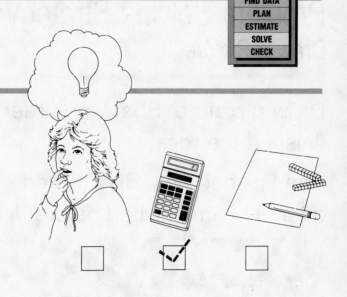

Solve the problem.
☑ the way you did it.

1. Megan hit 19 on the dart board 3 times in a row. How many points did she score?

   ____ points

   □ ☑ □

Try a ▢.

ON/C | 1 | 9 | + | 1 | 9 | + | 1 | 9 | =

2. Aaron scored 19 points. Then he scored 3 points. How many points did he score?

   ____ points

   □ □ □

3. Adam did 24 chin-ups. Then he did 35 more. How many chin-ups did he do?

   ____ chin-ups

   □ □ □

Problem Solving Strategy
Draw a Picture

UNDERSTAND
FIND DATA
PLAN
ESTIMATE
SOLVE
CHECK

Draw a picture. Show the order they finished the race.

Ann finished first. Bill finished after Jill. Tim finished before Jill.

More Practice, page 430, set B   Chapter 17

WRAP UP

MATH WORDS

Match. Then add or subtract.

1.	Count on by ones.	$29 - 2 =$ ___
2.	Count on by tens.	$87 - 50 =$ ___
3.	Count back by ones.	$35 + 3 =$ ___
4.	Count back by tens.	$46 + 20 =$ ___
5.	Make ten, add extra.	$25 + 7 =$ ___

MATH REASONING

Write the missing numbers.

6.
```
  5 6        8 □        □ 9
- 3 □      - 4 3      - 5 5
-----      -----      -----
  2 1        4 2        2 4
```

7.
```
  6 3        □ □        8 □
- □ 2      - 3 4      - 5 5
-----      -----      -----
  1 1        6 2        3 2
```

Name _____

CHAPTER REVIEW/TEST

1. Write the number as you count on. Write the sum.

    22, ____ , ____ , ____

    22 + 3 = ____

2. Write the number as you count back. Write the difference.

    38, ____ , ____

    38 − 2 = ____

3. Count on by tens. Then write how many in all.

    27
    + 20
    ———

    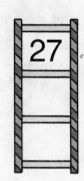

4. Count back by tens. Then write the difference.

    62
    − 30
    ———

    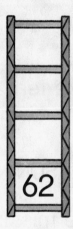

5. Draw tens and ones to show the sum. Add.

    12
    + 13
    ———

6. Cross out tens and ones to subtract.

    34
    − 21
    ———

    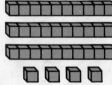

7. Josh found 9 balls. Nancy found 20 balls. How many balls did Josh and Nancy find?

    ____ balls

ENRICHMENT
Finding Another Solution

Sara sold 1 seashell on Monday.
She sold 2 seashells on Tuesday.
She sold 4 seashells on Wednesday.
She sold 8 seashells on Thursday.

How many seashells did she sell
on Friday? Fill in the table to find
the answer.

Day	Monday	Tuesday	Wednesday	Thursday	Friday
Shells Sold	1	2	4	8	

Sara sold _____ seashells on Friday.
Now do the problem another way.

| Draw a picture. | or | Use counters. |

Did you get the same answer?
Ring one.   yes   no

Name _____

CUMULATIVE REVIEW

Add.

1.
$$8$$
$$+8$$
○ 15
○ 16
○ 17

2.
$$9$$
$$7$$
$$+2$$
○ 18
○ 17
○ 19

3.
$$8$$
$$+6$$
○ 14
○ 15
○ 16

4. Find the double-plus-one fact.

○ $7 + 3 = 10$
○ $7 + 8 = 15$
○ $7 + 7 = 14$

Subtract.

5.
$$17$$
$$- 9$$
○ 9
○ 8
○ 7

6.
$$16$$
$$- 8$$
○ 7
○ 8
○ 9

7. Find the add-to-check fact for $12 - 5 = 7$.

○ $7 + 6 = 13$
○ $7 - 5 = 2$
○ $5 + 7 = 12$

8. Find the related subtraction fact.

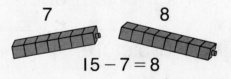

7   8

$15 - 7 = 8$

○ $15 - 15 = 0$
○ $8 - 7 = 1$
○ $15 - 8 = 7$

9. Choose the correct answer.
Glenn has 11 books.
He has read 6 of them.
How many does he have left to read?

○ 5 books
○ 17 books
○ 6 books

Name _____

Multiplying Equal Groups of Five

Cut out the flower cards.
Put them in the gardens below. Paste.
Count by fives. Write how many in all.

1.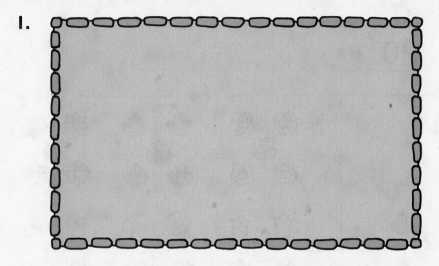

4 fives = _____

2.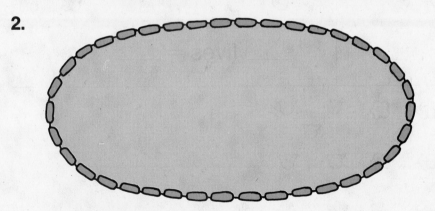

3 fives = _____

3.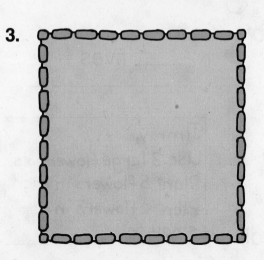

2 fives = _____

Count by fives. Write how many in all.

1.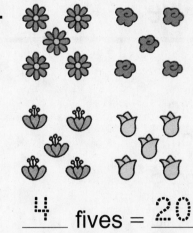

   _4_ fives = _20_

2.

   ____ fives = ____

3.

   ____ fives = ____

4.

   ____ fives = ____

5.

   ____ fives = ____

SHOW WITH COUNTERS

6. Use counters to solve. How many flowers did he plant?

   He planted ____ flowers in all.

   Jimmy,
   Use 3 large flower pots.
   Plant 5 flowers in each.
   Plant 2 flowers in a small pot.

Name _____

Problem Solving
Understanding the Operations

UNDERSTAND
FIND DATA
PLAN
ESTIMATE
SOLVE
CHECK

Color the apples to show the story.
Finish the subtraction sentence.
Answer the question.

1. 12 apples are in the bag. 7 are
    yellow. The others are red.
    How many apples are red?

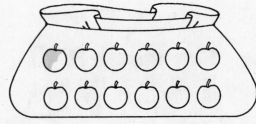

$12 - \boxed{7} = \boxed{5}$ ___5___ apples are red.

2. 10 apples are in the bag. 4 are
    yellow. The others are red.
    How many apples are red?

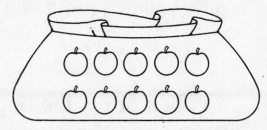

$10 - \boxed{} = \boxed{}$ _____ apples are red.

3. 12 apples are in the bag. 8 are
    red. The others are yellow.
    How many apples are yellow?

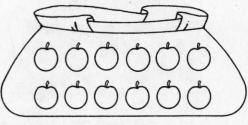

$12 - \boxed{} = \boxed{}$ _____ apples are yellow.

4. 14 apples are in the bag. 9 are
    yellow. The others are red.
    How many apples are red?

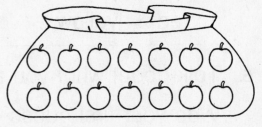

$14 - \boxed{} = \boxed{}$ _____ apples are red.

Chapter 18   More Practice, page 431, set B   (three hundred seventy-nine) 379

Probability

Work with a partner. Use 5 red and 5 yellow
cubes. Fill a bag with the numbers given.

1. 5 cubes are in the bag.
4 are red. 1 is yellow.

Are you more likely to pick a red
or a yellow cube? Ring one.

red   yellow

2. Try it. Shake the bag.
Pick a cube. Tally.
Put the cube back
in the bag. Do this
10 times.

Red	Yellow

3. 6 cubes are in the bag.
4 are yellow. 2 are red.

Are you more likely to pick a red
or a yellow cube? Ring one.

red   yellow

4. Try it. Shake the bag.
Pick a cube. Tally.
Put the cube back
in the bag. Do this
10 times.

Red	Yellow

5. Talk about what you picked out of the bag.

Was your first guess correct? Ring one.   yes   no

Was your second guess correct? Ring one.   yes   no

Understanding Division
Sharing

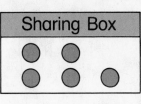

I more for you,
I more for you,
and I more for you.

Work with a partner. Use counters.
Share the number of seeds. Make an
equal group for each person. Write
how many are in each group.

Sharing Box

1.
6 bean
seeds

3 people

Each gets

__2__ seeds.

2.
9 carrot
seeds

3 people

Each gets

____ seeds.

3.
10 marigold
seeds

2 people

Each gets

____ seeds.

4.
12 pumpkin
seeds

3 people

Each gets

____ seeds.

5.
14 tomato
seeds

2 people

Each gets

____ seeds.

6.
12 lettuce
seeds

2 people

Each gets

____ seeds.

Sharing Box

Use counters. Share the number of seeds.
Make an equal group for each person.
Write how many are in each group.

1. 10 tomato seeds
2 people

Each gets __5__ seeds.

2. 18 radish seeds
3 people

Each gets ____ seeds.

3. 16 bean seeds
2 people

Each gets ____ seeds.

4. 12 corn seeds
4 people

Each gets ____ seeds.

5. 20 pumpkin seeds
4 people

Each gets ____ seeds.

6. 15 pepper seeds
3 people

Each gets ____ seeds.

PROBLEM SOLVING

Solve. Use punchout coins to help.

7. Fran has 20¢ in nickels. How many
nickels does she have? ____ nickels

8. Will has 25¢ in nickels. How many
nickels does he have? ____ nickels

Understanding Division
Separating

Work with a partner.
Use counters. Show the
amount of fruit in the
box. Make equal groups
for each bag. Write how
many bags are full.

3 in one bag
and 3 in
another bag.
2 bags are full.

Grouping Box

1.

6 oranges

3
in each
bag

___2___ bags are full.

2.

18 oranges

3
in each
bag

_____ bags are full.

3.

16 pears

2
in each
bag

_____ bags are full.

4.

20 apples

4
in each
bag

_____ bags are full.

Grouping Box

Use counters. Show the amount of fruit.
Make equal groups for each bag.
Write how many bags are full.

1.

    bags are full.

2.

   _____ bags are full.

3.

   _____ bags are full.

4.

   _____ bags are full.

MIDCHAPTER REVIEW/QUIZ

Tell how many in all.

1. **Count by twos.**

   3 twos = _____

2. **Count by fives.**

   2 fives = _____

Use counters. Show the number of seeds.
Make an equal group for each person.
Write how many are in each group.

3.

   3 people

   Each gets _____ **seeds.**

4.

   6 people

   Each gets _____ **seeds.**

Fractions
Halves

I out of 2 is yellow.

Cut out the garden shapes below.
Put the shape on the garden. Paste.
Write the fraction for one part.

1.

one half planted $\dfrac{1}{2}$

2.

one half planted $\dfrac{1}{2}$

3.

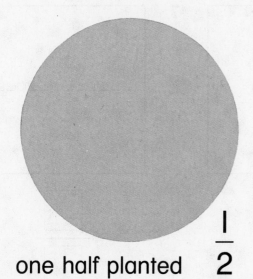

one half planted $\dfrac{1}{2}$

4.

one half planted $\dfrac{1}{2}$

Color one half of each shape.
Write the fraction.

I out of 2 is shaded.
That is $\frac{1}{2}$.

1.

$\frac{1}{2}$

2.

$\frac{}{}$

3.

$\frac{}{}$

4.

$\frac{}{}$

5.

$\frac{}{}$

6.

$\frac{}{}$

7.

$\frac{}{}$

More Practice, page 432, set A

Fractions
Thirds and Fourths

These gardens are divided into equal parts.

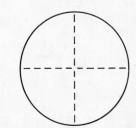

Use your fraction pieces. Show the part of the garden to be planted. Color a smaller circle to match.

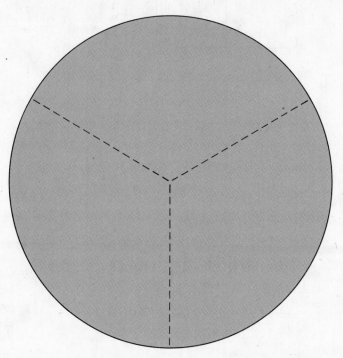

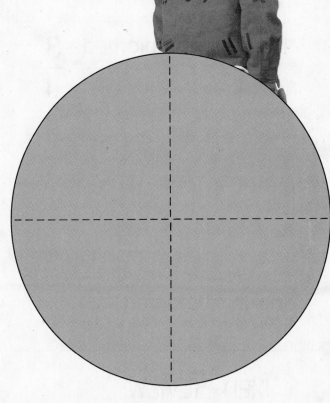

I. Plant I part.
3 parts in all.

one third
$\dfrac{1}{3}$ of the equal parts

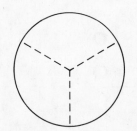

2. Plant 2 parts.
3 parts in all.

two thirds
$\dfrac{2}{3}$ of the equal parts

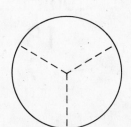

3. Plant I part.
4 parts in all.

one fourth
$\dfrac{1}{4}$ of the equal parts

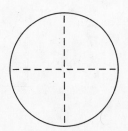

4. Plant 3 parts.
4 parts in all.

three fourths
$\dfrac{3}{4}$ of the equal parts

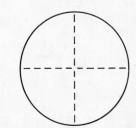

Color the garden.
Show how much has been planted.

1.
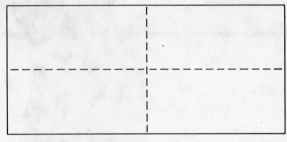

three fourths planted $\dfrac{3}{4}$

2.
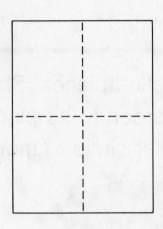

one fourth planted $\dfrac{1}{4}$

3.
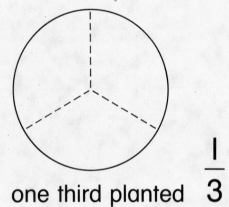

one third planted $\dfrac{1}{3}$

4.
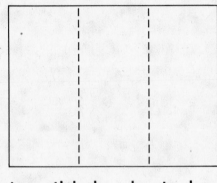

two thirds planted $\dfrac{2}{3}$

MIXED REVIEW

5. Count the money.

_____ ¢

6. Write the time.

_____

7. Add.

$$7 + 7$$ _____

$$9 + 6$$ _____

$$8 + 8$$ _____

8. Subtract.

$$18 - 9$$ _____

$$16 - 8$$ _____

$$14 - 9$$ _____

Name _____

Fractions
Using Sets

I of the 4
is red.
I fourth is red.

Work with a partner. Lay out
two-color counters to show the
tomatoes. Color to match.
Say the fraction.

1. I of 2 is red.

$\dfrac{1}{2}$ one half

2. I of 3 is yellow.

$\dfrac{}{}$ one third

3. I of 4 is red.

one fourth

$\dfrac{}{}$

4. 2 of 3 are red.

$\dfrac{}{}$ two thirds

5. 2 of 4 are red.

two fourths

$\dfrac{}{}$

6. 3 of 4 are yellow.

three fourths

$\dfrac{}{}$

Color to match.

1.

one half $\dfrac{1}{2}$
red

2.

two thirds $\dfrac{2}{3}$
green

3.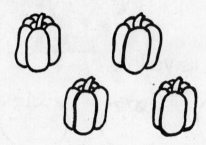

two fourths green $\dfrac{2}{4}$

4.

one fourth red $\dfrac{1}{4}$

5.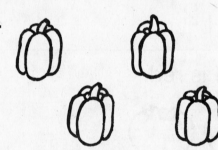

one third $\dfrac{1}{3}$
yellow

6.

three fourths red $\dfrac{3}{4}$

PROBLEM SOLVING

7. Solve. Color to show the story.

10 peppers are in the bag. 6 are
green. The others are red.
How many peppers are red?

$10 - \boxed{} = \boxed{}$

_____ peppers are red.

Name _____

Problem Solving
Finding Missing Data

 zinnia seeds 10¢
 bean seeds 5¢
 corn seeds 20¢
 sunflower seeds 30¢
 marigold seeds 15¢
 tomato seeds 25¢

Solve. Use the data from
the seed packets to help.

1. Alice bought 1 packet of snow peas for
   15¢ and 1 packet of sunflower seeds.
   How much did she spend?

   She spent _____.

   15¢
   +30¢
   45¢

2. Eric bought 1 packet of peppers for
   20¢ and 1 packet of zinnia seeds.
   How much did he spend?

   He spent _____.

3. Jon bought 1 packet of cabbage seeds
   for 10¢ and 1 packet of corn seeds.
   How much did he spend?

   He spent _____.

4. Kristina bought 1 packet of carrot seeds
   for 40¢ and 1 packet of bean seeds.
   How much did she spend?

   She spent _____.

UNDERSTAND
FIND DATA
PLAN
ESTIMATE
SOLVE
CHECK

Problem Solving Strategy
Use Logical Reasoning

Read the clues. Write each name.

Bruce laughed at Sue's .

Sara is wearing a .

Dick is wearing a .

Joan gave Eric a .

Name _____

WRAP UP

MATH WORDS

1.

   How many groups of two are there? _____

   How many groups of five are there? _____

   How many are there in all? _____

2.

   Share the berries so each bird
   gets the same number. Use
   counters to help.   Each gets _____ berries.

3. Color
   one half.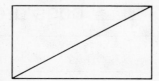

4. Color
   one fourth.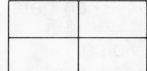

MATH REASONING

5. Tammy has 10 marbles. Hans
   has 5 marbles. Jane has
   6 marbles. To play a game,
   each needs the same number
   of marbles. Share the marbles
   so each has the same number.
   Use counters to help.

   Each gets _____ marbles.

Name _____

CHAPTER REVIEW/TEST

Tell how many in all.

1. Count by twos.

4 twos = _____

2. Count by fives.

2 fives = _____

3. Make an equal group for each person. Write how many in each group.

 5 people

Each gets _____ apples.

4. Make an equal group for each bag. Write how many bags are full.

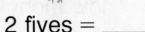 3 in each bag

_____ bags are full.

Match.

5.

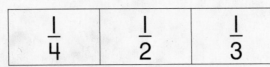

| $\frac{1}{4}$ | $\frac{1}{2}$ | $\frac{1}{3}$ |

6.

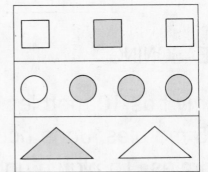

$\frac{3}{4}$

$\frac{1}{2}$

$\frac{1}{3}$

7. Zoe bought 1 packet of corn seeds for 15¢ and 1 packet of lettuce seeds. How much did she spend?

_____
+ _____
_____

She spent _____.

Name _____

ENRICHMENT
Relating Multiplication and Division

Work in a group. Use cubes to show each train below. Fill in the blanks to match. Then snap off each group of cubes. Fill in the blanks to match.

1.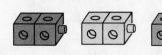

_____ twos = _____

_____ shown in _____ groups of _____

_____

2.

_____ twos = _____

_____ shown in _____ groups of _____

_____

3.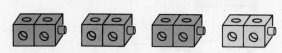

_____ fives = _____

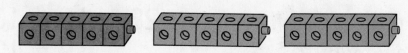

_____ shown in _____ groups of _____

CUMULATIVE REVIEW

1. Subtract.

$$\begin{array}{r} 18 \\ -9 \\ \hline \end{array}$$

- ○ 9
- ○ 8
- ○ 7

2. Find the add-to-check fact.

$$\begin{array}{r} 17 \\ -8 \\ \hline 9 \end{array}$$

- ○ $7 + 8 = 15$
- ○ $9 + 8 = 17$
- ○ $9 + 7 = 16$

3. Which belongs in the same fact family?

$7 + 7 = 14$

- ○ $14 - 8 = 6$
- ○ $14 - 7 = 7$
- ○ $7 - 7 = 0$

4. Subtract.

$14 - 9 = \underline{}$

- ○ 5
- ○ 7
- ○ 6

Add.

5.

$$\begin{array}{r} 43 \\ +30 \\ \hline \end{array}$$

- ○ 83
- ○ 63
- ○ 73

6.

$$\begin{array}{r} 15 \\ +22 \\ \hline \end{array}$$

- ○ 27
- ○ 37
- ○ 39

7. Count back by tens. Choose the answer.

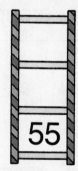

55

- ○ 75
- ○ 53
- ○ 35

$55 - 20 = \underline{}$

8. Subtract.

$$\begin{array}{r} 67 \\ -34 \\ \hline \end{array}$$

- ○ 42
- ○ 33
- ○ 34

9. Choose the correct number sentence.

There were 28 🍓 in the basket. Conchita ate 15. How many 🍓 are left?

- ○ $28 - 15 = 13$
- ○ $27 - 14 = 13$
- ○ $28 + 15 = 43$

Resource Bank and Glossary

Data Bank   398

Calculator Bank   401

Computer Bank   405

More Practice Bank   409

Glossary   433

Contents   397

Data Bank

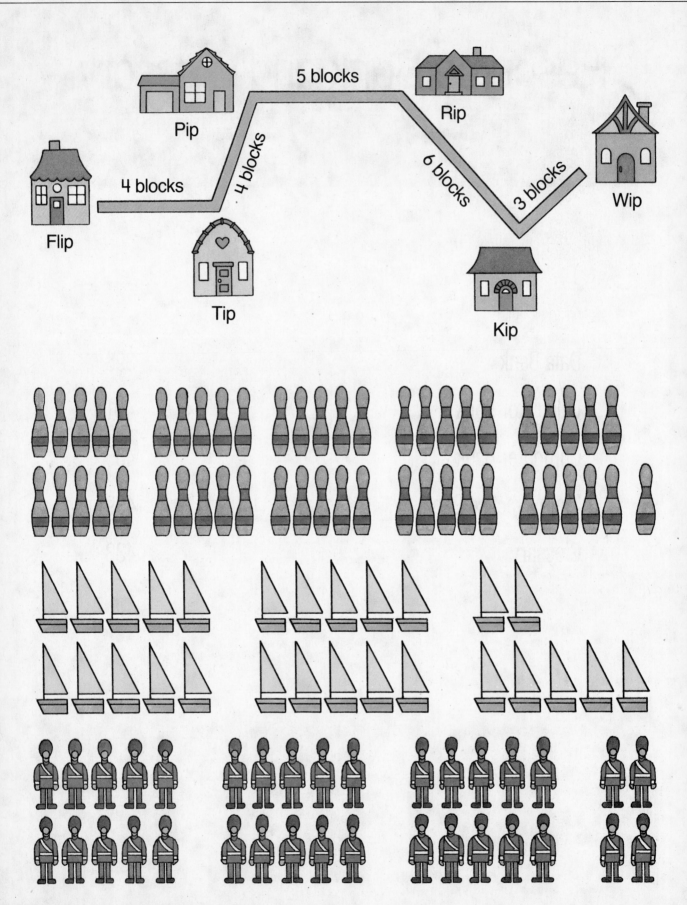

5 blocks

Pip

Rip

4 blocks

4 blocks

6 blocks

3 blocks

Wip

Flip

Tip

Kip

Data Bank

44¢

36¢

42¢

March, Year 2000

Sunday	Monday	Tuesday	Wednesday	Thursday	Friday	Saturday
			1	2	3	4
5	6	7	8	9	10	11
12	13	14	15	16	17	18
19	20	21	22	23	24	25
26	27	28	29	30	31	

Data Bank

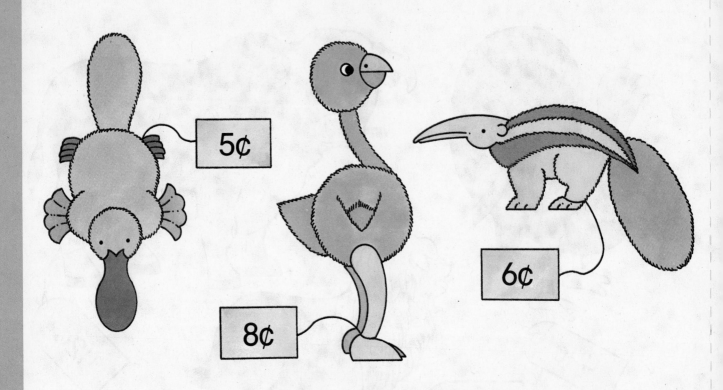

5¢

8¢

6¢

Dinosaur Lengths

40 feet

20 feet

30 feet

Name _____

Getting Ready to Calculate

1. Press the keys shown. Write what you see.

Press	See
ON/C	
1	
ON/C	
12	
ON/C	
1234	
5	
6	
ON/C	

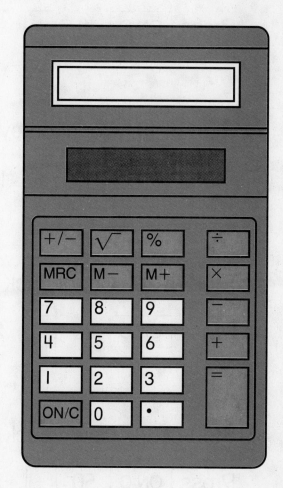

ACTIVITY

2. Press ON/C .

Press 1 2 3 4 5 6 7 8 9.

Ring the last digit you see.

Name _____

Counting On and Back

1. Start at 0. Count on by 1s. Write what you see.

Press [ON/C] 0 [+] 1 [=] [=] [=] [=] [=] [=]

⋮
_____ , _____ , _____ , _____ , _____ , _____

2. Start at 10. Count on by 10s. Write what you see.

Press [ON/C] 10 [+] 10 [=] [=] [=] [=] [=] [=]

_____ , _____ , _____ , _____ , _____ , _____

3. Start at 20. Count back by 2s. Write what you see.

Press [ON/C] 20 [−] 2 [=] [=] [=] [=] [=] [=]

_____ , _____ , _____ , _____ , _____ , _____

4. Start at 50. Count back by 5s. Write what you see.

Press [ON/C] 50 [−] 5 [=] [=] [=] [=] [=] [=]

_____ , _____ , _____ , _____ , _____ , _____

ACTIVITY

5. Ring the numbers that do not belong.
Start at 12. Count by 4s.

8   12   16   20   22   28   32   36   41   44

Name _____

Adding Whole Numbers

Say each addition sentence as you
press the keys. Write the sum.

1. Say   "Five   plus   three   equals."

   Press | ON/C | 5 | + | 3 | = | [   ]

2. Say   "Ten   plus   four   equals."

   Press | ON/C | 10 | + | 4 | = | [   ]

3. Say   "Twenty   plus   seventy   equals."

   Press | ON/C | 20 | + | 70 | = | [   ]

4. Say   "Six   plus   four   plus   five   equals."

   Press | ON/C | 6 | + | 4 | + | 5 | = | [   ]

ACTIVITY

| 9 | 5 | 8 |

5. Work with a partner.

   Use two and one set

   of punchout number cards.
   Mix the cards. Each player
   takes three cards. Find the sum.
   The player with the greater sum
   wins. The first player to win six
   games is the champion.

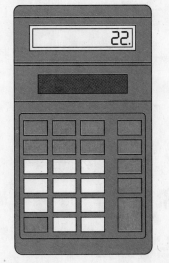

Name _____

Subtracting Whole Numbers

Say each subtraction sentence as you
press the keys. Write the difference.

1. Say   "Nine minus four equals."

    Press | ON/C | 9 | – | 4 | = |

2. Say   "Fifteen minus eight equals."

    Press | ON/C | 15 | – | 8 | = |

3. Say   "Twenty minus six equals."

    Press | ON/C | 20 | – | 6 | = |

ACTIVITY

Write each difference.
Connect the answers in order.

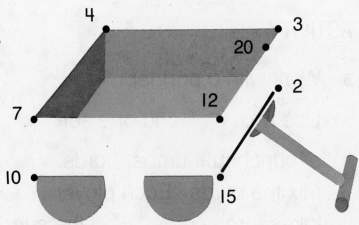

4. $9 - 7 =$ ___

5. $6 - 3 =$ ___

6. $11 - 7 =$ ___

7. $10 - 3 =$ ___

8. $18 - 8 =$ ___

9. $30 - 15 =$ ___

10. $24 - 12 =$ ___

11. $32 - 12 =$ ___

Name _____

Turtle Marathon

Write the number of corner turns each
turtle needs to make to finish the race.

Turtle 3 _____   Turtle 2 _____   Turtle 6 _____   Turtle 5 _____

Turtle 7 _____   Turtle 1 _____   Turtle 4 _____

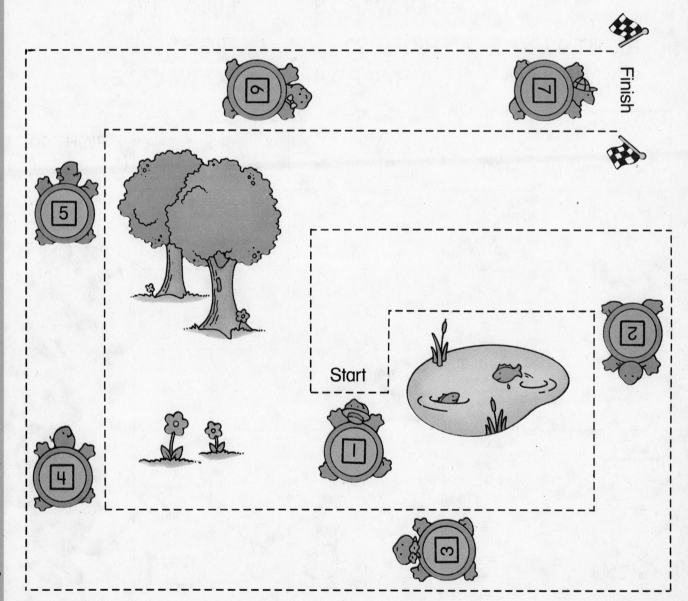

Name _____

Turtle Village

Cut out the turtle. Start in the HOME box. Follow the directions. Color each picture where the turtle stops.

1. FORWARD 3

2. RIGHT 90
   FORWARD 3

3. RIGHT 90
   FORWARD 5

4. RIGHT 90
   FORWARD 6

5. RIGHT 90
   FORWARD 4

6. RIGHT 90
   FORWARD 5

Name _____

My Square

A square has 4 equal sides. □

Draw your own square.

1. Draw a △ at any dot to start.
2. Connect some dots to make a straight line.
3. Count the spaces between the dots.
4. Draw the other three sides.

Write your directions on another sheet of paper.

Name _____

Turtle Goes Fishing

The turtle is fishing. Follow the directions.
Connect the dots to help the turtle catch
the fish. Cut out the turtle above to help.

1. BACK 2   5. BACK 3
2. LEFT 90   6. RIGHT 90
3. BACK 4   7. FORWARD 1
4. RIGHT 90

More Practice Bank

Name _____

Set A   For use after page 2.

Ring the bird that does not belong.

1.

2.

Set B   For use after page 4.

Color to continue the pattern.

1.

2.

Set C   For use after page 12.

Write numbers to show the pattern.

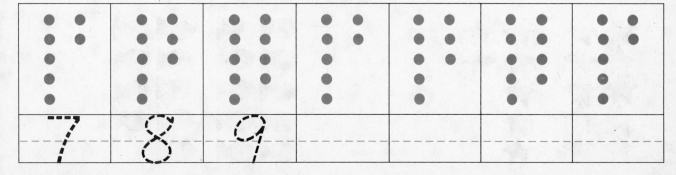

7   8   9

More Practice Bank   (four hundred nine)   409

Name _____

Set A   For use after page 18.

1. Count on. Write the missing numbers.

2. Count back. Write the missing numbers.

Set B   For use after page 20.

Barry had his toy cars lined up on
his shelf as shown. Continue his pattern.
Ring the car that comes next.

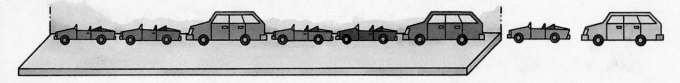

Set C   For use after page 30.

Write the number in all.

1.

2.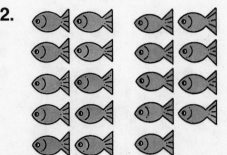

More Practice Bank

Name _____

Set A   For use after page 32.

Ring enough coins to pay.

1.

2.

Set B   For use after page 38.

1. Count. Write how many.

   Alex ЖII _____   Marty ЖI _____   Silvia III _____

2. Color the graph to show the tallies.

Number of Shells Found

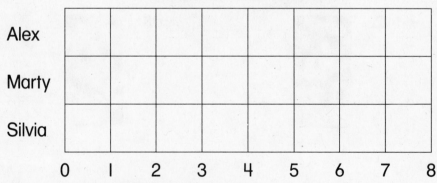

3. How many more shells did
   Alex find than Silvia?   _____ more

4. How many fewer shells did
   Marty find than Alex?   _____ fewer

More Practice Bank

Name _____

Set A   For use after page 50.

Write the sum.

1.

$3 + 2 =$ ___

2.

$2 + 4 =$ ___

3.

$3 + 3 =$ ___

4.

$5 + 1 =$ ___

Set B   For use after page 60.

Write what you see. Add.

1.  ____
   ___+___

2.  ____
   ___+___

3. 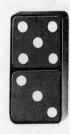 ____
   ___+___

Set C   For use after page 62.

Add.

1. $3¢ + 4¢ =$ ___ ¢
   in all

$2¢ + 5¢ =$ ___ ¢
   in all

$2¢ + 2¢ =$ ___ ¢
   in all

More Practice Bank

Name _____

Set A   For use after page 72.

Subtract.

1.

   $3 - 1 = \underline{}$

2.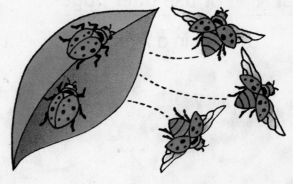

   $5 - 3 = \underline{}$

Set B   For use after page 76.

Subtract.

1. $\begin{array}{r} 3 \\ -\ 2 \\ \hline \end{array}$

2. $\begin{array}{r} 6 \\ -\ 3 \\ \hline \end{array}$

Set C   For use after page 82.

Subtract.

1.

   $6 - 2 = \underline{}$

   and

   $6 - 4 = \underline{}$

2.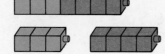

   $7 - 3 = \underline{}$

   and

   $7 - 4 = \underline{}$

3.

   $8 - 2 = \underline{}$

   and

   $8 - 6 = \underline{}$

Name _____

Set A For use after page 85.

4 owls sit in a tree.   2 fly away.

Ring the question you would ask.

How many owls are there in all?

How many owls are left?

Finish the
number sentence.

____ ◯ ____ = ____

Set B For use after page 92.

Add zero or count on.

$$
\begin{array}{cccccc}
5 & 0 & 2 & 8 & 1 & 9 \\
+1 & +7 & +6 & +2 & +8 & +0
\end{array}
$$

Set C For use after page 96.

Add.

$$
\begin{array}{cccccc}
2¢ & 9¢ & 7¢ & 0¢ & 3¢ & 8¢ \\
+6¢ & +3¢ & +3¢ & +8¢ & +4¢ & +1¢
\end{array}
$$

More Practice Bank

Name _____

Set A   For use after page 114.

Add. Ring sums of 10.

$$\begin{array}{r} 4 \\ +6 \\ \hline \end{array} \qquad \begin{array}{r} 8 \\ +2 \\ \hline \end{array} \qquad \begin{array}{r} 4 \\ +4 \\ \hline \end{array} \qquad \begin{array}{r} 1 \\ +9 \\ \hline \end{array} \qquad \begin{array}{r} 5 \\ +5 \\ \hline \end{array} \qquad \begin{array}{r} 6 \\ +6 \\ \hline \end{array}$$

Set B   For use after page 124.

Add.

1.
$$\begin{array}{r} 8 \\ +4 \\ \hline \end{array} \qquad \begin{array}{r} 4 \\ +5 \\ \hline \end{array} \qquad \begin{array}{r} 5 \\ +7 \\ \hline \end{array} \qquad \begin{array}{r} 0 \\ +9 \\ \hline \end{array} \qquad \begin{array}{r} 7 \\ +4 \\ \hline \end{array} \qquad \begin{array}{r} 5 \\ +6 \\ \hline \end{array}$$

2.
$$\begin{array}{r} 7 \\ +5 \\ \hline \end{array} \qquad \begin{array}{r} 6 \\ +6 \\ \hline \end{array} \qquad \begin{array}{r} 5 \\ +2 \\ \hline \end{array} \qquad \begin{array}{r} 4 \\ +8 \\ \hline \end{array} \qquad \begin{array}{r} 6 \\ +0 \\ \hline \end{array} \qquad \begin{array}{r} 5 \\ +4 \\ \hline \end{array}$$

Set C   For use after page 126.

Add.

$$\begin{array}{r} 3 \\ 4 \\ +2 \\ \hline \end{array} \qquad \begin{array}{r} 6 \\ 3 \\ +2 \\ \hline \end{array} \qquad \begin{array}{r} 2 \\ 0 \\ +5 \\ \hline \end{array} \qquad \begin{array}{r} 5 \\ 2 \\ +2 \\ \hline \end{array} \qquad \begin{array}{r} 1 \\ 4 \\ +3 \\ \hline \end{array} \qquad \begin{array}{r} 5 \\ 3 \\ +3 \\ \hline \end{array}$$

Name _____

Set A   For use after page 128.

Use the table to answer the question.

How much do 3 🐌 cost?

snails 4¢ each

snails	1 🐌	2 🐌	3 🐌
cost	4¢	8¢	____¢

3 snails cost ____¢.

Set B   For use after page 134.

Estimate how many units long.

Use 📎 to measure.

1.

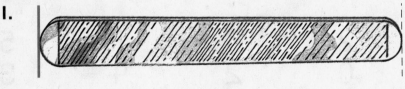

estimate ____ units

measure ____ units

2.

estimate ____ units

measure ____ units

More Practice Bank

Name _____

Set A   For use after page 138.

Use your ruler. Measure.
Write the length or height.

1.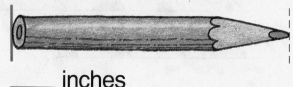

_____ inches

2.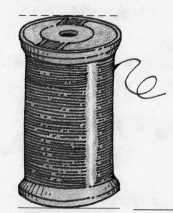

_____ inches

3.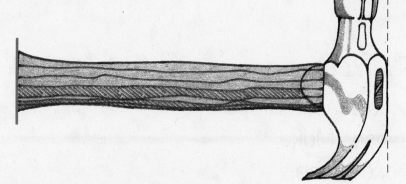

_____ inches

Set B   For use after page 140.

Use your foot ruler. Measure.
Ring the best answer.

1. your chair height

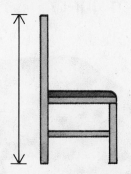

longer than 2 |1 2 3 4 5 6 7 8 9 10 11 12|

2 |1 2 3 4 5 6 7 8 9 10 11 12|

shorter than 2 |1 2 3 4 5 6 7 8 9 10 11 12|

2. your chair width

longer than 2 |1 2 3 4 5 6 7 8 9 10 11 12|

2 |1 2 3 4 5 6 7 8 9 10 11 12|

shorter than 2 |1 2 3 4 5 6 7 8 9 10 11 12|

Name _____

Set A   For use after page 142.

Ring 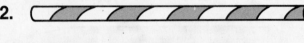 the longer one.
Ring 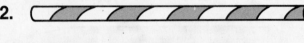 the shorter one.

1.

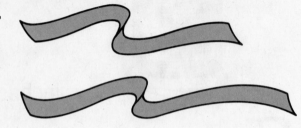

2.

Set B   For use after page 151.

Ring the answer if it makes sense. Cross out if it does not make sense. Make an estimate that does make sense.

1.

The baby snake is
10 centimeters long.

How long is the
snake's mother?

<u>12</u> centimeters

____ centimeters

2.

The puppy weighs
6 pounds.

How much does the
puppy's mother weigh?

<u>24</u> pounds

____ pounds

More Practice Bank

Name _____

Set A   For use after page 162.

Subtract.

1.

7	9	8	10	11	5
− 1	− 2	− 1	− 2	− 2	− 2

2.

6	11	9	10	7	8
− 1	− 2	− 3	− 3	− 2	− 2

Set B   For use after page 170.

Subtract.

8	9	10	5	7	6
− 4	− 9	− 5	− 0	− 3	− 3

Set C   For use after page 186.

Write how many.

1.

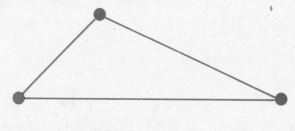

_____ sides

_____ corners

2.

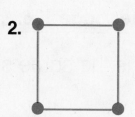

_____ sides

_____ corners

Name _____

Set A For use after page 192.

Write how many pegs inside, outside, and on.

1.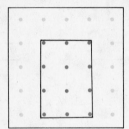

_____ inside

_____ outside

_____ on

2.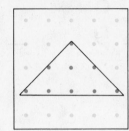

_____ inside

_____ outside

_____ on

Set B For use after page 194.

Draw a line to make
two matching parts.

1.

2.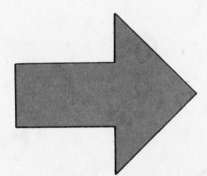

3.

Set C For use after page 196.

Ring the one that is the same size and shape.

More Practice Bank

Name _____

Set A   For use after page 197.

Use your inch ruler.
Write how many inches.

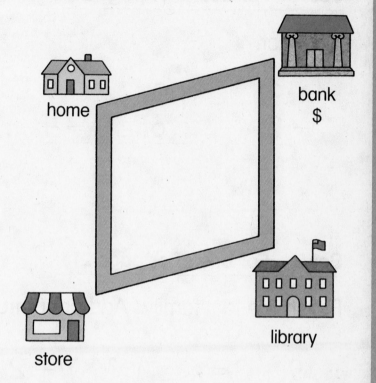

home   bank $

store   library

1. How far is it from
   home to the library?

   _____ inches

2. How far is it from
   home to the store
   by way of the bank?

   _____ inches

Set B   For use after page 198.

Color the one that comes next.

1.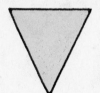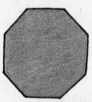

2.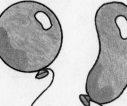

Name _____

Set A   **For use after page 204.**

Subtract.

9	10	9	10	9	10
− 5	− 6	− 4	− 8	− 6	− 7

Set B   **For use after page 216.**

Finish the fact family. Add or subtract.

1. $9 + 3 = $ ___   2. $7 + 2 = $ ___   3. $6 + 4 = $ ___

   $3 + 9 = $ ___ $2 + 7 = $ ___ $4 + 6 = $ ___

   $12 - 3 = $ ___ $9 - 2 = $ ___ $10 - 4 = $ ___

   $12 - 9 = $ ___ $9 - 7 = $ ___ $10 - 6 = $ ___

Set C   **For use after page 218.**

Subtract.

11	11	12	10	6	8
− 8	− 5	− 9	− 8	− 4	− 6

Name _____

Set A   For use after page 226.

Ring groups of ten. Write how many tens and ones.

1.

Tens	Ones

2.

Tens	Ones

Set B   For use after page 240.

Show how much money. Color enough dimes. Color enough pennies.

1.

2.

Name _____

Set A For use after page 248.

Count. Write how many.

1.

   37

   ____ , ____ , ____ , ____ ,

2.

   23

   ____ , ____ , ____ , ____ ,

Set B For use after page 260.

Start at the top of the ladder.
Write as you count ten more.

1.
   67

2.
   39

3.
   22

4.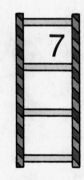
   7

Set C For use after page 264.

Count and color the frogs.

 second    fifth

More Practice Bank

Name _____

Set A   For use after page 272.

Use coin punchouts. Cover each
coin as you count. Write the amount.

1.

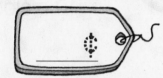

2.

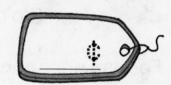

Set B   For use after page 276.

Count the money. Write the amount.

      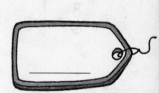

_____ , _____ , _____ , _____ , _____ ,

Set C   For use after page 284.

Count the money. Write the amount.

1.

_____ , _____ , _____ , _____ , _____

2.

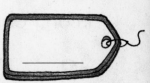

_____ , _____ , _____ , _____ , _____

Name _____

Set A   For use after page 294.

Show the time on each clock.

1.

   8 o'clock

2.

   10 o'clock

Set B   For use after page 298.

Write the times.

1.    ____:____

2.    ____:____

3.    ____:____

Set C   For use after page 302.

Ring the answer.

1. Valentine's Day is

   on a _____.

   Tuesday   Friday

2. Washington's Birthday

   is on February _____.

   12   15   22   29

FEBRUARY						
Sun.	Mon.	Tues.	Wed.	Thurs.	Fri.	Sat.
			1	2	3	4
5	6	7	8	9	10	11
12	13	♡14	15	16	17	18
19	20	21	22	23	24	25
26	27	28				

More Practice Bank

Name _____

Set A   For use after page 310.

Add.

8	9	9	4	7	9
+9	+6	+9	+9	+9	+5

Set B   For use after page 316.

Add.

5	9	2	4	9	4
3	4	8	6	9	0
+5	+5	+7	+5	+2	+4

Set C   For use after page 325.

Ring the number if it is correct.
Cross out if it is wrong. Write the
correct number sentence.

7 koalas are playing.
3 koalas are eating.
How many more koalas
are playing?

__10__ more koalas are playing.

____ ◯ ____ = ____

Name _____

Set A   For use after page 332.

Ring the subtraction doubles.
Then subtract all.

1. $10 - 5 =$ _____ $9 - 6 =$ _____ $16 - 8 =$ _____

2. $8 - 4 =$ _____ $18 - 9 =$ _____ $10 - 4 =$ _____

Set B   For use after page 340.

Subtract. Use the
add-to-check fact to help.

1. $\begin{array}{r} 5 \\ + 7 \\ \hline \end{array}$ $\begin{array}{r} 12 \\ - 5 \\ \hline \end{array}$ 2. $\begin{array}{r} 7 \\ + 6 \\ \hline \end{array}$ $\begin{array}{r} 13 \\ - 6 \\ \hline \end{array}$ 3. $\begin{array}{r} 4 \\ + 7 \\ \hline \end{array}$ $\begin{array}{r} 11 \\ - 4 \\ \hline \end{array}$

Set C   For use after page 347.

Write the number sentence for
the story. Write the answer.
Ring to finish the story.

7 dinosaurs are eating.
2 dinosaurs are sleeping.
How many more are eating?

____ ◯ ____ = ____

____ more are eating.

____ dinosaurs in all.

Name _____

Set A   For use after page 356.

Draw lines to make a ten.
Write how many in all.

1. 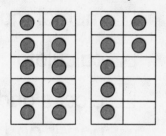 $\begin{array}{r} 17 \\ + 5 \\ \hline \end{array}$

2. 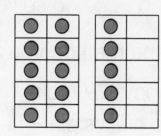 $\begin{array}{r} 15 \\ + 6 \\ \hline \end{array}$

Set B   For use after page 360.

Count on by tens.
Write how many in all.

1. $\begin{array}{r} 15 \\ + 20 \\ \hline \end{array}$ 15

2. $\begin{array}{r} 28 \\ + 30 \\ \hline \end{array}$ 28

3. $\begin{array}{r} 32 \\ + 10 \\ \hline \end{array}$ 32

Set C   For use after page 368.

Find the difference. Cross out
tens and ones to show it.

1. $\begin{array}{r} 36 \\ - 14 \\ \hline \end{array}$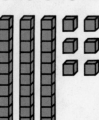

2. $\begin{array}{r} 48 \\ - 25 \\ \hline \end{array}$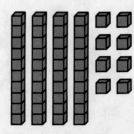

Name _____

Set A   For use after page 369.

Use mental math, blocks and paper and pencil, or a to solve the problem. ✔ the method you used.

Ian brought home 29 rocks. He gave 14 to his sister. How many rocks does he have left?

_____ left

I used

☐ mental math

☐ calculator

☐ blocks and paper and pencil

Set B   For use after page 370.

Draw a picture. Show the order they finished the race.

Tommy finished first. Tina finished before Elena. Rocky finished after Elena.

Elena   Rocky   Tommy   Tina

Name _____

Set A   For use after page 378.

Write how many in all.

1. _____ fives = _____

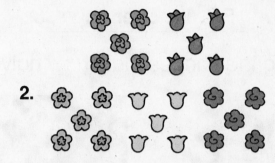

2. _____ fives = _____

Set B   For use after page 379.

Finish the subtraction sentence.

1. 13 apples are in the bag. 8 are red. The others are yellow. How many are yellow?

   13 – ☐ = ☐

   _____ apples are yellow.

2. 11 apples are in the bag. 6 are yellow. The others are red. How many are red?

   11 – ☐ = ☐

   _____ apples are red.

Set C   For use after page 382.

Share the fruit. Make an equal group for each person. Write how many are in each group.

1.

   10 apples   5 people

   Each gets _____ apples.

2.

   25 berries   5 people

   Each gets _____ berries.

More Practice Bank

Name _____

Set A   For use after page 386.

Ring the shapes that show halves.

 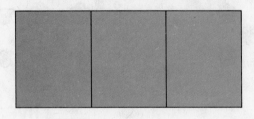 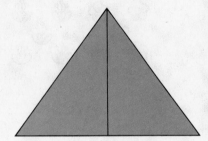

Set B   For use after page 388.

Ring the shapes that show fourths.

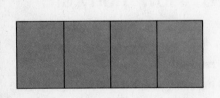 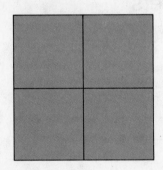 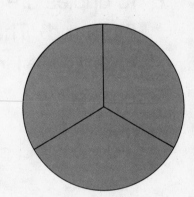

Set C   For use after page 390.

Ring the sets that show $\frac{1}{3}$ red.

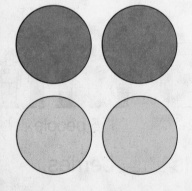 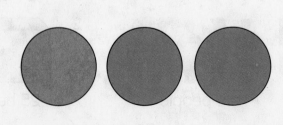 

Glossary

Add

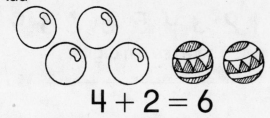

$$4 + 2 = 6$$

Addition sentence

$$3 + 6 = 9$$

After

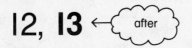

12, **13** ← after

Area

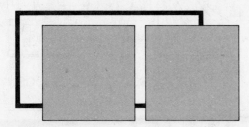

The **area** of this shape is 2 tiles.

Bar graph

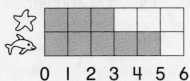

Sea Animals We Like

0 1 2 3 4 5 6

Before

before → **12,** 13

Between

9, **10,** 11 between

Box

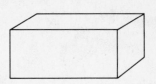

Calculator

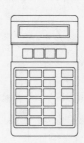

Calendar

MAY

Sun.	Mon.	Tue.	Wed.	Thu.	Fri.	Sat.
	1	2	3	4	5	6
7	8	9	10	11	12	13
14	15	16	17	18	19	20
21	22	23	24	25	26	27
28	29	30	31			

Capacity

The **capacity** of this glass is 1 cup.

Centimeter

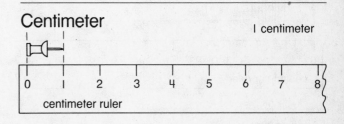

1 centimeter

centimeter ruler

0 1 2 3 4 5 6 7 8

Glossary

Circle

Cone

Congruent figures

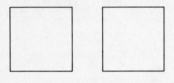

Corner

corner

Cube

Cylinder

Decimeter

I decimeter

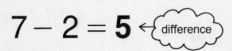

centimeter ruler

Difference

$$7 - 2 = 5$$

difference

Digit

0 1 2 3 4 5 6 7 8 9

There are ten **digits.**

Dime

10¢ or 10 cents

Divide

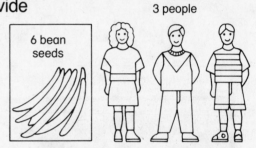

6 bean seeds

3 people

Each person gets 2 seeds.

Dollar bill

$1.00 or 100¢ or 100 cents

Dozen

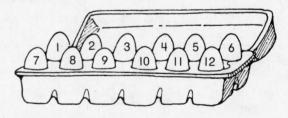

Even

2   4   6   8

Even numbers make pairs.

Glossary

Fact family

$$2 + 4 = 6 \qquad 6 - 4 = 2$$
$$4 + 2 = 6 \qquad 6 - 2 = 4$$

Fewer

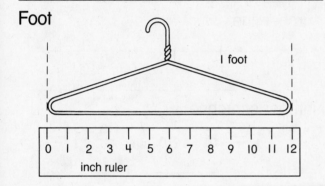

fewer

Foot

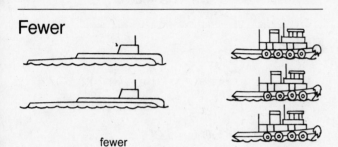

1 foot

inch ruler

Fractions

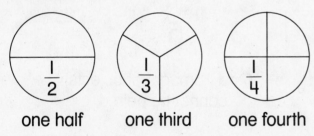

$\dfrac{1}{2}$ one half

$\dfrac{1}{3}$ one third

$\dfrac{1}{4}$ one fourth

Geoboard

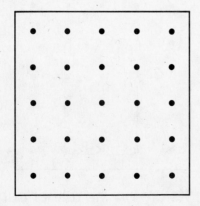

Greater than

17   13

Half hour

2:00 to 2:30

Hour

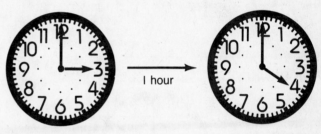

3 o'clock   1 hour   4 o'clock

Hour hand

The **hour hand** is pointing to the 9.

Inch

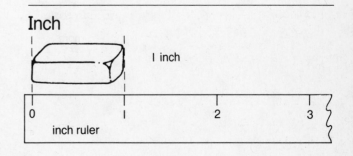

1 inch

inch ruler

Glossary

Inside

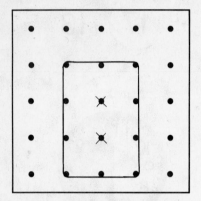

The Xs are **inside**.

Less than

Minute hand

The **minute hand** is pointing to the 12.

More

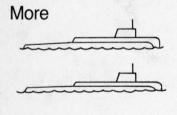

more

Multiply

3 twos = 6

Nickel

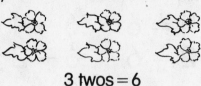

5¢ or 5 cents

Number line

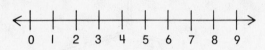

Number sentence

$5 + 3 = 8$ or $7 - 4 = 3$

Odd

1   3   5   7

Odd numbers of objects cannot be paired.

On

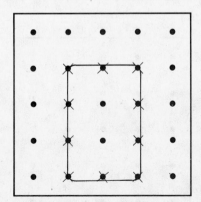

The Xs are **on** the rubber band.

Glossary

Ordinal numbers

first   second   third

Outside

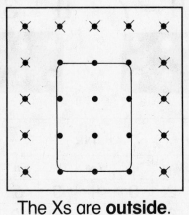

The Xs are **outside**.

Oval

Pattern

Penny

1¢ or 1 cent

Pictograph

Boats

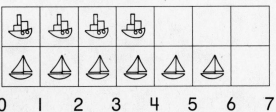

0 1 2 3 4 5 6 7

Quarter

25¢ or 25 cents

Rectangle

Ruler

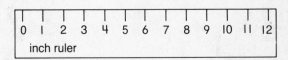

inch ruler

Side

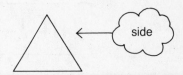

side

Sphere

Square

Subtract

$$4 - 1 = 3$$

Subtraction sentence

$$7 - 5 = 2$$

Glossary

Sum

$$1 + 3 = 4 \leftarrow \text{sum}$$

Survey

Do you like cats or dogs better?

Tally

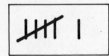

Temperature

°F

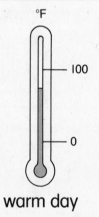

— 100

— 0

warm day

Ten-frame

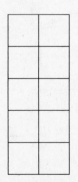

Triangle

Turnaround fact

$$3 + 4 = 7 \qquad 4 + 3 = 7$$

Week

JUNE

Sun.	Mon.	Tue.	Wed.	Thu.	Fri.	Sat.
1	2	3	4	5	6	7
8	9	10	11	12	13	14

1 **week** is 7 days.

Weight

0	1	2
3	4	5
6	7	8
9	10	11
12	13	14

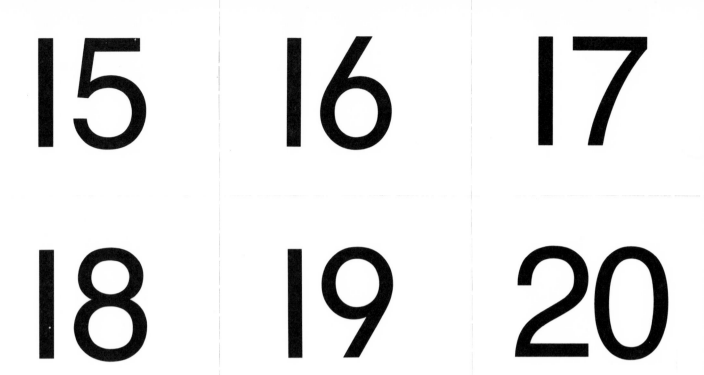

| 15 | 16 | 17 |
| 18 | 19 | 20 |

+

−

=

Signs

10-Frame

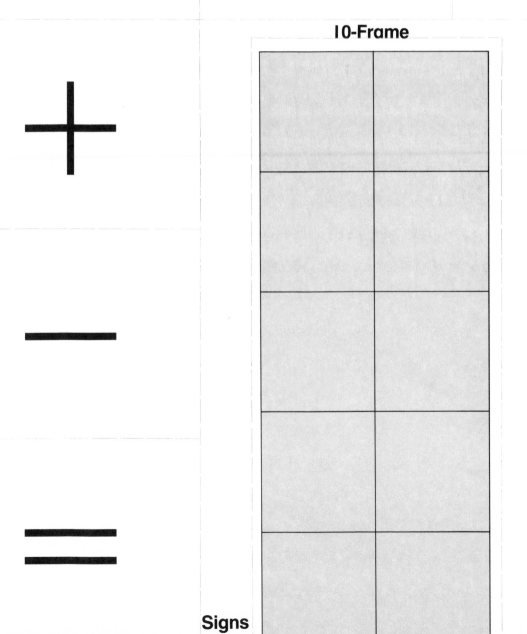

Use with page 1.

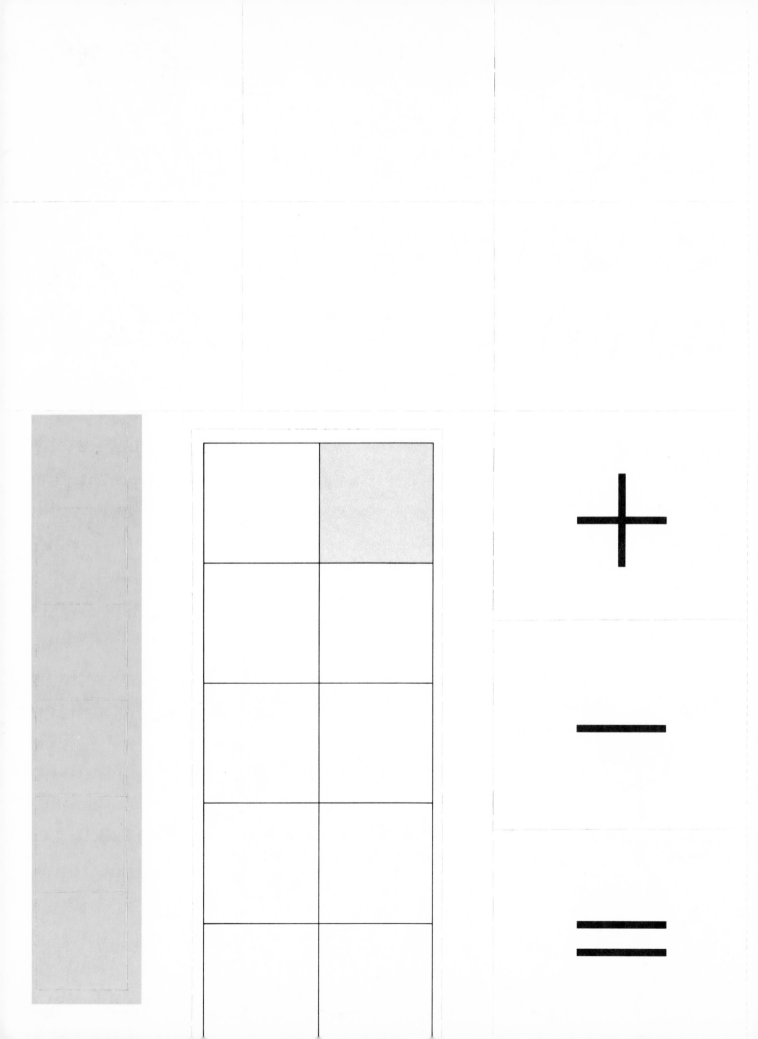

Coins

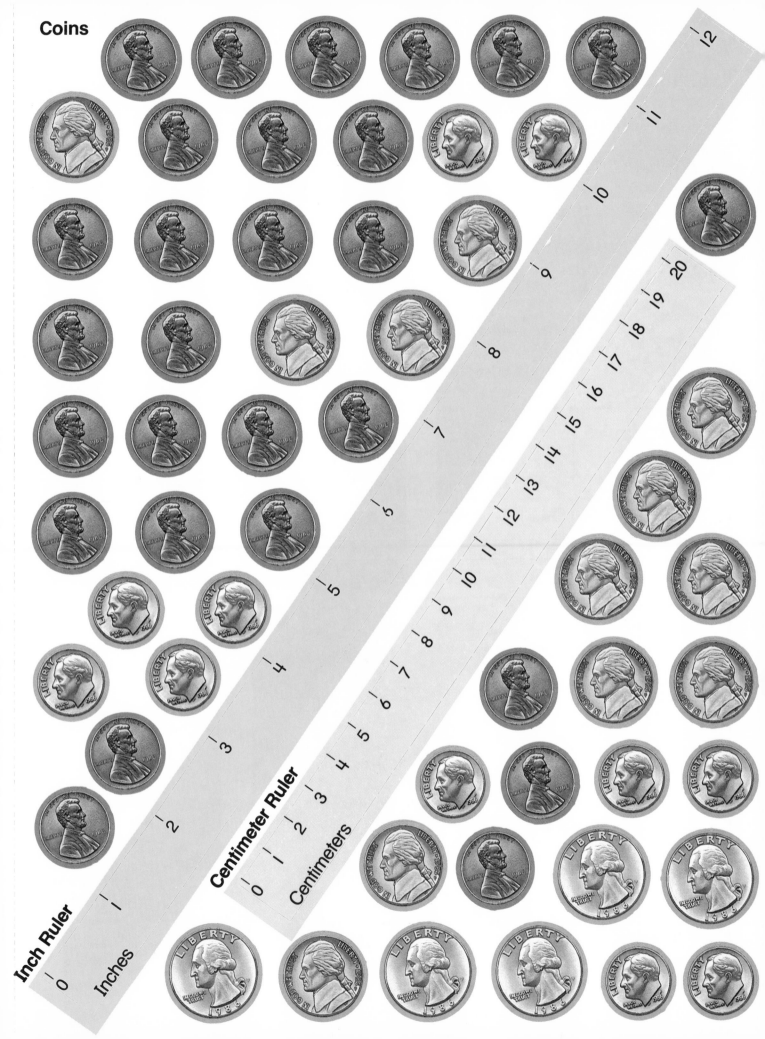

Inch Ruler

Inches

Centimeter Ruler

Centimeters

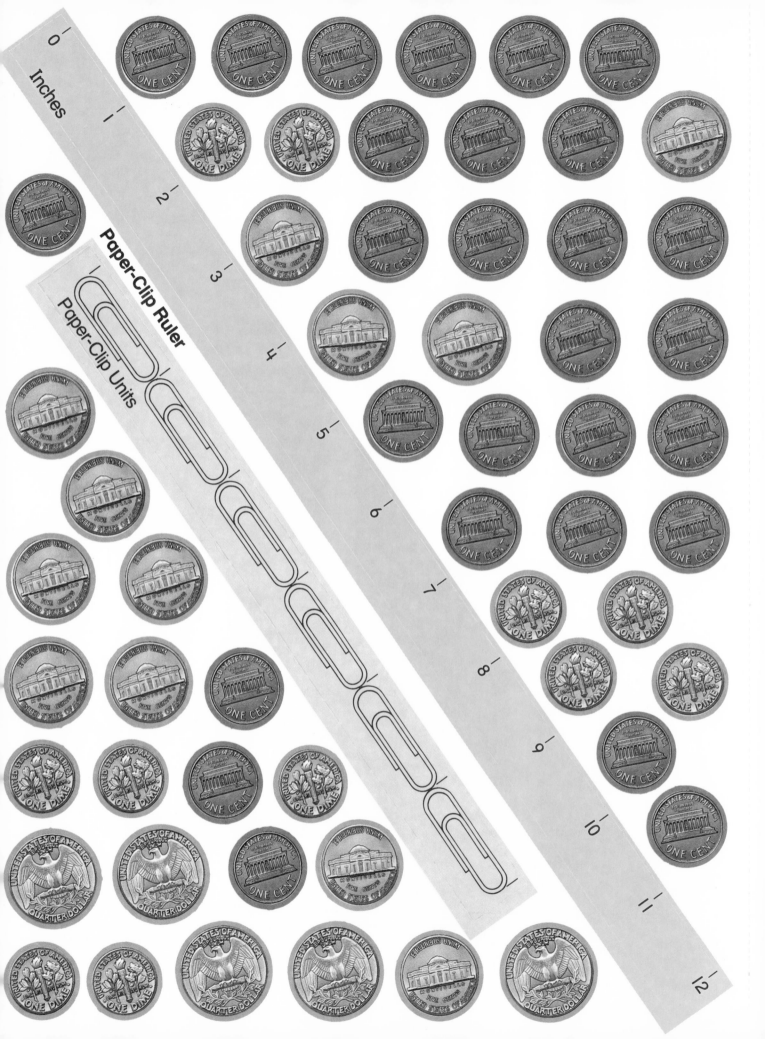

Counting Board

1	2	3	4	5	6	7	8	9	10
11	12	13	14	15	16	17	18	19	20
21	22	23	24	25	26	27	28	29	30
31	32	33	34	35	36	37	38	39	40
41	42	43	44	45	46	47	48	49	50

Money Cover-Ups

Punch out.

Punch out.

Punch out.

Punch out.

Money Cover-Up

Use with pages 144 and 187.

Use with page 51.

Punch out.

Clocks

Use with page 104.

1: 00

2: 00

3: 00

4: 30

5: 30

6: 30

7:00

8:00

9:00

10:30

11:30

12:30

6 + 4	7 + 2	3 + 6	8 + 2	2 + 8	Say the number **after.** 10
4 + 4	3 + 7	8 + 2	6 + 2	2 + 6	15
6 + 6	3 + 5	6 + 2	7 + 2	2 + 7	11
4 + 5	2 + 4	5 + 1	2 + 9	9 + 2	9
5 + 6	9 + 2	3 + 8	1 + 7	7 + 1	14
5 + 5	5 + 2	6 + 1	3 + 2	2 + 3	12

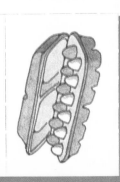

Use with pages
259–260.

Ladder Punchout

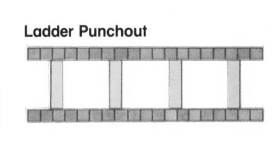

11	10	9	10
16	8	10	8
12	9	8	12
10	11	6	9
15	8	11	11
13	5	7	10

$$\begin{array}{r} 4 \\ +4 \\ \hline 8 \end{array} \qquad \begin{array}{r} 5 \\ +5 \\ \hline 10 \end{array} \qquad \begin{array}{r} 6 \\ +6 \\ \hline 12 \end{array}$$

9 − 6	10 − 8	9 − 3	7 − 3
11 − 9	9 − 4	7 − 2	10 − 3
12 − 9	10 − 6	8 − 3	8 − 3
9 − 7	10 − 9	6 − 6	11 − 3
8 − 6	10 − 7	8 − 2	9 − 3
8 − 5	9 − 5	7 − 3	12 − 3

| 6 + 5 | 4 + 5 | 5 + 6 | 5 + 4 |

4	$\begin{array}{r} 3 \\ + 6 \\ \hline 9 \end{array}$	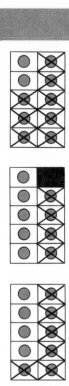	3
7	$\begin{array}{r} 2 \\ + 5 \\ \hline 7 \end{array}$		2
5	$\begin{array}{r} 3 \\ + 5 \\ \hline 8 \end{array}$		3
8	$\begin{array}{r} 6 \\ + 0 \\ \hline 6 \end{array}$	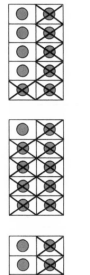	2
6	$\begin{array}{r} 2 \\ + 6 \\ \hline 8 \end{array}$	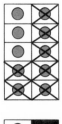	2
9	$\begin{array}{r} 3 \\ + 4 \\ \hline 7 \end{array}$	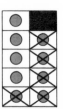	3

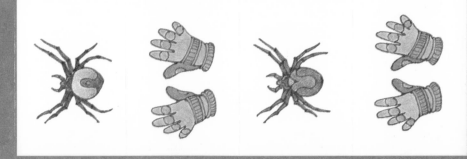

Add-to-Check
Facts

$$\begin{array}{r} 6 \\ + 7 \\ \hline 13 \end{array}$$

$$\begin{array}{r} 4 \\ + 9 \\ \hline 13 \end{array}$$

$$\begin{array}{r} 6 \\ + 8 \\ \hline 14 \end{array}$$

$$\begin{array}{r} 5 \\ + 8 \\ \hline 13 \end{array}$$

$$\begin{array}{r} 6 \\ + 9 \\ \hline 15 \end{array}$$

$$\begin{array}{r} 5 \\ + 9 \\ \hline 14 \end{array}$$

$$\begin{array}{r} 6 \\ + 7 \\ \hline \end{array}$$

$$\begin{array}{r} 7 \\ + 8 \\ \hline \end{array}$$

$$\begin{array}{r} 7 \\ + 6 \\ \hline \end{array}$$

$$\begin{array}{r} 8 \\ + 7 \\ \hline \end{array}$$

$$\begin{array}{r} 8 \\ + 9 \\ \hline \end{array}$$

$$\begin{array}{r} 9 \\ + 8 \\ \hline \end{array}$$

Say the number.

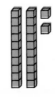

$$\begin{array}{r} 12 \\ - 5 \\ \hline \end{array}$$

$$\begin{array}{r} 11 \\ - 4 \\ \hline \end{array}$$

$$\begin{array}{r} 12 \\ - 7 \\ \hline \end{array}$$

$$\begin{array}{r} 12 \\ - 4 \\ \hline \end{array}$$

$$\begin{array}{r} 11 \\ - 5 \\ \hline \end{array}$$

$$\begin{array}{r} 11 \\ - 7 \\ \hline \end{array}$$

$$\begin{array}{r} 6 \\ + 6 \\ \hline \end{array}$$

$$\begin{array}{r} 7 \\ + 7 \\ \hline \end{array}$$

$$\begin{array}{r} 8 \\ + 8 \\ \hline \end{array}$$

$$\begin{array}{r} 9 \\ + 9 \\ \hline \end{array}$$

5 + 7 12	Say the tens. Say the ones. 40		13 − 6
4 + 7 11	26		13 − 4
7 + 5 12	17		14 − 6
4 + 8 12	22		13 − 5
5 + 6 11	32		15 − 6
7 + 4 11	14		14 − 5

  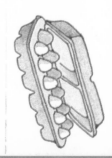

Use with page 344.　Use with page 342.

Use with page 331.

Related Subtraction Facts

13
− 4
9

15
− 6
9

14
− 5
9

17
− 8
9

12
− 3
9

16
− 7
9

Add-to-Check Facts

7
+ 8
15

8
+ 5
13

7
+ 9
16

8
+ 6
14

8
+ 9
17

8
+ 7
15

8

8

6

6

7

7

9

9

Use with page 227.

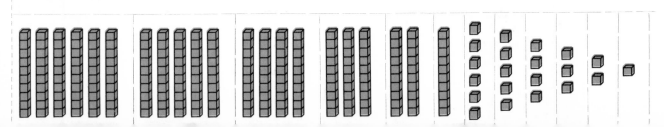

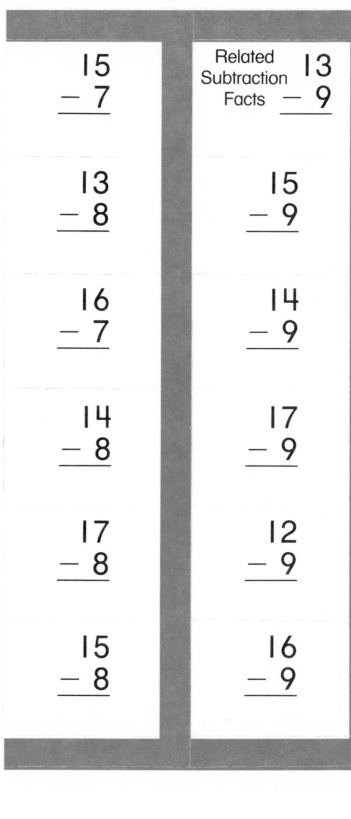

15
− 7

Related
Subtraction   13
Facts   − 9

13
− 8

15
− 9

16
− 7

14
− 9

14
− 8

17
− 9

17
− 8

12
− 9

15
− 8

16
− 9